Published in the USA by:
BearManor Media
PO Box 1129
Duncan, Oklahoma 73534-1129
www.bearmanormedia.com

ISBN 978-1-59393-229-9

Printed in the United States of America.
Book design by Brian Pearce | Red Jacket Press.

Your Friend and Mine, Andy Devine

by Dennis Devine

Kay —

It was nice meeting you in Santa Barbara —

Hope you enjoy my little Book —

Best Regards —

Danin Deoino

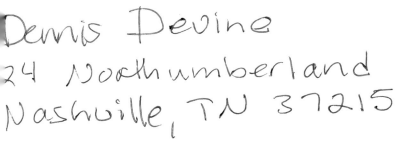

I dedicate this book
To the guys you rarely see

The stuntmen and others
Who were always there for me

With craftsmanship in making films
They only got faint praise

So thanks, you faceless warriors
For your talent, my glass I raise.

(AN OFT-QUOTED THOUGHT OF ACTOR ANDY DEVINE)

Acknowledgements

I would like to acknowledge the following individuals who made this book possible:

Nancy Cahoon — *Editing and Publisher Relations*

Crystal Dietz — *Editing*

Leslie Maxtone-Graham — *Photo Editing*

Other Contributors: Gary Witkin, Suzanne B. Day, Timothy A. Devine, Patrick Wayne, Steven Durr, Grace Kono-Wells, Lisa Chapman, Wade C. Hughan, Robert Boesch, the Andy Devine Museum, Kingman, AZ and the Western Heritage Museum, Oklahoma City, OK.

Table of Contents

Foreword 11
Prologue 13
Birthday at the Derby: 1939 17
Home on the Range: 1939 21
The War Years: 1942 23
Working Cheap: 1946 27
Father Smith: 1947 33
The Beginnings of Andy: 1905 37
Death and Discovery: 1924 41
Give Me a Break: 1929 45
Fat Contract and Romance: 1933 51
Radio: 1934 54
Extremes: 1935 62
Stagecoach: 1939 66
Universal Stinkers: 1940 68
Roy Rogers: 1947 71
Television: 1950 75
Special Films: 1952 77
New School: 1952 82
Trouble while Skiing: 1953 85
Happy Days: 1955 89
Down to Business: 1956 95
The Hotel: 1956 97
The Interview: 1956 101
Buster Brown: 1957 103

Lafayette Escadrille: 1957 .... **105**
Showboat: 1957 .... **116**
Decisions: 1957 .... **118**
New York: 1957 .... **122**
The Five Freshman: 1958 .... **125**
Embracing Success: 1958 .... **132**
Mortality: 1959 .... **137**
The Boys Club: 1959 .... **139**
Rome: 1960 .... **144**
Back to Work: 1960 .... **146**
Liberty Valance: 1962 .... **151**
The Military: 1962 .... **156**
Graduation and Work: 1962 .... **159**
Marriage: 1963 .... **164**
Taking the Plunge: 1966 .... **166**
The New Broom: 1967 .... **168**
D &S: 1968 .... **173**
The Candidate: 1968 .... **175**
Palos Verdes: 1969 .... **177**
The Sunset Years: 1971 .... **183**
Studio Village: 1972 .... **186**
Almost Famous: 1973 .... **188**
Trips, Trauma, Tributes: 1975 .... **191**
Up the Coast: 1976 .... **196**
Hitting the Jackpot: 1976 .... **199**
Odd Jobs: 1976 .... **203**
The Great Escape: 1976 .... **206**
Reagan for President: 1976 .... **210**
The Final Curtain: 1977 .... **213**
The Great Sendoff: 1977 .... **215**
Wishes Granted: 1977 .... **218**
Epilogue **221**
Credits **229**
Index **237**
Photo Index **245**

The last photograph of two old friends. They started working together as extras in 1926. They shared their first big hit as actors in the film Stagecoach, *circa 1939. This was their last film together,* The Man Who Shot Liberty Valance, *circa 1962.*

Foreword

I'm honored to write the foreword to this book because my dad loved Andy Devine. They first became friends as extras on the silent film *Noah's Ark* in 1926. Together they tasted real success in the film *Stagecoach* in 1939. Their final film together was *The Man Who Shot Liberty Valance* in 1962.

When I was interviewed by Larry King, he asked who Dad's favorite actors to work with were. Without hesitation I answered Jimmy Stewart, Maureen O'Hara and Andy Devine. Something special to me was that my older brother Michael and I remained friends with Dennis and his older brother Tad well after our father's passing.

Dennis has written a compelling and entertaining book. He captures firsthand the golden age of films and the demise of the studio system. This book flooded me with the richness of past experiences and relationships. I loved this book and so will you.

Patrick Wayne

Prologue

In December of 2011, Al Roker of *The Today Show* was clearing his throat when he commented, "Gee, I sound just like Andy Devine." This took place thirty-four years after my father's death. It's no wonder that people still remember this rotund, gravel-voiced, character actor. He was kind, approachable, and talented. It was odd, but most of his fans felt they knew him not as an actor, but more as a friend. As his youngest son I knew things weren't as easy for Dad as they seemed. His childhood was a struggle and his insecurities would stay with him forever.

This problem was magnified because he was under the watchful eye of his stern and ambitious father. After being moved from school to school, along came football, and he was very good at it. This new recognition improved his confidence, his grades, and his father's admiration. On the very day his father died, Andy would be "discovered" on, of all places, Hollywood Boulevard. This encounter would introduce him to many new friends and a life beyond his imagination.

The early days were difficult, but Dad would eventually achieve great success. Andy Devine would appear in more films than any actor — ever! (Please review his credits.) He would star in such diverse classics as *Stagecoach, Romeo and Juliet,* and *A Star is Born*. Because of his unique voice, he was on radio with Jack Benny for six years, *Lum and Abner* for five years, and broadcast a number of his own shows. He starred in two television series, *Wild Bill Hickok* for seven years, and *Andy's Gang* for five years. He also made many TV guest appearances and commercials. In 1957 he starred, to great acclaim, on the New York stage.

I admired my father but was independent of him simply because he was just so busy. He was the captive of his own success and was always working. Dad rarely gave me advice and seemed to be more of a friend than a father. But often he was wonderfully thoughtful. I just wish that he and my mom and even my older brother had been more involved in my childhood. Because of this detachment I dealt with school, athletics, and social issues all on my own. I never received an allowance and always had a job. I loved my freedom, and at home I lived alone upstairs, much like that of an apartment. But when the family did do things together it was special, because we always had so much fun.

I was in two feature films and was offered a contract by 20th Century-Fox. I considered following in Dad's footsteps, but after careful thought chose to attend college, pursue athletics, and enter the business world. Ironically a business opportunity would lead me to purchase the entire back half of the studio where Dad had been under contract. Up into the late sixties Dad had purposely turned down work. Now he wanted to get busy again, but the jobs were few. I was flattered that he asked for my help and together we went to work. We revamped everything and Dad achieved great success. But trouble was ahead.

Dad would be struck down by cancer, and all of our lives would change. What really happens to a family after the death of a famous patriarch? We were all forced to deal with success and failure, betrayal and redemption, humor and tears—but most of all survival. You'll get to know our entire colorful family and share in the complex but joyful relationship between a father and his youngest son. This narrative covers over sixty years in and around Hollywood, and you'll meet almost every show-business character who ever lived. It's all here and it's all true.

Clark Gable and Carole Lombard, circa 1939, at the Hollywood Brown Derby in the same booth where Mother went into labor. Please note the caricature of William Powell (upper right) looking down upon his former wife.

Carole Lombard, circa 1939, with my brother Tad on his birthday where she presented him with a new pony.

CHAPTER 1

Birthday at the Derby
1939

Clark Gable owned a Duisenberg, but tonight he was driving the station-wagon. He and his live-in girlfriend, actress Carole Lombard, were dining at the famed Hollywood Brown Derby with Andy Devine and his very pregnant wife Dorothy. Gable thought the fancy car would be a bit ostentatious for such company. He was in a festive mood because the very next day he would start work on the biggest film of his career, *Gone with the Wind*. Andy too was in a celebratory mood. He had finished shooting the film *Stagecoach* and it was to be released shortly. Dad was now at home and after viewing the breathtaking "rough-cut" knew this picture could become a classic.

The dinner was bittersweet for these four close friends. Carole and Clark, who would marry six weeks later, were very much in love. Not like you've read about, though. Yes, they were lovers, but most of all they were buddies. Although Carole was beautiful, she was also athletic and funny and "one of the boys." She could out-swear, out-drink, and out-shoot most men, and Clark loved her for it. The problem was that Carole had previously experienced difficulty getting pregnant. She loved kids and was desperate to have a child. Her dear friend Dorothy Devine was very pregnant and was a bulky presence at dinner. These two women were excited over the imminent delivery, and for whatever reason they mutually decided that the baby was going to be a girl, to be named Susie.

In those days The Brown Derby was the place to dine and be seen in Hollywood. It was owned and run by a fun-loving Montana cowboy named Bob Cobb. Cobb loved four things in life: celebrities, beautiful women, baseball and, most of all, his restaurant. And he was compulsive about the place. The food, the drinks, and the service were impeccable, and it was the most fun place in town. Cobb was handsome, well dressed, and exceedingly charming. The restaurant was always packed with celebrities, and Bob Cobb thought himself as big a star as any of his patrons. Bob's wife Sally was beautiful and as outgoing as Bob. Sally and Carole had recently hosted a baby shower for Dorothy. It was a lively happy party which was attended by all the girls.

Benny Massi was everybody's favorite waiter at the Derby where he spent forty-six years in service. He was kind, efficient, and humble. He

Mom (left), Dad (right) on the film Doctor Bull *with Will Rogers (center).*

walked that fine line between being a server and a friend. That night, as requested, Benny was serving the Gables and Devines in their favorite booth, number twenty-four. As dinner progressed, Dorothy felt a little kick from her baby, then another. As the men continued drinking and laughing and largely paying little attention to the girls, Dorothy whispered to Carole," I think my time has come." Excited and sensitive to pregnancies, Carole insisted they all go to the hospital. But wanting the party to continue Carole jumped up onto the seat of the booth and loudly announced to all the patrons that everyone was going to the hospital. "We'll make it a party, god damn it!" She had Benny call eleven taxi cabs, collect all the bartenders with booze and glasses, and ordered the kitchen to make sandwiches plus a big bowl of Cobb salad for which Bob would become famous.

It took but a few minutes to get to Cedars Hospital. Dr. Joe Harris and his associate Dr. Red Kroan were in attendance. Dr. Harris was unique in that, although he was an OB-GYN, he was also Frank Sinatra's primary caregiver — Joe Harris was the only doctor the singer trusted. The waiting room churned with celebrities, bartenders, waiters, and lots of onlookers enjoying the fun. Dorothy was admitted at 10:15 p.m. and her baby was delivered at 11:00. It wasn't Susie. It was a boy. It was me.

Mother and Will Rogers on the film Doctor Bull *circa 1933. Rogers was an old family friend as they were both from the same town, Oolaga, Oklahoma. This was the day that Rogers introduced my mother and father.*

Mother gave up her acting career to raise my brother and me. Here she is with my brother Tad, age 4, circa 1938.

CHAPTER 2

Home on the Range
1939

Bing Crosby was a very strange man. He was one of Dad's best friends, so close that Dad bought his first house across the street from Bing's estate in the Toluca Lake area of the San Fernando Valley. However, Bing had an odd way of treating people. He couldn't get enough of a person, but then without warning or explanation, he would cut a close friend off. He was a loner, a drunk, and a sociopath, but could be extremely charming when necessary. After three years, having had enough of Bing's erratic friendship, Dad sold the Toluca Lake house and moved to a ranch farther out in the valley in the town of Van Nuys. The ranch is where I came home to after my big birthday night, and that is where I would live until I finished high school.

Upon arriving at the ranch in Van Nuys, "Susie" did not have a name. My mother came from a large and opinionated family. They all lived close to us, and both the men and women were part of the film community, doing stand-in work, stunts, make-up, and horse wrangling. They all had different ideas as to what my name should be, but finally settled on Patrick Donald Devine. Then actor Dennis O'Keefe showed up at the house with a bouquet of roses. He adored my mother, who, in turn, felt a great fondness for this big, irresponsible, noisy Irishman. O'Keefe had no idea what the family members had already named me, but with his giant ego and the ability to sell his ideas, he talked my mother into a new name. As a result of his visit, my name became Dennis Patrick Devine.

Also at home was my brother Timothy, four and a half years older than I, with the full name of Timothy Andrew Devine. He was always called Tad, as those were his initials. When I was three years old, I moved upstairs to a large converted attic. It was private and airy, and all mine. Tad lived downstairs. Physically he matured quickly, and I quite slowly. It was like we were seven or so years apart rather than four. Tad went to Stanford at seventeen, became an All-American swimmer, and after graduation became a decorated naval officer. As children we were always going in different directions with different people. I always looked up to Tad, but I really didn't get to know him until both of us were adults.

My earliest memories are of my parents' friends. They were all young, attractive, funny, and fun-loving. Some were in films, some in the military (remember, the winds of war were gathering), and some were neighbors my parents' age. I thought everybody was like these friends. They flew planes, rode horses, rode motorcycles, and had parties. The best thing my parents did was let me hang around with these adults.

Our ranch in the San Fernando Valley was the perfect place for a kid to grow up. We had a cow, pigs, chickens, horses, dogs, and we grew our own crops. The ranch wasn't that remote and I found other playmates nearby. My mother was only twenty-three at my birth so she too was just a kid. As they got older, my brother and my mother were always riding horses or bicycles together, and many of our neighbors thought my mother and brother were brother and sister. Looking back I believe we were all growing up at the same time. I think my mother subconsciously knew this, and seemed to let things go their own way as to our rearing.

CHAPTER 3

The War Years
1942

I was old enough to experience the last part of World War II, and it excited me. There were lights-out drills, the neighborhood Civil Defense activities, and rag and paper drives. Because Dad was a celebrity, military men of all form and fashion visited our house. The most special among them were the Flying Tigers, or American Volunteer Group (AVGs). They were a collection of expert pilots who volunteered to fly for China in the late thirties before the United States entered the war. Many of the AVGs were transferred to the nearby Van Nuys Army Airfield after the U.S. entered the war.

Our house became the unofficial hangout for these exciting young men who came from varied cultural backgrounds. They all had different kinds of hide-and-seek games, varied recipes to share, and different cocktails new to my parents. The poker games at the Devine ranch were legendary. Some of the AVGs played well and some played poorly, but the fun and laughs were abundant. One family favorite was pilot Arvid Olson. He was such a bad poker player it was suggested that the nose of his airplane read *The Poker Player's Friend*. To be with these airmen was magical. They often took me to the airfield where they showed me their planes, taught me how to pack a parachute and introduced me to other new pilots.

In 1940 Dad was thirty-five years old and beyond draft age. However, he became close friends with Air Force General Barney Giles. Through General Giles, Dad volunteered to teach shooting for waist gunners in B-17s. With celebrities Robert Stack, Norris Goff, Phil Harris and Dad, they taught bird shooting from towers at March Air Force Base. Their gunners achieved more kills than any other group in the Eighth Air Force.

During the war fate did not ignore Hollywood. While working as an extra, Dad met another young extra named Ralph Brooks. Ralph would become one of Dad's very closest friends. He went by the nickname "Ish" and I knew him as "Uncle Ish." He was a dress extra. A dress extra has a great wardrobe (tuxedos, tails, suits, sport coats, etc.). The studio would pay him more to bring his own clothes so they could eliminate fittings, wear and tear, etc. Ish looked like an everyman. He played attorneys, bartenders, gangsters, doormen and so on. His lines would be "Right this way" or "What will it be?" or "Stick 'em up." Ish was one of the funniest men I've ever met, and I loved it when he came by the house. He appeared in 338 films, but was rarely credited. He always wanted to be a real actor, but just never got the break.

In 1944, at the age of thirty-three, Ish was classified 1-A by the draft board, but never received a draft notice. He thought at his age he was in the clear. Sorry. In late 1944 Ish was drafted, and there was nothing he could do about it. To make matters worse, he was sent to the infantry. There he was, a private, ten years older than his commanding officer, and substantially older than his fellow enlisted men. In the past his only real physical activity had been dancing in the background of movies. He was scared to death being thrown into battle with these young kids and enduring numerous and dangerous beach landings. To hear this older, very funny man tell these stories of his own harrowing experiences as a misplaced and aging soldier was hilarious and unforgettable.

In 1941 radio entertainer Norris Goff (*Lum and Abner*) found 120 acres in the north San Fernando Valley. Goff solicited Clark Gable, Phil Harris and Dad to join in on the purchase of this raw land they would call "The Hard Rock Land Company." The group planned to park their trailers and hunt pigeons and doves. However, campfires, drinking and spending time together were their main activities. Carole Lombard (who was now Mrs. Gable) was adamant that she purchase her own share. Because she was "one of the boys," the other men agreed. Sadly tragedy would strike. On January 16th, 1942 Carole was killed in an airplane crash near Las Vegas as she was returning with her mother from a U.S. War Bond drive.

Two weeks after her death, the "Hard Rock" partners were having drinks at Goff's Encino home trying to console Gable. Goff had a tendency to exaggerate, in a whimsical way, the nature of any and all wagers. Goff innocently and humorously challenged Gable to a pool game for a quarter of a million dollars. Gable reached into his coat pocket, pulled out a check and laid it on the pool table. "Here's mine, where's yours?" The check was for $225,000 payable to Gable for the life insurance policy the Government had placed on Carole. A few minutes later Gable picked up the insurance check and left Goff's house. After that night Gable would spend little time with those close friends. Actress Virginia Gray was a family friend and an "off-again, on-again" companion of Gable's for years. She explained to Dad that Clark missed his old friends terribly, but hated dealing with the memories. Gable told Virginia that those were the happiest days of his life. Sadly I would never meet those two famous, fun people who helped me celebrate my birthday.

As the war continued, Dad played in a film called *Ali Baba and The Forty Thieves*, starring Jon Hall, Maria Montez, and Turhan Bey. They were on an extended shoot in far-away Malibu Canyon where *M*A*S*H* was later filmed. Because of travel time and gas rationing, Dad thought it would be fun if we all moved to the Malibu Colony for the summer. Some of Dad's friends were already living in the Colony including Lana Turner, who was filming *The Postman Always Rings Twice*, and Bing Crosby. In the four months we lived in Malibu, Bing never came by.

There was swimming in the day, barbeques on the weekends, and sometimes horror films at night. While watching these films, with the waves crashing outside and the fog drifting in, I found it was really frightening to spend time with Dracula, Frankenstein and the Wolfman in that small dark beach house. Mostly I remember riding with Dad on his motorcycle on Pacific Coast Highway. Because of the gas shortage, many of Dad's friends bought motorcycles and formed a group called The Moraga Spit and Polish Club. The members included Ward Bond, Robert Taylor, Keenan Wynn, and directors Howard Hawks and Bill Wellman. They would ride together on Sundays and sometimes would take overnight trips to Vegas or Santa Barbara. The studios forbade these valuable artists from riding motorcycles; therefore there are no photos of the Moraga group. I also vividly remember the soldiers guarding the beach. One soldier told me about his brother. They had enlisted at the same time, and while he guarded Malibu Beach, his brother landed on Omaha Beach and remained in France. I was a little kid, but the soldier shared with me some of the horror his brother had endured. It was difficult for me to imagine that people were being killed while we were living in this wonderful cloistered environment.

Our Malibu house faced the ocean, with the garage and private drive to the rear. One day while waiting for my mother near the garage, I saw a strikingly beautiful young girl who was walking by holding hands with an older woman. As our eyes met she said hello, and I shyly responded. It was surely the first time I ever noticed a girl as pretty. Driving out we passed the two, and I asked my mother who she was. "She's the girl from *National Velvet*, she's Elizabeth Taylor. I believe she's staying here at the Colony."

Because Malibu was remote from the city, Dad and I would sometimes return to the ranch to check on things. On one of these trips, pilot Richard Bong stopped by our house. Stationed at nearby Burbank, he was test flying jets for Lockheed. He wanted to say hello as he was pals with our Flying Tiger friends. Bong was the flying ace of aces with some forty kills, and he was a recipient of the Medal of Honor. He gave me an autographed picture which I kept in my room. Ten days after our meeting he was killed on a test flight not far from our home. He seemed so young and confident with his curly blond hair and infectious smile. It was hard to believe this young hero was gone.

CHAPTER 4

Working Cheap
1946

The war was now over and things were returning to normal. I missed the servicemen and their comings and goings. They were all busy becoming generals, piloting commercial aircraft, or otherwise working in the airplane business. Back home we all had our chores, and one of mine was cleaning the dog run. The floor of the run was gravel, and raking dog poop in gravel is no easy task. On top of that, it was summer and summer in the San Fernando Valley is hot. One day while I was picking poop from pebbles, my brother walked by wearing dress slacks and a nicely pressed shirt. He came by to announce that he would be playing Dad's son in a new Universal picture. Although I was only seven, I could see that this was not a very good deal. While I was immersed in dog poop , my brother was off to become a movie star. I dropped my rake, ran into the house, found Dad, and begged to go to the studio. He said okay, if I could be ready in ten minutes. Firemen don't get dressed faster than I did that day.

Dad, my brother and I jumped into the station wagon for the twenty-minute ride to the studio. Entering a movie studio is exciting for anyone and, because Dad had been under contract to Universal for a number of years, he knew everyone. At the gate the uniformed guards practically saluted him. Inside the lot cowboys, soldiers, sheiks, and monsters drifted by. The commissary crowd included an indifferent clown puffing a cigarette while speaking with a man in a space suit and a fat policeman sharing dessert with a scantily-clad harem girl.

Nearby, in the imposing executive building, Producer Walter Wanger was waiting to meet my brother to assess his suitability for his part. Wanger greeted Dad warmly from behind his large desk. Dad and my brother sat down and started to make small talk. While they were occupied, I lost no time in sneaking around the producer's large desk, and then crawling up onto his lap saying, "I want to be in the movie and I'll work cheap." Wanger was startled, but paused, looked down, and chuckled, "As long as you work cheap." Thus began my limited film career. Wanger got up to open the door for our departure, and as we were leaving he said to Dad, "I think he'll make a better agent than an actor." Even at my young age I realized that I wasn't going to be handed anything. Had I not begged

Publicity photograph from the film Canyon Passage *circa 1946.*

to go, or not taken the chance of climbing up onto the producer's lap, I would still be at home cleaning the dog run.

The film was *Canyon Passage* and starred Dana Andrews, Susan Hayward, Brian Donlevy, Hoagy Carmichael, Ward Bond, Lloyd Bridges, and Dad. It was a location picture to be shot in Oregon near Crater Lake. I vividly remember the train trip to Oregon. We left at night on a train

While at the studio making Canyon Passage *we visited our old friend Glenn Strange who was playing Frankenstein's Monster in the film* Abbott and Costello Meet Frankenstein, *circa 1946.*

with a large steam locomotive and big steel sleeper cars. I could smell the steam and the grease and the creosote from the railroad ties. We had two sleeper rooms. I stayed with Mom, and my brother stayed with Dad. I remember looking out the train window from my bunk wondering where in the hell I was going. However, I knew that I was going to have a great adventure. Hell, it already was a great adventure!

As opposed to many Universal productions, this film greatly displayed its big budget. The studio had built an authentic western town with a bar, a bank, and many stores. There were a half dozen wranglers with forty or so horses. Twenty wagons were scattered among dozens of extras, including Indians, town folks, and even little children. We would be on location for six weeks, which is a long time. A location picture is like summer camp. You are away from home and living and dealing with people you don't know. It seems difficult as people become even more difficult when they are away from home.

Of the stars of the film, Susan Hayward was a trooper. As it happened, she had been incorrectly prescribed sleeping pills and was always taking naps whenever possible. Shooting a film is difficult and tiring, and she never complained. The sleeping pill error was realized just before we left for home. Hoagy Carmichael was well dressed and intelligent. He was kind of a laid back loner; he was cool and I even had a scene with him. Brian Donlevy was unique in that his appearance was deceiving. He was bald, overweight, wore dentures, and was extremely short. He commented that when making a film he would get up in the morning, put in his teeth, lace up his truss, apply his hairpiece, and step into his six-inch elevator boots. He hated wearing all that crap, and was self-conscious about his true appearance. He therefore rarely socialized, but was one of the most talented actors in films. Dana Andrews was my favorite. He was kind and

A scene from Canyon Passage.

fun, and we spent a lot of time together. He took me horseback riding, showed me how the camera and lighting worked, and explained what various people did. For some reason he gave me the nickname "Froggie." I later learned that he was an alcoholic, but at the time he was a wonderful companion to a little kid.

When we finished shooting the exteriors in Oregon, we returned to Los Angeles to shoot interiors at the studio. I went to the studio when I was on standby. This lasted about four weeks and just being around the place was exciting. I sometimes attended studio school where I felt I didn't belong because I found the teachers and kids all new and strange. However, I did go to the musical scoring sessions with Dad and they were unforgettable. Here were 150 musicians, all dressed casually, in this perfect room, playing great music with the film being shown on a giant screen in the background. It was on this day that I fell in love with film

Publicity photograph in the backyard of the Van Nuys ranch, circa 1940.

A photograph of the family visiting Dad on the set of the film Never A Dull
Moment, *circa 1950. This was the day I would meet Natalie Wood who lived
nearby in Van Nuys. We would remain casual friends for many years.*

music. With the immigrant western European composers, conductors, and musicians all coming to Hollywood in the late thirties to escape the anticipated tyranny, it was truly the golden age of film music.

Another memorable time at the studio was visiting the *Frankenstein* set. Universal had made a fortune off of this franchise, and kept making more and more of the films. They started off with *Frankenstein* in 1931 with Boris Karloff. Then *The Bride of Frankenstein* in 1935, *The Son of Frankenstein* in 1937, and so on. The final one in the series was *Abbott and Costello Meet Frankenstein* in 1947. Glenn Strange did a number of "B" westerns at Universal with Dad, and he became friends with my brother and me. When Dad, my brother and I arrived on the set, there was the monster sitting in a chair smoking a cigarette. I knew it was a movie, but at eight years old the monster was still frightening. Then the monster stood up and shouted, "Hey, it's Uncle Glenn." Glenn Strange went on to become famous playing Sam the bartender on *Gunsmoke*.

Canyon Passage opened to good reviews and moderate business. A problem was that both Dana Andrews and Hoagy Carmichael were also in the just-released *The Best Years of Our Lives*. It won Best Picture that year, and it was a film everybody went to see. And here were the film's two stars together once again. However, *Canyon Passage* did make money, which I'm sure was due to my reduced salary. The film was previewed in Studio City with a big party at the nearby Sportsman's Lodge. I enjoyed seeing all the grips and camera guys some six months after I had last seen them. They all thought I'd grown.

CHAPTER 5

Father Smith
1947

Public schools in Los Angeles in the late forties were much different from what they are today. The teachers were very strict, and corporal punishment was permitted, even encouraged. The students respected the teachers and administrators. My parents considered private school, but I wanted to go to the nearby public school with all my friends. It was Van Nuys Elementary School, and it educated me from kindergarten through the sixth grade. Severe dyslexia compromised my reading ability. I saw letters upside down and backwards, missed entire sentences, and transposed numbers. Through college I worked very hard to overcome this problem. On my own I enrolled in speed reading classes and eye exercise classes, and I forced myself to read as much as possible. My parents arranged for me to repeat the first half of the third grade, which postponed my graduation to the summer. Given my slow rate of maturation, this made a world of difference in my confidence.

Dad's time with Universal was coming to an end. He was still under contract but not working as much as before. He had more time to be a dad and we did everything. We would ride his motorcycle and go flying. That year Dad taught me to shoot and let me attend our annual dove hunt. Dad even drove me to Long Beach to see Howard Hughes' Flying Boat actually fly. Dad said that he met Hughes once at a party and was fascinated by him.

For my birthday my parents gave me a new lime green Schwinn bicycle. I pleaded with Mom to let me take it to school so I could show my friends. She finally agreed, but on my way home three older boys beat me up and took my new bike. I came home bloodied and heartbroken, but with no sympathy, my mother informed me there would be no new bike. So I went to the police impound yard and bought a used bike for one dollar. I took the bike apart, fixed everything and repainted the frame. A kid at school offered me twenty bucks for it, and that was the beginning of my bicycle business. My parents would never need to buy me a bike ever again.

In post-war California schools were being built everywhere as people were moving by truckloads to the Valley. As a result of this influx, I encountered greater ethnic diversity than I had previously been exposed to. I'll never forget sitting on the grass with two close friends and saying," I've heard there are Jewish kids in this school." They replied, "We're Jewish!" This sparked my religious curiosity which extended to numerous houses of worship. Every Sunday and some Saturdays I was off on my bike to "hear the pitch." I went everywhere from tent shows to Orthodox Synagogues. I was then introduced to Father Smith.

As a young chaplain, Harley Wright Smith was wounded in World War I. I remember the large scar at the back of his neck. His family had left him a modest estate, and he wanted to come to California. He started his first Episcopal ministry in actor Edward Everett Horton's Encino barn. Within ten years he had one of the biggest and most beautiful churches in the San Fernando Valley. He was quite a salesman. When I met him he was in his mid-fifties, bald headed, a twinkle in his eye, and a ready smile; everyone loved him. My mother would insist my dad go to Easter services, and Father Smith would always ask my father to stand so he could be introduced. After the introduction Father Smith, in front of the congregation, would then wish Dad a Merry Christmas, explaining he wouldn't see Andy again until the next Easter. Father Smith's delivery was perfect, and church laughter was everywhere.

My first "crush" was a pretty young girl in church named Mary. She sang in the choir and was about eighteen. Mary was very nice and involved in all Church activities. Three years later Father Smith and Mary would become husband and wife. He was fifty-eight years old and she was twenty-one. Father Smith now had a large and influential congregation in addition to his personal wealth. He was a humble man, but the Church thought he was acquiring too much power. The marriage was the clincher. The Church moved him to the slums of Watts to a disorganized congregation in a rundown building. Father Smith never complained and made his new congregation flourish. I realized then that politics were evident in all aspects of life.

Father Smith liked to claim that he was the "Devine Family Chaplain." As the years went by, whenever there was a family event such as a wedding, funeral, or christening, I would pick up Father Smith and drive him to the destination. Our talks in the car were profound. Philosophy, history, politics and even sex were discussed. He made me think, and I grew a little each trip. I truly loved the man. Father Smith would live into his nineties, and he and Mary would be married some thirty-eight years and produce four children. Through the years, when things were not going well, I would think of Father Smith. It made me feel better, and somehow I felt he was there with me.

Father Smith acted as sort of my mentor, but here I was ten years old without much supervision. When Dad was working he was gone and I was on my own. I was still poor at reading and, although I really tried, school continued to be difficult and it frightened me. I didn't want to be put in a special school or be kicked out. The only thing that helped my confidence was being so self-sufficient. But somehow I had to beat this reading thing as I was tired of being afraid of school.

In addition to childhood fears, I was curious about Dad. I knew all about Mom's family as they all lived nearby and all were happy to voice their opinions, share their values, and wear their feelings on their sleeve. As a result, they had few secrets. But with Dad it was different. Although he would tell a humorous story or two about his childhood, he spoke very little about his life in a serious way. And how many children really know that much about their parents anyway? However, I feel parents have the obligation to their children to tell them all about themselves.

On the surface Dad seemed to be simple and uncomplicated. In reality he was complex with many fears. But I had no real idea about anything. What were his parents like? Was he a happy kid? Was he good in school? How did he get along with his older brother? On top of all of that, I had no idea of how he got into the movies. How did he meet Mom? Why was he so passive about my upbringing? These and many other things were what I dug into. It took time to uncover the truth, and here is what I found.

The stern, capable and ambitious Thomas Devine, Sr. at the desk of his hotel in Kingman, Arizona. Circa 1925.

CHAPTER 6

The Beginnings of Andy
1905

My grandfather, Tom Devine, was a barrel of a man. He was strong and stern and smart. Tom got his toughness from his immigrant father, who had come to the United States from County Tipperary, Ireland. Tom was raised in Michigan and trained as an engineer. He married as a young man and sired a daughter named May. After a few years of marriage Tom's wife died, and Tom with daughter May moved to Flagstaff, Arizona for work. A versatile fellow, Tom was also a blacksmith and knew the lumber trade. He lived in Flagstaff for five years, and while there married the popular Amy Ward, the granddaughter of Commander Herman Ward, the first commandant of the Naval Academy and the first naval officer killed in the Civil War. In 1900 Amy gave birth to Thomas Jr., and in 1905 little Andrew arrived.

In 1906 Tom got an offer to move to Kingman, Arizona to manage the railroad switching yard. After a few years in Kingman, Tom fell under a train and lost his leg. The compensation package from the railroad allowed him to buy the local hotel and bar, which he successfully operated. He also became active in politics and was elected Mojave County Treasurer. While in office Tom successfully lobbied to have the new interstate highway, Route 66, run through Kingman rather than a small town to the north called Las Vegas.

May and Tom Jr. were both good kids and caused few problems for their parents. Andy seemed to need more care and attention. One day seven-year-old Andy was playing on the couch while his mother was hanging curtains. One of the rods went into Andy's mouth, injuring his throat. When everything healed, Andy was left with a distinctly raspy voice which in later years would become his trademark. Andy was academically average in school, but good at sports. Most of all he loved playing pranks, and he had a million friends.

In the lobby of his father's hotel, Andy nailed the traveling salesmen's bags to the floor and then yelled "Train!" As they grabbed their bags, the bottoms came apart, and samples flew everywhere. Although Andy was well liked, he still seemed basically directionless. So the elder Devine sent Andy to Los Angeles to attend Harvard military school, but he was quickly expelled for fighting with the Headmaster's son. After the failure in Los Angeles, Tom Sr. sent Andy to Kansas to be near Tom's sister and to attend a private school and possibly get into a junior college. Andy fared better there primarily because of his involvement with football, and eventually he did get into junior college. But even in college, Andy couldn't stay grounded. He attended two colleges, ending up at Santa Clara University in California where he again excelled in football. But he had given no thought to career choices. This deeply troubled his ambitious father and his strident and proper

Andy Devine, age 4. This was about the time that an errant curtain rod would give him his renowned raspy voice.

mother, who all her life had been surrounded by successful and disciplined people. Dad was insecure because he never believed he could satisfy his demanding parents. That's why he worked so hard at being likeable. It became a trait that he mastered.

In early 1924, Tom Sr. was diagnosed with stomach cancer. He asked Andy if he would move back to Kingman to help the family. Dad was thrilled that his father wanted his help. He also found out that he could attend Arizona State Teachers College which was nearby and had a football team. Andy was up to the task and made his ailing father proud. He provided the needed help and starred on the football field. His grades improved, so much so that Andy was elected freshman class president. However it was a bit of a hollow victory. You see Andy had been in and out of so many schools he was twenty-one and still a freshman. But as

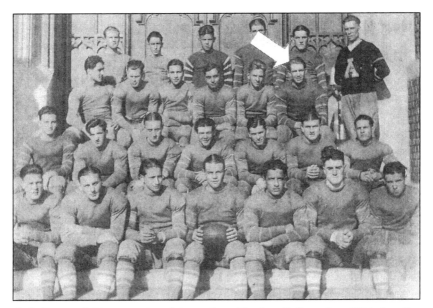

Andy Devine (white arrow) at Arizona State Teachers College, circa 1926. In a few weeks Dad would be working in Hollywood.

The Hotel Beale located on Andy Devine Avenue. I'm sure my grandfather is rolling over in his grave knowing that his hotel is located on the street named after his "screw-up" of a son.

Tom and Andy's relationship grew stronger, Tom's cancer would advance whereby surgery was his only option. The nearest qualified surgeon was in Long Beach, California. Because of his newfound respect for his son, Tom asked Andy if he would join him on the trip to Long Beach. Andy agreed, unaware of how grave the situation was.

The train trip from Kingman to Long Beach took most of the day. It was the first time that Dad and his father had really spent uninterrupted time together. I believe Tom knew how difficult his situation was and finally opened up to his son. It was something that the stern and judgmental Tom had never attempted — being vulnerable and compassionate. I believe Dad learned to love his father more on that trip than ever before. Tom also confided to Andy that if something happened, his banker would handle the money and the sale of the hotel. Andy's mother Amy would get the bulk of the estate, and she would move to Kansas to live with her sister.

I can only imagine what it was like for Dad to see his father taken into surgery. While waiting, all Andy could think about was his domineering mother and how much he resented the fact that she was not there. Then he thought about his own future and what he would do if his father didn't make it. The doctors finally came out. Tom had died on the operating table, and Andy was devastated. His strong father was the anchor of the family. Whether he liked it or not, he was on his own, and there was nothing he could do about it. Although Andy feared his mother, he always looked up to her. What he would never know was that to his unemotional mother, he was the favorite.

CHAPTER 7

Death and Discovery
1924

Not knowing of his mother's true feelings, Andy did not want to return to Kingman to face her. He was sure she was carrying her own guilt, and he didn't want to get in the middle of anything unpleasant. He felt good that he had become closer to his father, and thought it ironic that he, the screw-up, would be the last family member to see his father alive. He never felt more alone or scared. Tom Sr., always organized, had made all the arrangements for his body to be taken back to Kingman, just in case. There was Andy in Long Beach with no father, no future, and only a small amount of money. So he said, "What the hell. I've always wanted to see Hollywood, so I'm going." On the very day his father died, Andy left Long Beach on the Red Car to visit that legendary place he'd always dreamed of seeing.

Wearing his college football jacket, he stepped off the Red Car at Highland Avenue and Hollywood Boulevard. As Andy was walking down Hollywood Boulevard (a street that would honor him with not one but two stars), a car pulled up. The man inside the car asked, "Hey, kid, you look big. Do you play football?" "Can't you see my jacket?" "You want a job?" Andy, often never thinking about the consequences of his actions replied, "Sure." The man handed Andy his card and told him to use it to enter Universal Studios. Andy got back on the Red Car for the trip from Hollywood through the Cahuenga Pass to the San Fernando Valley and Universal Studios.

At the main gate, sure enough, the card got him in. The guard looked at the card and told Andy he should see the casting director, and showed him the way. Andy got to the casting director's office, and the meeting was matter of fact. The casting director looked him over and said that he'd do, and then told him that he would be doing extra work, with the exteriors being shot at the University of Southern California. The casting director also said that they would take him to the school and that he would appear in football gear with other USC players.

When he arrived on the campus, Andy casually met two of the USC players he would know for the rest of his life. They were Ward Bond and Marion Morrison; Marion would later change his name. The film was a series of silent shorts (two reels), which were usually shown in conjunction with a full-length feature film. The series was called *The Collegians*, and Andy worked on the series part-time for two years (1926-27). He discovered he liked this work with its interesting people who were funny and unpredictable.

Although the money from Universal was adequate, Andy still needed to find other ways to support himself. He heard of a traveling football team called the Los Angeles Wildcats who were semi-professionals with no home stadium. Andy tried out for the team and was hired, but he wanted to keep open the possibility of returning to play more college football. So he changed his name to something not too Irish. In 1926 "Jeremiah Schwartz" played for the Los Angeles Wildcats. In later years, as Dad would become famous, many columnists and authors thought Jeremiah Schwartz was his real name. It was even represented on Hollywood Squares. Dad was also an accomplished swimmer, and as a result, got a job as a lifeguard for the County of Los Angeles. His tower was on the border of the City of Santa Monica, which had just started its own lifeguard service. It was headed by Captain George Washington Watkins who became a lifelong friend. Cap, as he liked to be called, was charming, and dedicated to the lifeguard service. Dad eventually introduced all of us to Cap, and as kids would spend the weekend at Cap's cliffside home in Malibu which was built of old shipwrecks which had washed ashore over the years. It was "Robinson Crusoe" come to life, and we thought going to Cap's was better than going to Treasure Island.

In 1927 Dad was still working part time as a lifeguard and part time on *The Collegians* when he got a small uncredited part in a film called *Lilac Time* with Gary Cooper. It was just a few days work, but it was real film work. Dad moved in with a screenwriter named Arnold Belgard. Arnold became a good friend and knew many film people who tried to get Andy work. However, the odd jobs continued. Andy worked part time for the Lighthouse service, both on ships and in lighthouses. He ran a miniature golf course, did day labor, and continued part time with the County Lifeguards. He landed another minor uncredited role in a picture called *The Man Who Laughs*, which is considered to be one of the finest silent films ever made.

Things were not going well, and money was short. It was at this time that Dad met Florence. She was kind, and I can only speculate that she filled the void left by his own mother's detachment. Florence worked at the phone company and wanted to get married. Andy figured he had nowhere else to go, so after a short courtship, he and Florence got married. The marriage lasted only a few months and they separated. Divorce was quick for these two young people who had gotten married for all the wrong reasons. They must have both realized that financial security and companionship weren't enough to sustain their relationship. There must have been some shame involved, because Dad never went into any detail regarding this marriage, even after I was an adult. When I would ask him about it, he would quickly change the subject. I do know that Florence never contacted Dad in later years after he became well known.

After the divorce Andy moved into a single room in the Padre Hotel on Highland near the Hollywood Bowl. Things could hardly have been worse. His sister May had died of cancer, and his mother who had moved to Kansas was not well. Brother Tom was becoming very successful in the meat packing business, which made Andy all the more regret his own failures. Dad was broke, lonely, ashamed, and did not know what to do. Knowing Dad's insecurities, I can just imagine what he was going through. Dad was a proud man who hated to be alone. And here he was all alone, with no family, no future, and no money.

So Andy was going to show 'em and prove to all of them they were right. He was going to commit suicide. In this small barren room there was a gas stove with a connection to the wall. Andy decided to write his mother a long letter trying to relieve her bitter disappointment in him. He then took what sleeping pills he had and unhooked the gas pipe from the wall. After about four hours he awoke in a haze trying to figure out what had happened or not happened. Why was he still here? As Andy got his bearings, he decided to go outside, take a walk, and try to get some sense of things. Exiting his small room to the corridor, he noticed a sign hanging on the outside door knob reading "Gas Shut Off for Non-payment." He went back into the room, sat on the bed, and said to himself, somewhat philosophically, "Well, I'm not rich enough to live, and I'm too damned poor to kill myself." Andy then destroyed the letter to his mother. The next day he got a call to work on a picture called *Finders Keepers*. It was 1928. At first Dad kept this story to himself, but over the years as he became more successful, he would frequently recount this sad but ironic story to numerous interviewers.

Later in 1928 Dad would meet a lifelong friend. The picture was *Noah's Ark*, one of the last big budget silent films. *Noah's Ark* was already in production when the first talking picture, *The Jazz Singer*, was released. *The Jazz Singer* was a big hit, so the producers created partial sound for *Noah's Ark*. The flood scene was monumental with 300 extras. The casting director wanted only men over six feet four inches tall to play the King's guards. As the men stood in line, Andy put his hands on the shoulders of the man in front of him so Andy could appear taller. The man in front of him, standing on his toes, turned and said, "Easy, chum, I'm tall enough, but I don't need to be shorter." They both got the jobs, and on this disastrous film that killed three extras in one day, the two became lifelong friends. Over time they made many films together, with their last one some thirty-three years after *Noah's Ark*. The man was Marion Morrison, whom Dad had met briefly on *The Collegians*, but now he was called John Wayne.

CHAPTER 8

Give Me a Break
1929

Things started to pick up. Andy did five feature uncredited films plus a separate two-reel series. The work was steady and the money was tolerable, but Andy was still doing extra work and silent bits. He wanted to do more. When doing extra work, casting directors would sometimes draw names "out of a hat." Andy figured that three names were better than one, so he submitted three. They were Andy Devine, Andrew Vabre (his middle name) and Phillip Space. During this time Dad met a most unique and interesting man who was older but struggling in the same way. The two became friends and then roommates. George "Slim" Summerville would become a famous character actor, and they would remain close until Slim's untimely death in 1946. Slim's other friend was also named George. He was a former vaudevillian who was married, but was always hanging around their apartment as though he lived there. Contrary to his future film persona, he was very sophisticated, well read, and really loved to talk, and talk, and talk. His name was George Hayes, but because he talked so much everyone called him "Gabby." Little did Andy know that in the future Gabby Hayes, this literate man from the east, would often vie for the same roles as he himself.

In 1930 work again became scarce. The studios didn't want to make silent films, and the banks were reluctant to finance costly talking pictures. Andy made only one picture, and it was his last silent film. This was *Dawn Patrol* for Warner Bros., directed by Howard Hawks. The film attempted to cash in on the success of another World War I flying picture, William Wellman's *Wings*, which won the Academy Award for Best Picture. During the filming Dad fell in love with flying.

The Spirit of Notre Dame was a talking picture all about football. Andy was twenty-six and was still in good physical shape. Because he was experienced and likeable, Andy was asked to interview for his first speaking role. Although Dad desperately wanted a speaking part, the prospect frightened him. He also reflected upon his ailing mother in Kansas and her disappointment in him. If only he could get a part, any speaking part, maybe that could square things with Mom. Andy had never had an acting lesson, but he had now been around actors for five years. He thought the thing to do was just to be yourself. The irony here is that to be an actor,

This is Dad's first publicity photo, circa 1931, which he sent to his mother. She would keep this photograph on her nightstand until her death. What Dad would never know was that he was always his mother's favorite.

you must "play" someone else, but to get the job, you must be your relaxed, natural self. Actors train for years just to appear nonchalant. Finally Dad said, "What the hell, this ain't Shakespeare. It's just a football movie."

Well, the interview didn't go well — it went great! Andy not only got a part, he got the fourth lead. The film starred Lew Ayres (who also starred in *All Quiet on the Western Front*), William Bakewell, Sally Blane,

The Collegians, *Dad's very first job in Hollywood, circa 1926. Dad is second from left.*

and Andy Devine. Of special interest was the film appearance of the four horsemen All-Americans as themselves. In addition, Notre Dame coach Knute Rockne would play himself in the film. In March 1931, Rockne was flying from South Bend to Los Angeles for the final meeting prior to production, when his plane crashed, killing all aboard. They recast Rockne's part with actor J. Farrell MacDonald.

Andy got along well with everyone, especially the football players. The director liked him so much that he built up his part. A director's dream is for actors to be on time, know their lines and not be a pain in the ass. Andy met such expectations to the letter. The picture was a hit, and Universal offered Andy a one-year contract which he gratefully accepted. The first thing the studio did was loan him out to Columbia Pictures to play a prison inmate in a film called *The Criminal Code.* In "loan outs," a studio puts an actor, director, or a screenwriter under contract at a fixed weekly price. Reasonable guidelines within the contract protect the artist against excessive hours, objectionable types of material, unnecessary risks, etc.

However, after the contract is signed, "Your ass is mine." The studio negotiates all your contracts and, when not using you, tries to rent you out for as much as possible. You go when and where you're told. As a result,

The premiere of A Star is Born *circa 1937 with writer/director William A. Wellman. From left to right: Dorothy "Dottie" Wellman, Cecilia Wellman (Wellman's mother), Dorothy Devine, William Wellman, and Andy Devine.*

you would see Fox contract players at Universal and Warner contract players at Fox. Andy ran this labyrinth without an agent, which was foolish, but soon that would change. After the release of *The Spirit of Notre Dame*, Andy sent a letter to his mother in Kansas along with a photograph of himself from the film. On the photo was the inscription," Mother, hope all my love will cover all the heartaches and worries of the past. With all my love, your son, Andy." That framed photograph was on Amy Ward Devine's nightstand when she died later that year.

It was 1932 and Universal was going to get its money's worth out of Andy. That year alone he made eight pictures for Universal, plus numerous loan outs to Paramount, Columbia and 20th Century-Fox. With all this work, Andy was learning his trade. Some parts were small and

Stagecoach, *circa 1939.*

The Man Who Shot Liberty Valance, *circa 1962.*

insignificant while others were substantial. Of note were *Law and Order* with Walter Huston, in a screenplay written by his son John Huston, and *Impatient Maiden* again with Lew Ayres. Andy's most prestigious film that year was the big budget *The Man from Yesterday*. The film starred Claudette Colbert and Charles Boyer. Andy had a substantial part and received co-star billing. He knew he was in demand and felt confident and comfortable before the camera.

CHAPTER 9

Fat Contract and Romance
1933

It would be a banner year for many reasons. Andy's contract was up for renewal, and Universal had made a fortune off him. He had high hopes for a much bigger contract. After some careful shopping for an agent, he chose Myron Selznick, a former producer who had decided to go into the agency business. Selznick was smart, knew the business and was the brother of producer David O. Selznick. Of course it helped that David was married to Irene Mayer, daughter of Louis B. Mayer, Chairman of M-G-M. Myron got Andy a fat new contract at Universal, and things got better, a lot better. Why? Studio executives think if they're paying an actor more money, then they must put him in bigger and better pictures so they can make bigger profits off of him. That year Andy made seven feature films, all with big stars and co-star billing. He made three films at Universal and loan outs to Paramount, M-G-M, Fox, and RKO.

Of the seven films he made in 1933, two had great significance. *Midnight Mary* starred Loretta Young, under William Wellman's direction. Loretta became a close friend and they got along famously during the filming. Wellman was unique. Known as Wild Bill, he was one of the most outrageous men in Hollywood. He ran away from home at seventeen, flew combat in World War I, directed the first Academy Award-winning picture *Wings*, drank a bit, liked to fight a bit, and had been married four times. Dad truly loved him. Wellman already knew Andy, and when he arrived on the set for the first day of shooting, Wellman introduced him to Loretta by saying, "Stay away from Andy. He's got crabs," (which Dad had). For the rest of their lives, whenever the elegant Loretta would see Dad, she would say with a wink, "How are the little fellas?" Andy and

Wellman would go on to make nine pictures together, and the two men and their wives and children would remain friends forever.

The second significant film of 1933 was *Dr. Bull*, starring Will Rogers and directed by the legendary John Ford. A young girl on the set knew Will Rogers as she too was of Cherokee Indian heritage and was from the same town of Oologah, Oklahoma . She had a small part, but was one of the most beautiful girls Dad had ever seen. While this girl was speaking to Rogers, Andy drifted over to stand near them. Rogers, feeling a little uncomfortable, finally introduced Andy to Dorothy House. It was lunch time, and Rogers suggested that the three of them have lunch together. During lunch Andy was so taken by her beauty and her fresh, enthusiastic view of life that he told her, "Someday I'm going to marry you." Andy was twenty-eight years old, and she was still in high school.

Dorothy House came from a wild and wooly family of six children — three boys and three girls. Her father Jack was a dashing cowboy from Oklahoma with Cherokee blood. He appeared in rodeos from California to Madison Square Garden. Once when Jack was down in Ensenada, Mexico, he met a pretty senorita who accepted his invitation to go for a picnic near the river. One thing led to another, and before long the two were swimming naked when the girl's boyfriend found them and confronted Jack with his pistol. Jack drew his own pistol from under a blanket and killed the man. Unfortunately, the dead boyfriend was Ensenada's Chief of Police. Jack's close friend, Hussong, a bar owner, hid Jack in the attic of his saloon for over a week. Hussong found a fast horse for Jack to ride in the dead of night to Tijuana.

Jack did not return to Mexico for a very long time. Instead, he made his way to Colorado and married a school teacher from Canada. The couple then moved to Los Angeles where Jack had leased some horse property in Burbank. He started supplying the movie studios with horses and wranglers and stuntmen. After a while, Jack brought in cutting horses from Colorado to train and sell as polo ponies. In fact Jack and his three sons were the only nationally ranked all family polo team in the United States. Jack knew Will Rogers, as they both came from the same Indian reservation. Rogers helped Jack establish his presence in all phases of the Hollywood horse business. In 1930 the Los Angeles flood wiped out Jack's Burbank stables, so he purchased property near Griffith Park and built his own home and stables. As his studio business flourished, Jack started involving his children in movies as stuntmen, makeup men, stand-ins, extras, and bit players. It was Dorothy's role as a bit player which led to her meeting Dad.

The courtship didn't go well. Dorothy's parents thought he was too old and she too young. Her brothers were all tough horsemen and gave Andy a hard time, especially her oldest brother Newt. But Andy would not be denied, and in time, even without Dorothy's graduation from high school, her family came around. Andy and Dorothy were married in Las Vegas in October of 1933. The marriage would last until Dad's death some forty-three years later. Over time there would be adjustments to the marriage for both of them. However, Mom was a wonderful asset to the up and coming Andy. She was fun, adventurous, and had a wonderful personality. Everybody loved her, and therefore they liked and respected Andy even more.

CHAPTER 10

Radio
1934

The year started with a bang, as Andy did eight films, four with Universal, and one each with Fox, Warner Bros., RKO, and Paramount. His parts were getting bigger and the films were getting better. He worked with such stars as Ginger Rogers, Irene Dunn, Mary Astor, and Gloria Stewart (remember her from *Titanic*?). Andy was looking for a home. He had become close friends with Bing Crosby, and Bing told him about a small Spanish house across the street from his estate in the Toluca Lake area of Los Angeles. Andy bought the house and he and Mom moved in. Bing also encouraged Andy to join the nearby Lakeside Country Club which was an interesting place. Because many of the actors were under contract, the studio would often require an actor's presence at the studio in the morning, even if he had nothing to do. If by noon an actor had been given no assignment, he could go home. Lakeside was located ten minutes from Warner's, Universal, Republic and Disney. At 12:30 the club would be jumping with everyone who wasn't working. Besides Bing there would be Bob Hope, Gene Autry, and The Marx Brothers. Even the "Munchkins" showed up after the wrap party for *The Wizard of Oz*. There was lunch, golf, and stories with drinks around the big table. Times were good, and Dad was having the time of his life.

In November of that year Dorothy gave birth to my brother Timothy, twelve months after they were married. However, Andy's friends, in kidding him would ask, "Now, Andy, when you married that high school girl in Vegas, did you two stop on the way there or on the way back?"

Andy's contract at Universal was for films only and his weekends were free. In 1935 radio was the rage, and it was performed live on Sunday afternoon. Therefore, radio work didn't conflict with Andy's studio contract. Among the most popular radio performers were Fred Allen and Fibber McGee and Molly, but the highest rated was Jack Benny. In spite of later issues, Bing Crosby was the person who got Andy into radio. In 1935 Bing had his own show, sponsored by Woodbury Soap. Bing announced to his radio audience that next week Andy Devine would be his guest. Well, the Woodbury Soap people hit the ceiling, stating that Andy's raspy voice was unacceptable, and they refused to have him on the show. The next week Bing showed up with Dad and told the sponsors

On radio with Jack Benny, Bing Crosby and others, circa 1942.

that if Andy didn't go on, then he wasn't going on. Because the show was live, the sponsors had to give in. Dad was an enormous hit and that was the start of his very successful radio career.

Because of the Crosby show, Dad would commence a six-year run as a regular on the Sunday afternoon Jack Benny radio program that was sponsored by Jell-O. Dad found out that acting with your voice and read-

With "Froggy the Gremlin" from his television series Andy's Gang, *circa 1956.*

ing off of a script are totally different, but realized he was very good at it. Live radio required more voice inflection, precise timing, and the ability to deal instantly with mistakes and accidents because it was live. Jack Benny was a real vaudeville pro with impeccable timing. He really couldn't do much, but what he did, he did perfectly. Benny was smart, down to earth, and kind. Although he portrayed himself as a tightwad, he paid very well and gave very expensive gifts. He and Andy would never be close friends, but they enjoyed working together, and it was on the Benny show that Dad met Phil Harris.

Wonga Phillip Harris was from Nashville and had a captivating persona. Just seeing him made you smile. He became a band leader and took his band from coast to coast, developing quite a following. After a while he became a singer in his own band. He really couldn't sing; he would just do these up-tempo tunes and kind of talk-sing and let his personality shine through. Everybody, including Benny, loved him, and he was on Benny's show for many years. Benny, Andy, and Harris even made a film together. It was called *Buck Benny Rides Again*. It was the dumbest movie you'll ever see, and it was wonderful! Dad spent a lot of time with

As Captain Andy in the New York musical presentation of Showboat, *circa 1957.*

his San Fernando Valley friends. Norris Goff, whom Andy met through Benny, was the wealthiest of the group which included Harris and Gable. For years he had a radio show called *Lum and Abner*, and his contract called for him to be paid $5,000 per week. Goff purchased nine holes of a defunct country club and built a fabulous home. On the remainder of the estate he built a large pool area, stables and a horse arena. Goff would later sell the property to John Wayne.

These men hunted, fished, and drank together. Very late one evening, after a night of drinking, they all decided to go fishing. Goff's houseman drove the four to Lake Sherwood where they all got into a rowboat and continued drinking. Suddenly they started seeing various brightly colored animals. There were pink monkeys, bright yellow pigeons, and green tigers. They thought they were hallucinating and threw the remaining booze overboard. As the sun was slowly coming up, a boat came from around the bend and an assistant director admonished the men for being in the way. The man explained they were in the principal shooting of the film *Jungle Book*. When asked about the rainbow-colored animals, the assistant responded they were just props. The four rowed back to the car. No booze, no fish, hangovers to come. The men voted — Gable rowed.

Personal appearance at Barnum & Bailey Circus with renowned clown Emmett Kelly.

Andy appeared on Goff's live radio show *Lum and Abner* for five years. Often Andy did both *Lum and Abner* and the Benny show on the same Sunday. During this time Andy met the Jell-O ad rep for the Benny show. This little rumpled man from Chicago worked for an agency that specialized in food products. He had a quick wit and a great personality and he and Dad became close friends. He confided in Dad that very soon

Left: Bing Crosby in black-face. Right: Mom and Dad.

he planned to start his own agency. Their friendship would have a large impact on Dad's television career in years to come. The man's name was Leo Burnett.

The network then gave Andy two of his own musical variety shows. They were called the *Melody Round-up* and *The Fitch Bandwagon*, which was sometimes co-hosted with Phil Harris and Cliff Arquette. Legend has it *The Fitch Bandwagon* was canceled after one year because old man Fitch died, and when young Fitch took over, he told the agency that he didn't want to advertise on Sunday because "that's when everyone is playing polo."

Live radio shows continued to be very popular until the early fifties when television took over. To see the broadcast of these old radio shows was thrilling. They were all set in theaters at the radio network complex. These theaters held about 300 people, and the patrons would wait in line, purchase tickets, and then enter the theater about 45 minutes before the show started. Inside the theater was a full orchestra with a conductor, two sound effects men (walking on gravel, closing doors, etc.), and the "warm-up" man. The warm-up man would come out about twenty minutes before the show and advise the audience about making noise and other simple rules. He would go over the plot of the day's show in humorous fashion and introduce the guest stars. Then he would tell a few jokes and

Hoagy Carmichael at the piano.

get everybody ready. He would then introduce the principal stars, and they would take their places before their respective microphones. A large sign on the wall would light up, ON THE AIR. The orchestra would play the show's theme song, and the actors would begin. It was all very exciting for both the audience and the actors who were performing live. The best part were the screw-ups. The actors had to be very quick and have confidence in one another. An actor might "flub" a line which would change the entire context of the story. Could the other actors save him? Mostly yes, but after an actor had "winged it," there were great sighs of relief and laughter at the commercial break. The studio audience loved it, as they felt personally involved with the actors and part of this live, high wire act.

Ken Murray and Bob Hope

CHAPTER 11

Extremes

1935

While Andy was making a big impact on radio, his film career was progressing. He made a total of seven films, three for Universal, and two each for Fox and Paramount. It was becoming evident that the better pictures were coming from the other studios, and that Universal was now using Dad for his marquee value and sticking him in wherever they could. That year Andy made *Farmer Takes A Wife* with Henry Fonda and Janet Gaynor. Andy found Fonda, who was from New York, a bit formal and serious. On the set Fonda liked to take long naps while sitting in his chair. Andy told Fonda there was a grip who didn't like actors, and when an actor was asleep the grip would come over and piss on his shoes. The next time Fonda was asleep, Andy came over and dropped little pebbles on Fonda's shoes. Fonda woke up, jumped in the air, and yelled, thinking he'd just been pissed on. Everyone got a laugh and Fonda was a good sport. Andy and Gaynor became close friends, and in the next two years they made two more pictures together, including *A Star is Born*. Also that year Andy made two pictures with his old roommate "Slim" Summerville.

Andy and Dorothy had moved into their Toluca Lake house and were adjusting to having son Timothy. Dad was spending a lot of free time with Crosby, fishing and playing golf, and Mom was getting to know Bing's wife Dixie and was dealing with her alcoholism. When Bing Crosby married Dixie Lee, she was only eighteen and was a bigger star than he was. Dixie was a knockout. However, soon after the marriage, things took off for Bing, and he wanted Dixie to give up her career to concentrate on him, the house and future kids. Mom, at twenty-one, was only four years younger than Dixie, but was ill-equipped to deal with her famous neighbor's issues. Years later, as things deteriorated between Bing and Andy, Dixie had a party at our Van Nuys ranch. She called it the "Crapped on by Crosby" party. It included everyone who had been cut off or betrayed by

Bing throughout the years. The event had quite a turnout, and everyone had a great time, especially Dixie. Dixie continued drinking a lot, as did Bing. They had a tumultuous and sometimes unhappy marriage. Dixie died in 1952 at the age of forty of ovarian cancer.

The year 1936 was highlighted by further extremes. Andy made five pictures and, as the parts got larger, the list of films got shorter. That year also established Andy, like Walter Brennan, as an actor who could go from big budget "A" list films to B pictures with ease. Andy made a second picture with Janet Gaynor, *Small Town Girl*, which was again directed by Bill Wellman. Then the impossible happened. Irving Thalberg (the boy wizard of M-G-M) personally chose Andy for a major role in *Romeo and Juliet*. This role firmly established Andy as an "A" list actor. First, he was chosen by Thalberg. Second, he was co-starring with the most accomplished actors in films. Third, *Romeo and Juliet* would have the largest budget of any M-G-M film ever produced. On top of that, Thalberg's wife Norma Shearer was to star. The all-star cast included Leslie Howard, John Barrymore, Edna May Oliver, Basil Rathbone, C. Aubrey Smith, and…Andy Devine. Dad worked on the film for eight weeks and became a close friend of Norma's. That year her husband Irving Thalberg died of pneumonia as a result of a congenital heart condition. About twenty years later our family would run into Norma and her new husband Marty Arrougé on a skiing vacation. She and Dad reminisced, and I skied with Marty.

Over the years both Norma and Marty would remain my personal friends. It all took place when I was driving home through the back streets of Beverly Hills. One day I saw Marty and Norma walking together holding hands. They were very close, but she was losing her eyesight. I stopped to say hello and then we would walk together for a couple of blocks. This ritual would continue for a number of years and was pure joy.

To appreciate extreme contrasts, immediately following *Romeo and Juliet*, Dad was cast in a film called *Yellowstone*. It was another low budget stinker from Universal where Andy played a robber trying to steal hidden money at the Yellowstone Lodge. The film takes place in wintertime, and the robbers are caught when a geyser erupts, freezing the culprits. When under contract to Universal, remember, they own you. It was during this time that Mom and Dad were invited to numerous social events. Dad at thirty-one was still a physical presence. He was very coordinated and very strong. At one particular party a man came up from behind Dad, put his arms around him and said, "I understand you're one of the toughest men in Hollywood." Without turning around, Dad replied," You better believe what people tell ya." The man released his grip and Dad turned around. When Dad faced the man, he didn't know who he was. The tall slender man extended his hand and said, "I'm Howard Hughes, and I've always wanted to meet you." Dad was fascinated by this famous, bright, unorthodox man. They talked airplanes and movies and motorcycles for hours. Dad had an unforgettable time, but never spoke to Hughes again.

There were now both good and bad films under Dad's belt, but in the next few years he would make some of the most revered and long-lasting films ever made. Even the Universal parts were getting better. The most significant film of that year was *A Star is Born*. The film was written by William Wellman (who also directed), Dorothy Parker, and Robert Carson. Throughout Wellman's long career the Academy would nominate him numerous times for directing. However, his only win was for the screenplay of this film. The film starred Janet Gaynor, Fredric March, Adolphe Menjou, and Andy Devine. Dad had a real shot at this picture as Wellman had become a close friend, and his agent Myron Selznick was the brother of the producer. The picture opened at Grauman's Chinese Theatre in Hollywood and Radio City Music Hall in New York on the same day. It was a big hit and won numerous awards, including color photography, as it was the first feature film in color. Of course, this timeless story has been remade twice.

The next film was *Double or Nothing* with Bing Crosby and Martha Ray. Dad and Bing were still close which made the shoot fun. It was the story about a dying millionaire who wanted to give away his fortune if he could find an honest person. It was during this time that Dad joined a neighborhood group called The Toluca Lake Marching and Chowder Society. It was made up of composer Johnny Mercer, composer and arranger John Scott Trotter, comedian Jerry Colona, actor Tyrone Power, Bing Crosby, Bob Hope and others who lived nearby. About once a month or so they would gather and put on a show. It was really just for fun. However, there would usually be some charity tie-in to help with Crosby's image.

The year rounded out with *The Road Back*, a takeoff on *All Quiet on the Western Front* and *You're a Sweetheart*, a musical with Alice Faye and George Murphy. Andy started putting on weight as he was living a very social life, eating whatever he wanted, and drinking more than usual. He felt that life was moving just a little too fast and, because of this, decided to sell the Toluca Lake house. He and Mom decided to buy a ranch farther out in the Valley as they both wanted to start living a simpler life.

Dad was sensitive, and intuitive. He wasn't particularly ambitious, but succeeded because he was so damn likeable. He cared little about a man's station in life, but was profoundly influenced by a person's true intellect. I have been with him when he was bored to tears speaking to a Harvard-educated Cabinet Member, yet intimidated when speaking with a wise plumber. Because of his god-given talent, his career just seemed to fall into place. He was extremely honest, with little sense of ego, and that's another reason why people were drawn to him. I knew that if he was aware I did something wrong, he would counsel me. But if I did something intentionally wrong, he would punish me.

The year was good for films. It started out with *In Old Chicago* for 20th Century-Fox. At the time it was the most expensive film ever made by Daryl Zanuck. The film starred Tyrone Power, Don Ameche, Alice Faye, Brian Donlevy and Andy. It was about Mrs. O'Leary's cow and the Chicago Fire. The film was a big hit with the final fire scene being as big as the fire scene in *Gone with the Wind*. The next film was *Dr. Rhythm* with Bing Crosby. During the making of the film, Bing got into a serious auto accident while drinking, and as a result he was required to spend nights in jail. It became a humorous studio ritual for the police to pick Bing up in the afternoon and deliver him back the next morning. The remainder of 1938 was filled with four more pictures at Universal, and one each at Fox and Paramount.

CHAPTER 12

Stagecoach

1939

Andy had worked for director John Ford on *Dr. Bull*, the film where he met my mother. Ford was a tyrant and didn't like actors. He was quoted as saying, "All actors are crap!" Westerns were still out of favor because of the big budget flop *The Big Trail*. The film put Fox Pictures into bankruptcy (it then became 20th Century-Fox), starred John Wayne and almost ended his career.

Ford fell in love with a short story called "The Stage to Lordsburg." He enlisted his long time collaborator Dudley Nichols to write the screenplay, which Ford loved. At the same time Ford had become familiar with Monument Valley in southern Utah, and thought it would be the perfect place to shoot this picture. The problem was money. Because westerns were out of favor and financing was impossible, Ford was at an impasse. The studios might compromise if they could get Gary Cooper, but at his price they couldn't afford to shoot in Utah. Most westerns were shot in and around the outskirts of Los Angeles and looked cheap.

Ford went to producer Walter Wanger (the man whose lap I had occupied) and convinced him that the exteriors in Utah were as important as any big star. Ford further stressed that this was an ensemble piece, and the supporting players were as important as the lead. Although he tried to hide it, Ford had great affection for John Wayne, as he had known him since he was a grip and an extra. After some conversations about using Lloyd Nolan, the studio cast Wayne as the Ringo Kid. Wayne was paid less than any of the other principal actors.

For the stage driver Ford wanted Ward Bond, who was a Ford favorite. However, Bond didn't know how to drive a "six-up" team, and they didn't have time to teach him. Dad was suggested as he had the experience with a team of horses and had the hand strength needed. Ford remembered Andy from *Dr. Bull* and recalled he wasn't difficult. Great effort went into casting the other parts because Ford knew the shoot would be rigorous and uncomfortable and only wanted actors he had worked with before.

The exterior shoot in Utah was rough. It was late 1938 and Monument Valley was in the middle of nowhere. It was all dirt roads, lousy accommodations, cold, dusty, and windy with creatures. But the "dailies" were breathtaking and everyone in the company got along and had confidence in Ford's judgment. Upon returning to Los Angeles, Ford showed the "dailies" to studio executives. One of the most dramatic scenes was the Indians chasing the stagecoach across the dry lake bed. At the screening a studio vice president asked Ford, "Why didn't the Indians just shoot the horses?" Ford replied, "Because that would be the end of the picture!"

The entire cast returned to Los Angeles to shoot interiors. Ford had his own style of shooting interiors. He would use low ceilings to confine the actors. Since interior lighting usually comes from above, it required Ford to light indirectly. Planned or not, this created a film noir interior atmosphere. Ford felt that with the interiors being claustrophobic, the exteriors would be more grand. The remaining exteriors were shot at Corrigan Ranch outside Los Angeles. The day they floated the stagecoach across the river it was difficult and dangerous. At the end of the day Dad wanted to celebrate. It was January 24th, 1939, and he wanted to take his very pregnant wife to dinner at the Hollywood Brown Derby. He called Gable to see if he and the girlfriend he adored could join them.

Dad was going to ride the crest of *Stagecoach* which would become a blockbuster. He was gaining unexpected status in Hollywood and wanted this momentum to continue. But a big problem loomed ahead that was so subtle no one could see it. It could end his career and this problem would be…

CHAPTER 13

Universal Stinkers
1940

At Universal Dad was still under contract. They were paying him a lot and were working him a lot, and they would put him into anything. They didn't care about his career; like any chattel, they only cared about how much money he could earn for the studio. In the year 1940 alone Dad made eleven films. Eight were for Universal with three loan outs to Fox, Warner's, and Paramount. The loan outs were great. Dad worked with James Cagney, Pat O'Brien, Fred McMurray, and Marlene Dietrich. The highlight was *Buck Benny Rides Again* at Paramount. It was special because it was just so damn much fun. The Universal stinkers were *Tropic Fury*, *Danger On Wheels*, *Hot Steel*, and on and on. Universal would cast a film with whatever contract player was available, irrespective if the actor was the correct physical type. Actually it was pretty funny. Dad's last Universal picture in 1940 was *Trail of the Vigilantes*. It starred the slightly built Franchot Tone, known for drawing room melodramas, and the diminutive Russian-born Mischa Auer, both playing the lead cowboys. Why? Because all other contract actors were working.

On the home front Dad was taking stock of himself as he continued to gain weight. He now weighed over 300 pounds. He quit drinking and never drank again. He started working out at Frankie Van's gym at Universal, and watched his diet. He actually lost weight, but it would be a battle he would wage the rest of his life. Norris Goff and Gable also had weight problems, and the three would kid each other continually. Somebody gave Dad a weight-loss machine called a "Tiger-Stretch" which had the motto, "Have you ever seen a fat tiger?" Whoever was in possession of this cumbersome machine would give it to one of the other two at Christmas. If the possessor thought the gag was too current, he would simply wait a year or two. The owner would take the thing apart and disguise it as anything but what it was, so as to sustain the surprise.

The pieces of the machine would be wrapped and sent by some of the finest stores in Beverly Hills, New York, or god knows where, just to fool the recipient. This charade went on for many years and gave many laughs to all involved.

The winds of war were blowing and Dad was very busy. He made nine pictures in 1941, but one big thing changed; no more loan-outs and there would be no more loan-outs for the next six years. I really don't know why; however, I can only speculate that Universal had put him in so many second-rate films that it cheapened his marquee value. Other studios would not pay the price that Universal was asking, because they were paying Dad very well. Dad had his own philosophy and that was, "Just keep working." He told me this many times as he said making a film is a collaborative effort, and you couldn't tell if a film was good even after you've shot it. He said even good films can fail because of release dates, competition, or external factors that are beyond anyone's control. Dad said low budget films with a sound script can be good if there is competent directing and the principal players have chemistry.

Irrespective of the material, Dad was meticulous when reading and blocking a script. He had this red and blue double-ended pencil and with a ruler would go through an entire script drawing a neat red box around his dialogue, then underlining the key words. In the script, when others were speaking to him, he would draw a neat blue box and underline those key words. Dad said that sometimes a really good script would just grab him and he would beg to do the part. His favorite scripts were, *A Star is Born*, *Stagecoach*, *The Red Badge of Courage*, and *The High and the Mighty*.

Dad didn't get the part in *The High and the Mighty*. I think both Wayne and Wellman (who co-produced) wanted Dad, but thought he was just too physically large to play either the dying millionaire or the tormented navigator. I read both the book and the screenplay, and thought the film would be terrific, but difficult. Remember, ninety percent of the film was shot inside an airplane, and to keep the drama high was no easy task. Wellman (who was nominated for an Academy Award) did a masterful job. Dimitri Tiomkin's score (which won the Oscar) kept the drama high and made the film a classic. The film cost about one and a half million, and at eight and a half million was the highest grossing film that year. Wayne, Wellman, and (author) Gann had a percentage of the profits, and all did very well financially.

In 1941 Dad would make nine more films for Universal, most of which were the standard fare, the exceptions being *The Flame of New Orleans* with Marlene Dietrich and *Badlands of Dakota* with Robert Stack,

Richard Dix, and the infamous Francis Farmer. That year Dad made six more films with Richard Arlen, with such titles as *Lucky Devils*, and *Road Agent*. The voluptuous Maria Montez was one of Dad's frequent co-stars at Universal. She really couldn't act or sing or dance. She mainly stood around and wore as few clothes as the censors would allow. As a child I had a picture taken sitting on her lap; I wasn't looking into her eyes. She developed quite a following until she put on a little too much weight and Universal sent her packing.

During the war years everyone was on edge. Although Universal made numerous second rate films, the studio was strong financially, and wanted to continue productions. Dad had been under contract for eleven years and had made some eighty films. In 1944 Dad's agent, Myron Selznick, died at the age of forty-five. At five foot six inches tall, Selznick had become one of the most powerful agents in Hollywood and was actually wealthier than his more famous brother David. Upon Selznick's death, Dad immediately hired the Louis Shurr-Al Melnick Agency to represent him. Their biggest client was Bob Hope, but they had numerous clients like Dad. Their claim to fame was discovering both Kim Novak and Debbie Reynolds. "Uncle Al" would represent Dad until 1967, when Dad and I would change everything.

Dad hated confrontations and never had any disputes with the studio. However his present contract was coming to an end. In late 1945 he went to speak with producer Walter Wanger. Dad liked Wanger and the feeling was mutual. Dad asked Wanger if there was anything better on the horizon or would it just be more of the same. Wanger said that Universal would be making the biggest budget film it had made in ten years. He said it would have an all-star cast and Dad would be in it. Wanger said it would be a location picture to be shot in Oregon and thought there might be a small part for Dad's oldest son. The film would be called *Canyon Passage*. After fifteen years it would be the last contract picture Dad would make for Universal. After all that time of being under contract, Andy Devine was going to be cast aside. Although he was well known, the old insecurities surfaced as he had no idea what the future would hold.

CHAPTER 14

Roy Rogers
1947

Dad's Universal contract was coming to an end; however that wasn't good enough. The studio wanted to get rid of him right now. I was only eight years old when Dad asked me if I wanted to go with him to the studio. Not Universal but another studio, Paramount. Adjacent to the Paramount lot was a facility called Western Costume. It was owned by a conglomerate of studios who would all share the costumes. It was a smart idea and eliminated duplication. When Dad and I got there, we were met by Lon Chaney, Jr. who was also on the chopping block. Dad and Lon were to wear horse and bear costumes and never be seen. The studio thought this would be so humiliating that Dad and Lon would refuse, thereby nullifying their contracts. Not Dad. He wore the costume, did the movie, and no one knew who was inside the horse. His contract was fulfilled. On the way home from his horse costume fitting, Dad explained why he was doing this. "A deal's a deal, and money is money, and no studio is going to take advantage of me." But his contract finally ended.

Now Dad was out of work. Herbert J. Yates owned Republic Studios, whose stock-in-trade were "B" movies, usually westerns. During the late thirties, his biggest star was Gene Autry, the singing cowboy. In early 1940 Gene walked out on his Republic contract as he joined the Army Air Force as a pilot. The military was Autry's out as he hated Yates and wanted to terminate his contract. Few people know this, but Gene Autry was a true military hero. As a command pilot, he flew numerous and dangerous combat missions in B-24 "Liberator" bombers. With Autry gone, Yates needed a new singing cowboy. Yates found two from the western singing group The Sons of the Pioneers. Yates was going to pick either Bob Noland or Leonard Slye to replace Autry. For whatever reason, Yates picked Slye and changed his name to Roy Rogers.

During Dad's last years at Universal, he sort of "worked his way down" to Republic's level. Republic was interested in signing Dad to a short-term contract. They wanted him to be a new and fresh sidekick for Rogers. For financial security, Dad liked contracts, so he signed with the knowledge that Herbert J. Yates had a terrible reputation. But who among the studio heads was a saint? The year 1947 was truly a time of turnabouts. That year Dad did three pictures with Rogers which were shot very fast (in about three weeks). Then Dad was "loaned back" to Universal for three more films with Jon Hall.

In Dad's contract with Republic, it was stipulated that Rogers' horse Trigger would have second billing to Rogers, but ahead of all other actors. This contract requirement amused Dad. Studios don't own horses; independent contractors provide them. This is what my grandfather did. Fat Jones was the largest supplier of horses and wranglers in the movie business. A golden palomino stallion named Golden Cloud made his film debut as Olivia de Havilland's (Maid Marion) horse in *The Adventures of Robin Hood.* Rogers was told he could go to the various stables and pick a horse he liked and felt comfortable riding. He picked Golden Cloud. The horse was beautiful, smart, and with his handler could do numerous tricks. Republic rented the horse for Rogers' first picture, then Rogers personally purchased the horse for $2,500, on the installment plan of $200 per month. Rogers renamed him Trigger, and the horse would appear in some 188 films. Trigger would become the most famous animal that ever lived.

During '47 and '48 Dad made eight pictures for Republic. Six were with Rogers and two with an actor known as "Wild Bill" Elliott. Elliott was a taciturn actor with a great voice (there's a combination). He had this judgmental look and kind of strolled through a film staring at people. During Dad's brief time at Republic, he befriended a young writer. This young man was thirty-four, from New York and had written some plays, short stories, and radio scripts. He came to Hollywood, not to write for films, but to try and sell his completed novel. It was about his time in the infantry in World War II. He got a job on the Roy Rogers films as a script rewrite boy just to eat. On low budget films, when shooting a scene, a script rewrite boy follows the director, and when a line is misspoken (but it doesn't affect the scene or the plot) he just rewrites the script.

Dad liked this well-built Jewish kid from Brooklyn. They frequently had lunch together, and Dad introduced him to as many people as possible to further his career or perhaps help him sell his book. Dad liked him because he was smart and loved to tell stories. Dad said to him, "If you can write like you can bull shit, you'll go far." Within a few months the young man published the novel about his war experiences. It was called *The Young Lions*, and the man's name was Irwin Shaw. Dad never told me this story, but in 1982 at a bar in New York City, Irwin Shaw did.

I had briefly met Irwin Shaw a year before. I was meeting some friends at our hotel bar and there was Irwin Shaw sitting by himself in a large corner booth. I introduced myself and Shaw asked me to join him.

Roy Rogers and Andy Devine in Under California Stars, *circa 1948.*

Because of my last name, he asked me if I was related to Andy Devine. He went on and on about what a wonderful guy Dad was and the fun they had on the Roy Rogers films. Within a few minutes, my friends from Chicago joined me. Because of Shaw's fame in writing "Rich Man, Poor Man," they enjoyed meeting him. Shaw then explained he was there to meet his literary agent.

Within moments this diminutive, very well dressed older man with interesting glasses arrived. I was well aware of who he was, but my friends from Chicago had no idea. The agent's name was Irving "Swifty" Lazar. Shaw was now on his third round of drinks, and when he introduced Swifty to my Chicago friends, he slurred his name a bit and my friends thought his name was Shorty. They slapped him on the back and said,

"Hi, Shorty!" which thoroughly pissed off Swifty Lazar, and Shaw could have cared less.

Swifty then admonished Irwin Shaw, saying he and his friends were a "bunch of assholes" and that he was going to 21 to meet Richard Nixon. After he left, we all had a great laugh. When it was time to leave, I said my goodbyes, and Irwin Shaw shook my hand and with his other hand placed on my shoulder, he looked at me and said, "I'm a Jew with a heart of an Irishman. And you're an Irishman with a heart of a Jew." We embraced and I never saw him again.

In 1949 *The Last Bandit* was the last picture Dad would do for Republic. It starred Bill Elliot, Forrest Tucker, and Jack Holt. It was better than most Republic films as it took six weeks to shoot rather than three. At the end of the film they told him his contract was up and they would no longer need him. After some twenty years of having a long term contract as a safety net, Dad was really on his own and didn't like it. In addition, because of the advent of television and the "Red Scare," film production had cut way back, and few were working. Dad made the comment to a reporter, "I love being an actor, because you get two vacations a year. Unfortunately they're both six months long."

CHAPTER 15

Television
1950

In 1950, after the termination of the Republic contract, Dad quickly got two movies. They were *The Traveling Saleslady* with Joan Davis at Columbia and *Never a Dull Moment* with Irene Dunne, Fred McMurray, and Natalie Wood at RKO. Although Natalie lived nearby in Van Nuys, it was on this film that I first met her. She would attend (infrequently) both Robert Fulton Jr. High and Van Nuys High. In the late fifties when I was doing my film at Warner Bros., she would often come to visit. We simply talked like two kids about our friends and high school things, rather than two people (one famous, one not) working as actors at a studio. She was unpretentious, a little shy, and very nice.

That year Dad's agent got a call from a producer nobody had heard of. His name was William Broidy. He had the rights to the name Wild Bill Hickok and wanted to make a television series of the same name. He had an agreement with an extremely handsome former RKO contract player whose career was in the toilet named Guy Madison. Madison had run the gamut of pretty-boy roles, and he was such a wooden actor that bigger film roles would never come his way. However, in the fifties TV was often a safe haven for marginal actors. In addition, Broidy got him cheap.

He offered the second lead to Burl Ives, but Ives turned it down. He then offered the role to Dad, and Dad accepted, but for more money than Madison. However the problem was financing — Broidy didn't have any. Dad asked if he could help, and they said sure. So Dad called the little man from Chicago. Leo Burnett, whose agency was now flourishing, said, " For you, Andy, I'll get Kellogg's to buy the pilot and twelve more weeks if it's any good." Hats off to "Uncle Al," Dad's agent. He got Dad a nice piece of the show in addition to his salary. The show was a hit and ran for seven years. Kellogg's and the Burnett agency were on board the whole time.

Guy Madison was pleasant, uncomplicated, and vulnerable. He came from a small town (Pumpkin Center) and was discovered at nineteen just after he finished his tour of duty in the Merchant Marines. However, his lack of education or sophistication wasn't his real problem. It was his charisma; sadly, he didn't have any. If only he had been more like his long time stand-in and stunt double, Dick Farnsworth. Now there was an interesting man with an abundance of charisma. In his later years Dick Farnsworth became an actor and would eventually be nominated for an Academy Award. Another big problem for Madison was his wife. He was married to actress Gail Russell, who was as beautiful a woman as you have ever seen. However, she was a chronic alcoholic, just like her mother. She was working a lot, and because she was so young, the booze hadn't caught up with her looks. John Wayne took a very special interest in Gail and had her co-star with him in two films, *The Angel and the Badman* (1947) and *Wake of the Red Witch* (1948). However, her drinking continued and Guy asked Mom if she would help. So Mom brought her home and got her sober. Mom kept her busy and she stayed with us for over a week. Then she disappeared. Mom did this twice, then gave up. Madison finally divorced her, and she died at thirty-six, alone in a one-room apartment in Los Angeles.

On the Hickok series the ad rep for the Burnett agency was a man named Donald Tennant. Don was a creative genius and the creative head of this now large agency. A few of his creations were The Marlboro Man, The Jolly Green Giant, and The Pillsbury Doughboy. However, his first love was movies, and for Don it was a thrill just being on the set. For fun, Dad got him a small part as a bad man. His appearance on the screen was hysterical. Don and his wife Barbara became very close family friends, and in 1955 they named their newborn son Andy. Andy Tennant is now an established writer and director for television and motion pictures.

Dad was more popular than ever because of television. As a result, he was in big demand for guest spots on radio and television, plus there were numerous public appearances. However, there was a downside. He worked six to seven days a week, about twelve hours a day, and for over five years I rarely saw him.

CHAPTER 16

Special Films
1952

With all the films Dad had made, he had become very well known. But he never dreamed of the exposure that the *Wild Bill Hickok* television series would bring. Besides the weekly television show, there was a *Wild Bill* radio show, comic books, and games. Millions of Kellogg's cereal boxes would have Dad's name and likeness on the cover. There wouldn't be a place Dad could go without being recognized. The money would be better than ever, and he would have a contract which would give him the security he desired.

The *Wild Bill* series debuted in the fall, and they had a contract with Kellogg's for thirteen weeks. The show had been on for only a few weeks and the ratings were negligible. It was Halloween night and Dad got home around five, which was earlier than normal. All he wanted to do was take a shower and relax. But, no. Mother reminded him that last year he'd been out of work for eight months, and now he had all these television fans. Mom insisted that the Trick-or-Treat children should be greeted by Dad. So he put back on his sweaty, thirty-five pound buckskin jacket and his cowboy hat and prepared to welcome the children. Mom had picked some big red apples for Dad to give them as treats. I was standing near Dad when the first doorbell rang. When the door opened, we saw the cutest little kid dressed as a bumble bee. His big sister was close behind. Dad welcomed the little bumble bee, "Hi, partner." The kid replied, "Trick or treat." "Well, this is for you," and Dad dropped one of the big apples into the kid's open paper sack. The little kid looked into his sack, then looked up at Dad and said, " I don't know why an old fat man like you is wearing a cowboy suit, but you just broke all my cookies, you big jerk !" Dad politely closed the door and decided to take his shower.

There was another benefit that came with Dad's television contract. He could do any other outside work provided it didn't interfere with the series. During the years Dad was shooting the Hickok series he made seven feature films. Of these, four were memorable. It was a tribute to Dad's worth that in making these feature films the producers had to accommodate Dad's TV schedule which had contractual priority. The back stories behind the making of these films were memorable because they involved by far the most interesting people Dad had worked with.

I was in the kitchen at the house when the phone rang. When I answered, I heard a voice the likes of which I'd never heard before. It was as if the caller was God, doing Shakespeare. "H e l l o...May...I...please...speak...to...Mr. Devine." I asked who was calling, and the voice replied, "Well...this...is...his...old...friend...John...John...Huston." I called Dad and handed him the phone. They talked for almost an hour. When Dad hung up, I asked what that was all about. Dad laughed, shook his head and said John Huston is the absolute king of bullshit. He said that John went on and on about his love for his father (Academy Award winner Walter Huston) and how Walter truly loved Andy (they had worked together on the film *Law and Order*). John said when he bought the story *The Red Badge of Courage*, he had his father in mind for this part. But, because Walter had passed on, the only one for this part was "you, yes, you, Andy." However, and here came the money part, they could only pay so much because they had a tight budget.

Huston continued, "You know Walter would have understood and taken less money." Huston didn't know it, but Dad had already read the script and loved it. He told John to save his breath. "I'll do the picture, and I'll call my agent and tell him about the money." Two weeks later Dad worked for just three days on *The Red Badge of Courage* as the Happy Soldier. His performance was wonderful and it was something he was always proud of. In spite of Huston's bullshit, Dad liked him and saw him as a great talent.

My own encounter with John Huston had nothing to do with films. As an adult, I had been casually dating his ex-wife Celeste ("Ce Ce" was a character in her own right) and she told me what a cheap bastard and scoundrel John Huston was. I was flying back from New York and John Huston and I were both in a rather empty First Class. The flight attendants were extremely pretty and Huston completely dominated all their time. As I was departing the plane, Huston was still hustling the flight attendants. When I entered the terminal from the covered gangway, there was an electric car with the sign 'John Huston.' I said, "I'm John Huston and my limo is in front." When I got to my car, I thanked the Skycap and gave him a tip. He said he enjoyed my films.

Over the years Dad made numerous films with director William
Wellman. Dad had also made many films with John Wayne. John Wayne
and Wellman were business partners and had participated in, as well as
co-produced, a host of films together. But these three friends had never all
worked on the same film together. *Island in the Sky* would be the first and
only film the three would work on at the same time. It was a treat for Dad.

Island in the Sky was the first Ernest K. Gann book I ever read. I loved
his style of writing because you had the feeling that he had really been
there (which he had). It was a simple story about a C-47 plane that gets
lost near the Arctic Circle and the crew's effort to survive. While this
takes place, the crew's fellow pilots are in the air looking for their lost
comrades. I went to the studio once as I loved the airplane sets. I also went
with Dad the day he shot his swimming sequence (that's right, swimming)
at the Hollywood YMCA pool. Although Dad was large, I'd forgotten
what a good swimmer he was.

It was 1953, and I remember the night the film previewed. It was in
Westwood (near UCLA) and all the principals and their families were
invited. The Wellmans and most of their seven kids were there, and they
were like a force of nature. They were all attractive, loud, and made broad
gestures. They seemed to be supremely confident, and what I admired
most is they were all having such a good time. I hoped I'd get to know
them better some day. *Island in the Sky* did fairly well at the box office,
but more importantly, it established a solid relationship between Wayne,
Wellman, and Gann. Their next picture, *The High and the Mighty*, would
be a blockbuster.

In early 1956 Dad got a call from Jack Webb who was making a film
called *Pete Kelley's Blues.* Jack Webb was a journeyman actor who created
a radio show called *Dragnet.* It went on for many years and then became
a hit television series. Because of the show's high ratings, Webb had
leverage with the studios. He loved jazz and wanted to produce, direct,
and star in a Prohibition era crime drama set in a jazz club. His casting criteria were simple; he hired the people he liked, and he liked Dad.
Webb also liked Ella Fitzgerald and Peggy Lee, and he put these two
jazz icons into actual acting roles. Lee was so good she was nominated
for an Academy Award.

Webb hired every top jazz musician on the west coast to work on the
film, and the music was unbelievable. If it was an easy day, they would
play after work. Dad said you've never experienced better impromptu
jazz sessions in your life. Imagine sitting around with a dozen musicians
including, Dick Cathcart, Moe Schneider, Matty Matlock, and Nick

Fatool with Ella Fitzgerald and Peggy Lee taking turns singing. Jack Webb was in heaven. The rest of the cast included Janet Leigh, Edmond O'Brien, and Lee Marvin, plus numerous well-known character actors, including a young Jayne Mansfield. For a nice change, Dad played a well dressed cop who was a little crooked.

The film was released to mixed reviews and modest success. The problem with the film was Webb. He was a lousy actor because he was so stiff. On his TV show, *Dragnet*, he could get by playing a marionette police detective, but on the big screen he was terrible. Over the years I got to know Webb at a small bar and restaurant in West Hollywood called Dominick's. He was smart, funny and a really good guy. The irony was that, aside from his acting, Jack Webb was a top notch film director. Everybody including Dad thought so.

The last memorable film Dad did during the Hickok years was *Around the World in Eighty Days*. Mike Todd was a Broadway impresario who had gone broke a few times. He was a fearless salesman with an ego to match. He had a vision of making the blockbuster of all blockbusters. Show business is much like the real estate business in that the real control is in owning or controlling the "property." In real estate it is the land, in the film business it is the story (book, play, or screenplay). The trick is convincing the studio (the banks) that what you have is really valuable, and that's where the salesmanship comes in. Mike Todd obtained the rights to Jules Verne's book, and then got the studio to put up all the money to make the movie. I know nothing about Mr. Todd's financial situation but I assure you, knowing the business, Mike Todd didn't have a nickel in the deal.

In casting the film they got everybody in town, and it sort of became the thing to do. They paid little, but nobody wanted to be left out. Dad worked on the last part of the picture where the S.S. Henrietta is sailing to England. They used Catalina Island as England, and Dad was in the scene in which the crew was using the superstructure of the boat for fuel in order to complete the journey. David Niven, Shirley MacLaine, Victor McLaglen and Jack Oakie were aboard, and it was more laughs than hard work.

During the week that Dad was shooting near Catalina, Mike Todd came to town to see how things were progressing. In high school I got a job parking cars. Tony Duquette, the interior designer of the new Dorothy Chandler Pavilion in Los Angeles, was opening his refurbished studio in West Hollywood. The place was a converted trolley car station and was large and unique. For the opening Tony threw the biggest party Hollywood had seen in years. Every celebrity in town was in attendance, and there I was parking cars. Mike Todd showed up with his new girl-friend, the still married Elizabeth Taylor. He had a new white Cadillac convertible with, of all things, a chauffeur. They both looked silly getting in and out of the backseat. Later in the evening as they were leaving I retrieved their car. I went around and opened the passenger door for Todd and Taylor. Before they got in Todd, who had been drinking, couldn't find any tip money. Todd, looking over at Taylor, who was wearing a low cut dress, said, "Let's ask my girlfriend with the great tits if she has any money." I said, "It's really all right, Mr. Todd, you can catch me later." Todd grabbed me by my parking coat and asked me if I wanted to do something about it. "No, Mr. Todd, I'm just a parking stiff, and if you don't get in that car, I'm going to run down the street and you're going to have to fight someone else." Thankfully, he and Taylor got in the car.

CHAPTER 17

New School
1952

Robert Fulton Junior High School was brand new, with new buildings, new teachers, new rules, and new students. Because of where I lived, only a few students from my grammar school went to this new junior high. My days at Van Nuys Elementary School were comfortable because I had known my classmates for a long time. However, this new school would be more traumatic on many levels. It was small because it was new. Most of the students were from blue collar families or the farms in the northwest valley. Dad was famous, and as a result I was looked upon as a target. I had my share of fights, but after a while the fighting stopped as these kids got to know me or didn't want to mess with me.

I was always working and trying to save money. Once Mom purchased a great deal of fire wood, and it was just dumped out near our wood shed. It just sat there for about three weeks. It was a big job and finally Mother said she would give me fifty dollars if I would stack all that wood, as it looked like it would take forever. I went out and got four guys at five dollars each, and we stacked all the wood in six hours non-stop. Mom refused to pay me because she said I did it too fast. I went to Dad and told him the story, explaining that I'd worked my ass off and I'm out twenty bucks. Dad laughed so hard I thought he was going to fall over. He explained that my mother came from a long line of devious horse traders and maybe I'd learned something about character and with whom to do business. He was right. Then he paid me.

I also sold rakes door to door, worked in a hobby shop, and still had my bicycle reconditioning business. Mostly I worked at the public pool across the street. For years I cleaned the changing rooms, hosed off the decks, and picked up trash in the parking area. I loved to swim and was in the pool all the time. Sometimes we would play pool tag, and no one could catch me. I never thought about being a competitive swimmer though, as that was my brother's domain. I wanted to play football and baseball.

My brother was becoming well known as a star swimmer. My parents had hired a private coach named Ralph Flanagan, and my brother had won an event at the Los Angeles High School swimming championships. At the age of seventeen he was off to Stanford University, which had a nationally acclaimed swimming program. Everyone knew of my brother's accomplishments. Here I was, this awkward thirteen-year-old kid who was just trying to go through puberty as anonymously as possible. A humorous highlight of this attention bias was when Dad was honored on *This is Your Life*. Near the end of the show Ralph Edwards introduced my brother and me with, "And, Andy, here are your two sons. Tad, who is a student at Stanford University, an All-American swimmer, a son any father would be proud of. And your son Dennis. Good luck, Dennis."

Dad, to his credit, recognized that I too needed a little attention and suggested he take me to New York while he was doing the *Milton Berle Texaco Hour*. I was so excited about going to New York and looked forward to being alone with Dad. I taught myself to tie a conventional tie as well as a bow tie as I wanted to be ready. Speaking of bow ties, Dad had finally been invited to attend the Academy Awards. It is a black-tie affair, but Dad had no idea how to tie a bow tie. He called a friend to help. When the friend got to the house, he asked Dad to lie on his back. When Dad questioned this procedure, the friend replied, "Andy, remember, I am a mortician."

Dad and I flew to New York first class on a DC-6 with a fuel stop in Chicago. We had a suite at the St. Regis, and the first thing we did after we arrived was go to Luchow's German restaurant for dinner. This was Dad's very favorite place and he was in heaven. *Milton Berle's Texaco Hour* television show was number one in the country and was performed live. Dad met the writers the first day, rehearsed for three days, then did the show. The rehearsals were hilarious. Berle was a vaudeville comic and afraid of no one. He would scream at the writers, tell the director to sit down and shut up, then laugh out loud at one of his own jokes. All the time he was running around in circles wearing a cashmere bathrobe with a big towel around his neck and sweating buckets. Berle had this overweight valet who was as funny as Berle. The valet would follow Berle trying to light his cigar and at the same time trying to put a chair under his ass when he decided to sit down.

On the second day of rehearsals, Dad asked me to go back to the hotel and change into a nice shirt and blazer as we were having lunch there.

Dad and I were seated in a large corner booth and in five minutes in walked Berle with Jackie Gleason. Dad had never met Gleason but they got along great. Numerous fat man jokes. The interesting thing, and the genesis of this meeting, was how interested these two famous television performers were in the current status of motion pictures. Although both men had done some film work, neither had Dad's film experience, and both felt Dad approachable.

Berle and Gleason both knew the film business was on its ass but wanted to find out everything. How was the business going to rebound? Who were the good agents? Were there studio heads you could trust? Here I was at thirteen, listening to these famous men speak to each other so candidly. Needless to say, I kept quiet. Another thing I remember was the restaurant had a sandwich named after Berle, and Berle commenting to Gleason that if he ever got regular work (this was just before *Honeymooners*), perhaps he too could get a sandwich named after him. Gleason, who was Irish, responded that Berle's rabbi couldn't be too pleased since the principal ingredient of his named sandwich was ham, or was that just Berle's persona?

The rest of the time was a wonder. Robert Keaton, one of the Flying Tigers, was now a Captain for Pan American Airlines and was based in New York. His wife took me to all the tourist sites, and I dreamed of some day living there. That night Dad took me to "21" for dinner. I love snobby places, and "21" fit the bill; I just loved that place. Flying home I explained to Dad that I knew he took me on this trip because he felt I needed some attention. I told him that if he ever felt I needed more attention, just let me know, because I had the time of my life. Dad put his big arms around me and told me how proud he was of me and how he marveled at my self reliance. There were truthful tears all around. The following Monday I was back in school, not much older but a little bit wiser. I felt it inappropriate to tell any of my classmates where I'd been or what I'd done.

CHAPTER 18

Trouble while Skiing
1953

In the late forties my parents bought a small cabin at Big Bear Lake. Mom and I had taken up skiing and we loved it. The cabin was only a two-hour drive from Van Nuys, yet it seemed a world away. Both Mother and I became fairly good at this new sport, and I would travel to the other areas to race for a local ski club. However, I found it was a handicap to compete against the kids who lived in the mountains. One day in Mammoth after a race, a few of us had lunch and a discussion with Mammoth's founder, Dave McCoy and Jill Kinmont. McCoy was a god among ski coaches, and Kinmont was so pretty, so nice and so talented. It was a wonderful hour or two. Who would have thought that in a short time, this pretty girl would be on the cover of *Sports Illustrated* and then become paralyzed from a skiing accident? Brother Tad knew her better than I did. The summer after her accident she was rehabbing in Santa Monica and Tad's lifeguard tower was right in front of her rehab facility. Tad would often visit her, and one day he put her in his Austin-Healey sports car for a drive along the curving roads of Mullholland Drive. Apparently the two of them had an unforgettable day. As a quadriplegic Jill Kinmont would go on to become a successful teacher, wife, and painter. Being a champion comes from the inside. It always does.

One of my fondest memories was the day I skied with my mother in Big Bear. It was noon on a beautiful day and we were heading down the mountain for lunch. About halfway down the hill Mom took a sharp left into the trees. After skiing briefly through the trees we came to a clearing where a knapsack was hanging from a tree. There was a basket, a blanket, and a bottle of white wine chilling in the snow. After Mom spread the blanket, she opened the basket and pulled out cold pheasant, cheese, asparagus, and freshly baked sourdough bread. She opened the wine and poured it into stem glasses saying wistfully, "I didn't graduate from high school, and academically I really can't teach you very much, but I can teach you how to live."

Toward the middle of my eighth grade we decided to take a week's skiing vacation at Squaw Valley, California. It was a real treat, and the first people we ran into were Norma Shearer and her new husband, French skiing great Marty Arrougé. In addition, Norma's daughter Katy (Thalberg) was there with her boyfriend (and later husband) Olympic medalist and film director Jack Reddish. They were all fabulous skiers, and I was invited to tag along. They all were coaching me, and by the end of the week I was skiing like never before. However, the hand of fate knows no direction. On the last day I decided to race for the Golden Sun. It's a race against time. You start at a place on the mountain and if you get to the bottom within the allotted time, you win. Unfortunately I crashed, severely breaking my leg in two places.

I was in a hip cast for four months and a leg cast for six weeks. Because I was bedridden I couldn't attend school, so the school system provided me with a private teacher who would see me every day. To my good fortune the teacher was a reading specialist and was a wonderful help with my reading issues. Remember it was 1952 and there was no television; therefore all I could do was read. After the casts were removed I was immersed in rehab. The best thing I could do was swim both in the ocean and the pool across the street. All I did was swim, and swim, and swim.

Even with rehab, my leg was still stiff, but I returned to junior high and the ninth grade. It was great to see my old schoolmates, many whom I hadn't seen in eight months. Things had changed. The girls were filling out and it seemed everyone was smoking. I became involved in student government and enrolled in Mr. Sharp's ninth grade leadership class. My art teacher asked if I would illustrate the inside cover of the yearbook. I created a large steamboat (after all, it was Robert Fulton Jr. High) full of kids, heading toward an island oasis labeled 'Van Nuys High School.'

After I finished the yearbook my art teacher suggested I enter a city-wide art contest for a billboard promoting sober driving. The contest was open to all 9th through 12th grade students in the City of Los Angeles. Although I was still in junior high school, I was in the ninth grade and therefore eligible. I always thought a billboard should have as few words as possible. I drew the rear of a speeding ambulance, to the right was a hand pouring bourbon on the vehicle, and on the left was a hand pouring gasoline. The caption was "Don't mix 'em!" I couldn't believe it — I won the whole damn thing! The first prize was $500 plus commercial art classes. Billboards were in a few places around town, and it was exciting to look up and see what I had created.

The ninth grade was coming to a close, and many of my friends were going to the new Birmingham High School. However, again, because of where I lived, I was going back to Van Nuys High and would be reunited with my old grammar school friends. During graduation practice, we were selected by height, and I was seated next to this guy I'd never seen before. I learned he had just transferred from West Los Angeles and knew no one. We became friends immediately. His name was Mike Hooper, and he is one of the finest persons I've ever known. To this day we remain friends. We spent most of that summer hitchhiking to Santa Monica beach where I continually swam and bodysurfed. Mike's West L.A. friends became my friends, and they were much more "worldly" than us Valley boys. But high school was ahead, and I could hardly wait.

Even after the accident, Mother and I would continue to ski. Both of us would occasionally take skiing lessons from the local instructors. One of those instructors was a man named Hank Smith. Besides teaching skiing, Smith worked at Kerr's Sporting Goods Store in Beverly Hills. He was one of those men who could do anything. He taught skiing at Big Bear, tennis at the L. A. Tennis Club, and golf at the Los Angeles Country Club. Smith was in his early thirties, good looking, well spoken and without any particular direction. He started helping my mom and me improve our skiing. Then he slowly gravitated toward our entire family.

As I was entering high school, Smith moved into our maid's quarters next to the garage. The problem was I knew he was having an active, long term affair with my mother. They didn't know it, but I inadvertently caught them more than once, and I really didn't know what to do. It broke my heart. I was afraid to go to my dad, but felt by being quiet I was betraying him. My brother was at college and, because we weren't close, I thought it wise not to distract him or involve him in this mess. For over a year it ate me up, just dealing with it and keeping this secret inside. On occasions Smith and Mom would take trips together and insist I go along. I tried to avoid these outings, but if I resisted too much it might have caused problems. Of course, the only reason they insisted I go along was to act as their cover. I was their "beard" and it offended me. How dumb did they think I was? The clincher was one summer night we were having a cookout in our backyard and Smith, who had been drinking, was extremely rude and disrespectful to my father. That was it. If Dad didn't have the courage to stop this nonsense, I was going to somehow extract this man from our family. I was disgusted with my mother and wanted to bring her to her senses, but didn't want to start a family disaster.

While all of this was going on, I was turning sixteen. My parents purchased my brother a new sports car and gave me his old convertible which was pretty banged up. It needed extensive repairs and restorations. The car was my only transportation and it really wasn't useful until all the repairs were completed. I went to work to restore the car and knew it would take over a month. I worked night and day to get things finished. Because I'd always worked, I had saved over three thousand dollars. My plan was to confront Dad and without going into great detail insist Smith move out immediately. If Dad hesitated one inch, I would say nothing and would take my car with my savings and go to Texas. I would get a job and finish school. I knew how to hide and that would be their punishment.

When I restored the car I had to repaint the car entirely which also included a new top. My parents didn't know what color it was because they never asked. If I left they would be looking for a yellow car with a black top and now it was a white car with a white top. I refurbished some junk yard license plates and would use them until I got to Texas. When the car's restoration was finished, I knew I could go whenever I wanted. I then mustered up all my courage and sat down with Dad. I know I had anger and frustration in my voice, but I simply told him, "If that asshole doesn't move out right now, there will be severe consequences." I did not elaborate, nor did Dad question my demand. Dad simply got up and left the room. Smith was gone the next day. I was prepared, and this taught me that most battles are won or lost before they ever start.

I tried not to judge my parents or try to figure out their respective motives. Hell, I didn't even want to think about it. I blamed my mother for being indiscreet and compromising me. I blamed my father for being so passive and not having the courage to face the facts. I do know that after Smith was gone, it was a little chilly around the house. However, my parents slowly became closer and nothing like this ever happened again. These two people were weathering a storm and I thought it best to stay out of the way. Hopefully they would both grow and learn about themselves during this time. I tried to forgive them and hoped that as time went by the memories would fade away, but they never did. At the age of sixteen I felt more on my own than ever. I endured this long charade all by myself, as I never told my brother or anyone else…until this writing.

CHAPTER 19

Happy Days
1955

Seeing that there was no need to run away, I started high school. I arrived at Van Nuys High School in the middle fifties, and it was like something out of a teenage movie. Take *Rebel without a Cause*, *American Graffiti* or *Grease*, and all those clichés were part of my high school life. There were hot rods, drag races, duck tails, poodle skirts, and rock 'n roll. There were varied student groups within the school. This included boys clubs called High Hats, Jesters or "Ambassadors" and girls clubs called Damian's or Marquise, and it was all white. There were no minorities anywhere. There was no prejudice — we just never thought about it. It was a different time. Van Nuys Boulevard was the place for cruising, and Bob's Big Boy was the place to hang out. Because the school was so large (3,500 students), the sports teams were excellent.

During that time a number of future actors attended Van Nuys. Among them were Robert Redford, Natalie Wood, Stacy Keach, and Diane Baker. A special friend was entertainer Jimmy Boyd. He didn't attend Van Nuys but lived there and was always hanging around. We were born in the same month of the same year, and I always kidded him he was much older (two weeks). Although famous for his hit song "I Saw Mommy Kissing Santa Claus," Jimmy continued to work with the biggest and the best. As adults we remained friends through tennis, and we were always running into each other. He was one of the good guys.

The thing I remember most was that I had to deal with high school on my own. My brother was at Stanford and Dad was shooting the Hickok series, sometimes seven days a week. I really had no mentor as to what to do. However, it wasn't much different from my parents' lack of participation in junior high, except high school was bigger and the issues were more complex.

My first day orientation I obtained my class schedule and signed up for football. I was fifteen years old, five feet eight inches tall and weighed 140 pounds. They put me on the "B" squad, which was all right, as I just wanted to play. My problem was speed. I was quick, but my forty-yard time was lousy. I had the size of a defensive back, and the forty-yard speed of a lineman. I worked on my speed and it became better, but in truth, if you ain't got it, you ain't got it. I did not earn a letter and played some at quarterback, as I had the quickness and could throw well. Coach McCaffery told me I would have a shot at quarterback if I returned to the "B" squad the next year.

The teachers were very serious about their jobs and prided themselves on the number of students who went to colleges and universities. My reading was getting better, and I was very good in math. My friends Mike Hooper and Bob Peters followed me from junior high and proved to be trusted allies. Reuniting with my old grammar school friends was more of an adjustment than I'd imagined. I don't know what the problem was, but it took longer to become reacquainted.

One of my first new friends at school was a guy named Dan Kroan. He and his brother Rusty lived in an exclusive section of the Valley called Royal Oaks. One day I was at their house when their father came home. Dan introduced me to his dad who was a physician. Dr. Kroan said, "So you're Dennis Devine. Well, let me tell you a story. About fifteen years ago I was on call at Cedars Hospital. All of a sudden Clark Gable, Carole Lombard, and Andy Devine show up with a half dozen waiters and a room full of partygoers. They were all escorting this very pretty, very pregnant woman who was having a baby. It was the wildest and most fun group I'd ever encountered, and the most memorable delivery I'd ever had." Then Dr. Kroan patted me on the head and said, "I'm glad you've made it this far." Dr. Kroan and I remained friends well into my college days.

In the spring I decided to try out for baseball. I was pretty good, but our team was the defending City Champions, and the best I could hope for was Junior Varsity. During that year I had grown two inches and was now five feet-ten. I'd gained twenty pounds and weighed 160. At the tryouts I played great. No fielding errors, and I went two for three with good pitching. I was sure I was in. When Coach Ford read the team list, my name wasn't called. Afterward I asked him if it was for the Varsity, because surely I must have made the Junior Varsity. Ford replied, "Sorry, kid, you're just not that good. You didn't make the team, and that includes the JVs." I went home and up to my room, never coming down until the next morning. It's funny how differently people react to disappointment.

At first I felt sad and rejected, then pissed off. But somehow I knew there must be something I could do.

The next morning on the way to school I saw Assistant Football Coach Sias across the street from my house. He was in the parking lot of the public plunge where I worked part time. I asked him what he was doing, and he said he was the new swimming coach, and they were having tryouts that afternoon. He got in his car and drove away. It got me thinking. God knows I swim enough, but never competitively. I thought about my running speed and wondered if that would relate to swimming speed. It also occurred to me that good swimmers start when they're six or seven. I'm sixteen and starting to swim competitively. It sounded a little desperate. No, I'd just been cut from the JV baseball team. I was definitely desperate.

That afternoon I cut fifth period and purchased a racing suit. I got to the pool early to warm up and visualize the bottom of the pool and the walls. Coach Sias (who knew me from football) showed up with a bunch of kids and asked me what I was doing there. I politely said I'd like to try out for the team. At this point the way things were going I wouldn't have been surprised if he said you can't even try out, but he shrugged and walked off. He then asked everyone to warm up and go to the end of the pool. He told the "B" freestyle swimmers to line up for a one-lap straightaway swim. He put me in that group. I beat everyone by two body lengths. He then asked me to swim against last year's "B" City Champion, head to head. I beat him by one body length. He then suggested I swim against Cameron Avery, last year's All-City Varsity Champion. I almost beat him too. What do you know, I finally made a team. This ordeal taught me a few things. First, no matter what, you've got to keep trying. Second, you never know what skills you may possess. Finally, we all face obstacles, but it's not the end of the world. Disappointments often gauge what you're made of, and character is your most important asset.

I knew absolutely nothing about competitive swimming. Coach Sias had never coached swimming, but knew a little, as he had swum in college. More importantly was the help of Cameron Avery, last year's champion. He was a very good all-around athlete and a great guy. He was different from the other kids. He looked older and acted older, and he didn't hang around with any of the high school groups. He wasn't arrogant, but seemed above it all. He was a little mysterious, and I liked him.

I trained with the team, and we moved to a new larger pool at the Van Nuys Municipal Park. I learned how to do a flip turn and how to do a quick start. I also started learning the butterfly stroke. Although limited in knowledge, everyone tried to help me as much as possible. Coach Sias kept me on the "B" team, as he thought I might win the Valley League Championship. As to my parents, I didn't tell them what I was doing. This may sound strange, but I was a little embarrassed having them think I was trying to follow in my brother's footsteps. Well, I won the Valley League Championship in the 100-yard freestyle, and came in second in the relay. The next event was the Los Angeles City Championships at the Los Angeles Coliseum Olympic Pool.

One day after practice someone brought a football, so we all thought it would be fun if we played a game of water football in the shallow end of the pool. Ten minutes into the game I got kicked in the ear, and my eardrum broke. The ear was bleeding and I lost all equilibrium. Someone drove me to a doctor who brought in an E.N.T. specialist. They repaired the ear and it was covered with a large bandage. However, no swimming for three weeks. There goes the City Championships.

Five days later, with a smaller bandage on my ear, I went to the Coliseum pool to support my teammates who were trying to qualify in the heats. I was sitting in the stands watching the swimmers consult with their coaches. When they had free time they were studying, or stretching, but all seamed serious and organized. I realized there is a chance I may have some talent. But here I am, going into the summer before the eleventh grade, an average student, an average athlete, going nowhere. Most of my life I had been surrounded by successful people. They seem to have more money, more fun, and more fulfillment than many of the less ambitious parents of my schoolmates. It's time to grow up, get college-ready grades, get a good coach and try to accomplish something.

Summer was upon me and the first thing I did was get a job running a Union 76 gas station in downtown Van Nuys. It was on weekends and evenings which gave me time to train. I got a coach named Kris Kristensen. He ran a highly regarded swim school in nearby North Hollywood and was training some great swimmers. Frankly, I was surprised he took me. I also enrolled in a gym. It was a famous old place called Vince's. It was unique in that it had dark wood inside, with a lot of tattooed motorcycle guys. At first it was a little scary just to walk in there. I had read a book on swimming by "Doc" Councilman, of Indiana University, who advocated weight work. Not your bodybuilder stuff, but lighter weights with numer-ous sets, concentrating on specific muscle groups. The book also advocated running to build the wind and the legs. I worked out at Kristensen's three times a week and Vince's twice a week. I ran and swam on my own the other day. I knew time was against me, but I was committed. This wasn't my best shot — this was my only shot.

My parents now knew I was working out, but had no idea what I was specifically doing. I was strict about my regimen, and after only a month I could tell the difference. I had lost ten pounds, but was getting stronger. I did not want to compete that summer as I just wanted to learn and get in the best shape possible. At Kristensen's I was now swimming with the better swimmers and my times were really dropping. The months of summer were flying by and I felt good about my improvement. In September I made the decision to play "B" football. I remembered that Coach McCaffery spoke to me about playing quarterback and I realized that playing football would only be for a ten weeks. I never thought about getting hurt.

The eleventh grade started and I really applied myself. I was getting good grades and getting along well with my teachers. I was selected as the first string "B" quarterback. We won our first four games, and then Coach McCaffery benched me because he felt I had little leadership ability. After that we lost the next three games. McCaffery would play me, but only occasionally. After the season ended he sat me down and gave me this stern lecture on leadership. When he was finished, I told him I appreciated his concern, but respectfully disagreed with him. I don't know why I said this, but I suggested that to test my leadership ability, I would challenge him to a football game. He could pick half the team, whoever he wanted, and I would take the rest. We would play in the stadium in one week. To my amazement he agreed. I wanted a written list of his players the next day so there would be no misunderstanding. He said no problem, and the game was on.

The next day I received his list of players. The main reason I wanted the coach's list was as a motivational tool. We then made our own list breaking down the names with positions. There were some misfits, but good players, and after the first meeting we were all excited. Talk about getting even, those guys were ready to run through a wall. We'll have run-throughs, but no scrimmages, as we should all be fresh. We had meetings every day and each player got to submit one play. What amazed me was how thoughtful these former screw-ups had become. It was now a collaborative effort, and this new team became very close very fast. Pride is a wonderful tool.

The word got out and the large campus was buzzing. Even the Varsity guys were excited. I confirmed a rumor that Coach had arranged for all the cheerleaders and the pom-pom girls to form an entrance for his team. When I heard this I wanted to retaliate. I had a shop class with a guy named Jerry Pierce. I don't know how old he was, but he looked twenty-five and was a revered member of the Hell's Angels. Jerry owed me a favor, so I got him to get all of the Valley members of the Hell's Angels (100 strong) to take our team on the field. They were all waving their leather motorcycle jackets, and it was a sight to see. Guys from twenty to forty, tattoos, beards, earrings at a high school football game in the late fifties. When we came on the field between all those leather jackets, the stands went nuts. Coach McCaffery and his team couldn't believe their eyes.

We were really fired up and ready to play. We won the toss and elected to receive. We had a running back named Paul Masachio who was by far the fastest guy on the team. Problem was Paul couldn't catch anything and therefore never played. So I had this sure-handed guy receive the kickoff, then hand it to Paul. Paul then ran for an eighty-five yard touchdown on the opening play of the game. Our defense became a bunch of killers. Any guy who thought he could play linebacker, we put him in. We kept rotating guys to keep everyone fresh. We could do no wrong, and by halftime we were ahead 28 to 0. We did not score the second half because we played everyone at whatever position they always dreamed of playing. We had guards playing quarterback, and wide receivers playing running back. However, our defense didn't yield a score. After the game, McCaffery came up, put out his hand and said, "You got me." It was an unforgettable memory, but now it was time to get serious about working out and swimming.

CHAPTER 20

Down to Business
1956

Football season was over and now it was back to swimming in earnest. I returned to Kristensen and Vince's Gym. I never worked harder and started entering AAU meets. I was in way over my head as I had been swimming just a little over a year. Here before me were my goals — the guys I would have to eventually compete against. Swimming in these open AAU meets was a far cry from the competition in high school, and I didn't mind stinking up the pool. Although all of these swimmers had been competing for years, each week I was slowly gaining on them. It was like I was sneaking up behind them in the dark. For whatever reason I never felt better about what I was doing and it was so exciting to have a chance at success. For the first time in my life I felt like I had a shot, and no one was going to take it away from me.

One of the first athletes I remember from these AAU meets was a high school swimmer from El Monte named Lance Larson. I had read all about him, and he was great. At my fourth AAU meet I finally qualified — eighth in an eight-man final. As I was standing on the blocks, I looked over and there was Larson. He came in first, and I came in seventh (well, at least I beat somebody). Little did I know that in the future, this Olympic gold medal winner would become my teammate, my competitor, and my close friend.

In those early days I first met a person I wouldn't forget. He was a rather formal man who came up to me and introduced himself. "I'm Peter Daland, I'm a swimming coach." He said I had a nice stroke and looked comfortable in the water, but deduced that I hadn't had much formal training. He wished me luck, excused himself, and was gone. I don't think I saw him for another year, but in the future this formal man would change my life.

High school swimming formally started and I was swimming on the varsity. As luck would have it, our high school team was now training at

Kristensen's swimming school. I would work out with the high school team and then stay and work out with Kristensen. It was a perfect situation, and I was putting in a lot of mileage. Our high school team had become very good as we had inherited a number of former "age group" AAU swimmers. We had a shot at winning the City Championships. Coach Sias had learned a lot, and my friend Cameron Avery had come back for his senior year. I was swimming more butterfly, as it was becoming my best stroke.

We went undefeated in dual meets and easily won the Valley League Championship. The City Championships were very exciting. We came in second, but by the narrowest of margins. The Championships were at night at the Olympic pool near the L.A. Memorial Coliseum in downtown L.A. My parents were now becoming aware of my swimming efforts, but were more interested in what my brother was doing, and rightly so. His times were some of the best in the country, and he was planning to try for the Olympics. To enhance my brother's chances, he moved to Hawaii to train with famed swimming coach Soichi Sakamoto. He gave his best shot and narrowly missed making the 1956 team.

CHAPTER 21

The Hotel
1956

Few things in my life would change my outlook or values as much as my new job. My friend Mike Hooper asked if I'd like to go to work with him at the Beverly Hills Hotel. Mike's parents lived next door to the hotel's doorman, a man named Leon Smith. Smitty, along with his other duties at the hotel, hired and supervised all the parking attendants. I jumped at the chance as the hotel was an iconic, beautiful place and possibly a little more interesting than the gas station in Van Nuys. The other parking attendants were in college. They were all smart and good looking. We all had to be well groomed, polite, and on our toes. The money was good, and I was being exposed to a lifestyle far different from my own.

It's one thing to be the son of a film actor who lives on a farm out in the San Fernando Valley. It is quite another to be dealing with the most influential and wealthy people in the country. At the hotel, in dealing with guests, no job was mundane. I learned what responsibility was all about, what thinking ahead was all about, and what keeping your mouth shut was all about. For a kid of seventeen, the experience was unparalleled, as there was so much more to this job than just parking cars. I worked there for six years, and indeed it was an education. The patrons were unforgettable, as were my co-workers.

In addition to working at the hotel, I worked for Smitty at other venues. If we did a good job at the hotel, we would have the opportunity to work at private parties, studio functions, the Los Angeles Country Club or Ronny Jones Parking Lot. The L.A. Country Club was so exclusive it excluded any show business people as members. Smitty didn't even want it known that I was related to an actor. Ronny Jones Parking Lot was another matter. It was a front so that mobsters from the east coast could rent new Cadillacs with no questions asked. The lot was in Beverly Hills where Spago's Restaurant is now located.

I would work at the hotel on weekends and the other venues at night. It actually helped my studies. At a private party the people would arrive, then we would sit for three hours or more waiting for the guests to depart. During that time I would do what the college guys did. Pick a big sedan, sit in the back seat, and study without any distractions. However, on some evenings there were wonderful distractions. One summer night I was working a private party. After I had parked all the cars, I got something to eat and sat near the kitchen. Judy Garland, with seven musicians, entertained outside for two hours. She was in top form and unforgettable. That night my studies suffered a bit.

And oh the people. I had no idea there were so many characters in this world, prominent or otherwise. Believe me, every important person who ever lived would eventually come to or through that hotel. The most fun were the Academy Awards. The hotel would have a hundred or so guests going to the awards, with at least twenty nominees. Sharing part of the evening with these beautiful people looking their best was exciting. Many of them wanted to share the moment with someone. And there I was, the parking boy, sharing their thoughts and fears before I opened the door to their limousine. Irrespective of one's station in Hollywood, on this night everyone is a bit overwhelmed. As they departed with their drivers, I knew I would not see them again until possibly the next morning, when they would often share their experiences of the night before.

There was never a day at the hotel that was ordinary. Powerful people from all walks of life were commonplace. However, there were a few special people, and at my age I learned something different but important from each one of them. I was near the lobby, and Jack Benny came up behind me holding his violin case. He politely asked me if I would put it in the back seat of his car. Because I wasn't busy, I suggested I move his car to the shade so the violin wouldn't get too hot. He was so kind and enthusiastic when he commented how thoughtful I was. We started talking which went on for over half an hour. He seemed so much younger than his age. I was so impressed as to how curious he was. He was interested in everything and had a million questions. Jack Benny was having so much fun talking it didn't seem to occur to him that I was younger and at a different station in life. As a matter of fact, for a brief moment I felt we were just friends. Benny taught me that enthusiasm and curiosity seem an excellent tonic for staying young and happy.

Famed Hollywood columnist James Bacon was always at the hotel. After a while he found out that I was Andy's son, and we became friends. Jim loved what he was doing and confided in me one day, "I love to write, and I love to go to parties. Dennis, to me every day is Saturday." He would tell me about all the Hollywood scandals and he really knew 'em. I would always put his car in a special place. I was professional and we treated each other like contemporaries. We remained friends for many years as he lived into his nineties. Jim taught me the importance of mutual respect, and what a rare gift it is to do what you really love doing.

One Saturday morning the hotel was buzzing with a massive Jewish wedding. A hundred cars were entering the hotel all at once and it was a mess. Up the exit came a brand new Cadillac limousine. However the car was filthy and the driver was equally unkempt. I happened to be near the exit and challenged the man driving the dirty limo the wrong way. As he rolled down the window, I saw it was Howard Hughes. He apologized and said he had to get to his bungalow. I told Hughes to take off and I'd take care of everything. He took my hand, looked straight into my eyes and said, "You're really saving my ass." In the years that followed, whenever I would see Hughes he would always give me a little nod. Hughes taught me that even the most important people rarely forget a considerate act.

I didn't work at the hotel at night, except for special occasions. This night was a very special occasion. It was the Directors Guild black-tie dinner and all of the A-list Hollywood types were in attendance. As the guests were entering, I noticed director William Wellman and his wife Dottie had just driven up in their red, fifty-five T-Bird. I was busy and didn't have a chance to say hello, although they hadn't seen me since I was about thirteen. The dinner went on for three hours, and as the guests came out, I could see that Wellman was looking for his parking ticket. I remembered where their unique car was located and brought it up for them.

Dottie Wellman was driving as Bill had been drinking. As I opened the driver's door, she handed me a tip. I said, "It's all right, Mrs. Wellman, this one's on the house." She replied, "Why?" "I'm Dennis Devine, Andy and Dorothy's son." Dottie looked into the car to the passenger side where Bill was now sitting. "Bill, it's Denny, (that's what they called me), Denny Devine." She then put her arms around me and gave me a hug. As she was doing this, Bill got out of the car. In greeting me, he inadvertently put his hands on my shoulder, then my arm, "Christ, you're in shape and good looking." We then talked about my parents and how everyone was doing. We said our goodbyes and off they went; it was a very nice moment. Little did I know that in two days I would be meeting with Wellman, John Wayne, and producer Robert Fellows about co-starring in a film they were producing. Wellman taught me that a person never knows when opportunity will present itself. Actually, Wellman taught me a lot of things. I really liked Bill Wellman and his entire family. He was an unforgettable character.

CHAPTER 22

The Interview
1956

I didn't mention to Mom or Dad that I'd seen the Wellmans at the hotel over the weekend, but the following Monday Dad got a call from John Wayne. At first Dad didn't know what Wayne was talking about. Dad thought Wayne wanted him for a part. "No, Andy, this is not for you. We want to meet your son Dennis." Wayne wanted to set up the meeting so I could meet with his partners Wellman and Bob Fellows, as well as himself. He also wanted Dad to come with me. The next day Dad and I drove to their offices in West Hollywood. I was naturally apprehensive because of whom I was meeting and where in the world this whole ordeal might take me. When we got there everyone was thrilled to see Dad. They must have talked, laughed, and told stories for more than a half-hour. There was a specific reason why they wanted Dad to accompany me (so I'd feel more comfortable) and a specific reason why they asked Dad to leave the room (so they could deal with me directly). Dad understood how all this was playing out, and quietly went to the waiting room. I said little during their initial meeting with Dad, but gradually became more comfortable as I observed these men. That comfort would last about ten seconds.

As Dad left the room they closed the door behind him. They had arranged the chairs so that I was facing all four men. I sat there and realized I wasn't a kid anymore and now I'm at the grownups' table. These very famous and talented men were going to put up money and make a film that hopefully will turn a profit. And here I sit as they are interviewing me to see if I could contribute to this enterprise. Because I had no idea what I was doing, my only chance was to be as candid and truthful as possible. Wellman, a born leader, started the questioning and was purposely abrupt. He asked me about prejudice and blacks and uneducated people. Did I have a dog? I really don't think Wellman cared very much about my answers but wanted to see how fragile I might be. The others asked questions, but on a less personal basis. Wayne was primarily concerned about my age. I think I held my ground and told them what I really thought. The longer I was there, the more comfortable I became, and the more I admired these serious men.

As we spoke I learned that they wanted me to have the second lead in a small film called, *Good Bye My Lady*. It was a coming of age story about a boy and his dog. It was to star Walter Brennan, Phil Harris, and a new, young black actor named Sidney Poitier. The part I was to play was that of a fourteen-year-old kid. Although I was seventeen, I had a young face. However John Wayne was a little more blunt as to my appearance. Near the end of the interview Wayne observed, "He carries himself like a fighter and I'll bet he has hair on his dick. I thought we wanted a little kid." I didn't get the part as it went to Brandon DeWilde, who was famous for his role in *Shane*. The next day Wellman personally called me to give me the news. He said my interview went great, but I was just too old for the part. He was very kind and seemed sincere. He said that I would definitely be in his next film, a war story to be produced by Warner Bros. I unfairly wondered if Wellman would honor that promise.

CHAPTER 23

Buster Brown
1957

For years radio announcer Ed McConnell had a popular kids' show called *Smilin' Ed's Buster Brown Gang*. His producers were planning to put the show on television as McConnell was a big, jovial man whose appearance would still appeal to kids. On radio McConnell would tell stories and deal with his little friends, most notably Midnight the Cat and Froggy the Gremlin. Froggy was a troublemaker who would disappear when Ed would say," Plunk your magic twanger." The double entendre was obvious. In 1954 as they were getting ready to produce the television show, Ed had a heart attack and died.

For two years the producers tried to find a replacement for McConnell, then finally thought of Dad. They renamed the show *Andy's Gang* and kept the same radio format. The Brown Shoe Company continued as the show's sponsor because their best selling shoes were for children and were called Buster Brown Shoes. The television show was a hit and would continue for five years. Now Dad had two national television shows on at the same time.

After only six weeks the producer, Frank Farren, mentioned to Dad that he owned a sixty-five foot motor yacht, He told Dad that if he and the family would like to use it, it would be his pleasure. Well, it was summer and everyone was home, so Dad said great, we'll take it next week. So the whole family, plus Cap Watkins and his girlfriend Dori, spent one full week going to all seven of the California Channel Islands (a new one each night). Cap Watkins had a book on the history of each island which made it more personal and exciting. We went scuba diving, hiking, and beach combing. Most of the time we caught or dove for our own dinner. It was like we were a thousand miles from California. It was the best family vacation ever. Farren's Captain said that we used the boat more and had more fun than Farren had in the past four years.

Andy's Gang was doing well in the ratings. Dad had been doing the show for two years, and his contract called for fifty thousand a year. The format of the show was that he would introduce a dramatic episode for children and at the same time deal with the now little rubber television characters Froggy and Midnight. Dad could shoot about two shows in a day and his total filming commitment to the show was about three weeks. His contract was up for renewal, and his agent had negotiated an increase to sixty-five thousand a year. He had never made twenty grand a week doing anything. They did the negotiations face to face, and Dad thought he had just robbed a bank.

The Brown Shoe Company commercials would start with a little kid holding his dog and saying, "I'm Buster Brown, I live in a shoe. This is my dog Tige, he lives with me too." No sooner had Dad concluded his face-to-face negotiations than, Bang! The office door was thrown open and in walked Buster Brown. However, he wasn't a little kid. It was Jerry Maren, a fifty-five year old midget who was one of the original Lollypop Kids from *The Wizard of Oz*. He was wearing a tailored, charcoal gray, double breasted suit accompanied by a light gray homburg. "What the hell do you mean, one-hundred and twenty-five thousand? I know I only work two days a year, but its one-seventy or you guys can take that dog and those shoes and stick 'em up your ass!" The Brown Shoe people and the ad agency people looked at each other in amazement. Realizing his face was in three-million shoes, they nodded and gave him the money. When Dad departed, he didn't think he was taking advantage of anybody.

CHAPTER 24
Lafayette Escadrille
1957

It was my senior year and I was excited about the future. I was now five feet, eleven inches and weighed 170 pounds. I had continued working out and was in the best shape of my life. I knew I had little future in football, but it was so much fun and our team was going to be so good. The previous year our varsity had almost won the City championship, and the whole team was coming back, plus the transfers and the guys coming up from the "B" squad. We were loaded. I knew I'd play because coach Tucker was a good guy whom I'd known for years. He was on the sidelines when I beat Coach McCaffery and was smiling and laughing. I would play on special teams, come in with the "mop-up" guys when we were ahead, and run the "scout" team in practice. I knew my place and that was fine. Our first four games we went undefeated, and I was playing off and on as I had expected. My grades were really good and my classes were more interesting than before. I was elected President of the Knights, which was a student organization made up of all the school leaders (Student Body President, Class Presidents, Football Captain, etc.). I had a very pretty girlfriend that I liked and Mom and Dad were getting along well. I was happy as things were simple and predictable. Then the truly unexpected happened. I got a call from Warner Bros. I was told to show up in two days for an interview. It was Wellman making good on his promise.

The Warner Bros. studio was located in the San Fernando Valley. Each studio seemed to have its own style. Warner's was known for war films and gritty crime dramas like *Scarface, Pride of the Marines,* and *Casablanca.* In 1957 it was the end of the studio contract system. However, Warner's was a holdout as they were grooming young contract players to go into their lucrative television business. Warner's was smart by using these contract players to make inexpensive formula TV shows such as *Maverick.*

When I got to the studio, I met with Wellman, the writer and some suits. As we talked, one of the suits asked Wellman if I could act. In front of me Wellman replied, "Well, we'll find out." I was told to report the next day to one of the sound stages for a cold reading. A cold reading is where they give you a script you have never seen before and you read it aloud. That night I told Dad what was before me and he sat me down. Dad said the main thing is to relax. The sound stage and Wellman might be overwhelming, but it's your job to forget it and just be yourself. They aren't going to bite you. As a matter of fact, they want you to be good more than you do. As far as the context is concerned, just try to convey the thought behind what you are saying and don't worry about every word. Just have fun. Right!!!

Testing Andy Devine's 17-Year-Old Son Dennis For 'La Guerre' at WB

Dennis Devine, 17-year-old son of Andy Devine, will be tested next week by William Wellman for a leading role in "C'est La Guerre" at Warner Bros. Wellman wrote the original, and will also direct "Guerre."

Only thesping in pix actor has done previously was a bit in "Canyon Passage." Dana Andrews-Susan Hayward co-starrer filmed in 1946 by U.I. Youngster was cast as Andy Devine's son in this film.

Clipping from Variety.

I got to the studio and reported to the sound stage. There was a big round table with about twenty chairs. Each chair had a script in front of it on the table. Dad was correct, it was overwhelming. The large sound stage door was open, and various costumed people walked by. One by one these young, strapping, good looking men walked in and sat down. They looked like they knew what they were doing, and they were all in their mid to late twenties. It was 1957 and these guys weren't famous yet, but sitting down at the table were Tab Hunter, David Janssen, Clint Eastwood, Jody McCrea, Tom Laughlin, Will Hutchens, Bill Wellman, Jr. and others. Wellman Sr. gave a little talk as to what we were trying to achieve.

I figured Wellman would go to his immediate left or right so I sat 180 degrees from his chair, so I could buy some time and size things up. As the reading started this guy pulled up a chair behind me and patted my arm. "Hi, I'm Jim Garner. I'm a contract player here and I'm a friend of your Dad's from the Municipal Golf course. I heard you were going to be here and thought I'd sit with you." Garner continued, "Relax, I'm right here. This will be a piece of cake." I asked if he was in the film and he said he was, but his part was so small he wasn't asked to read at the table. When my turn came I was more relaxed as I had been watching the others do their readings. David Janssen was the best. He could really read lines. By now I really was relaxed and thought my reading went fine. In any event, I got the job. The next day were the wardrobe fittings. We took our fittings at the studio, and they were very thorough about it. I took my fitting with actor Will Hutchens. Because of all the working out I had large shoulders and Hutchens had extremely small shoulders. As we were being fitted, the wardrobe man commented, "Where does Wellman

Lafayette Escadrille, *circa 1957. I'm the next one up to bat, following Clint Eastwood. I am sitting to his right wearing the hat.*

find you freaks? Can't he hire normal actors?" Hutchens was thirty, but looked younger. He was likeable and capable. Two months later he had his own television series called *Sugarfoot.*

All of this came very fast and I hadn't notified my school as to what I was doing. I went to Mr. Cumerford, the boys Vice-Principal, who was familiar with this situation because of the other actors who attended Van Nuys. Because I was under eighteen, I had a teacher on set a few hours each day. I then went to Coach Tucker to explain the situation, and he got a big kick out of the whole thing. He said the team had been winning by thirty-five points each game so they could probably live without me. The team would hold out my jersey and it would be mine upon my return. I was told by the studio we would be leaving for location in a week.

Before the United States entered World War I, France was fighting Germany. Since before the American Revolution and the export of
inexpensive cotton, France has always been our ally. Air power had just
become a factor in war, and fighter planes were in their infancy. Flying
in battle was dangerous business, and casualties were substantial. A few
Americans, chasing the glamour and excitement, enlisted in the Lafayette

Lafayette Escadrille, *circa 1957. I'm to the left of David Janssen.*

Flying Corps and flew for France. Wellman was one such person, and the
film *Lafayette Escadrille* was a veiled story of his life.

Wellman's illustrious career was coming to an end, and he knew it. But
he was a romantic, a fighter, and a great storyteller. He wanted this film
to be his "*le grand denouement*" (his grand victorious finale). However, as
I said, the making of a film is a collaborative effort, and luck often plays
a very large part. Originally the story was approved, the screenplay had
been basically written, and James Dean was to star. It's a story about a rich
spoiled kid who gets in trouble, goes to France to fly, gets in trouble again,
and then finds redemption. Dean would have been perfect. However, in
late September of 1955 Dean was killed when his sports car hit a tree in
central California. With Dean there would have been a bigger budget,
bigger co-star and all the rest. Then Paul Newman was attached including the possibility of Bridget Bardot (she was 23 at the time). However,

Newman and Wellman didn't see eye to eye on many aspects of the film. Remember this was Wellman's baby, and he wanted to do it his way. Then Jack Warner wanted to shelve the project and make it later. I think this scared the hell out of Wellman as he was afraid of time and was afraid that the script and the film would be forgotten. His best and perhaps only chance was to make it now. So the budget was cut, Tab Hunter was cast and Wellman did the best he could with what he had.

We were to be on location in Santa Maria, California, which is a small coastal town in the central part of the state. The primary exterior shooting was at an airport that had only a grass strip. By the time the art directors finished with the buildings and the vintage airplanes arrived, it looked like 1917 France. Actors talk about "getting into character," and god knows I'm no actor, but it is difficult not to get into the moment when you put on your uniform and are surrounded by all of the period artifacts.

George Washington "Cap" Watkins.

Santa Maria was about two and a half hours northwest of Los Angeles, and the studio provided a bus for transport. I remember my friend Mike Hooper taking me to the studio for my departure as my parents were busy. While en-route to Santa Maria on the bus, I looked out the window at the ocean, and it reminded me of my other journey some eleven years before going to make the film in Oregon. But here I was again, on my own, trying to figure out how to survive this thing. I knew absolutely no one and was well aware that when directing a film, Wellman scared the hell out of everybody.

I reiterate that going on location is like going to summer camp. I laid low and did exactly as I was told. I was never late and was always prepared, which was easy as I didn't have that much to do. Although my observations were from a distance, I grew to greatly admire and respect Wellman the more I was around him. He wasn't unreasonable, he just couldn't stand bull shit. Making movies is no easy task, especially when there are so many moving parts. Outdoor sets, old airplanes, a large ensemble cast.

I had a number of small scenes which were easy, including one where I played the ukulele.

My last scene on location was the most amusing. I was to have crashed my plane in the roof of the field bakery. After the mock crash, with my plane's tail sticking out of the bakery's roof, I come out of the front door covered in flour and holding a loaf of bread. With debris in the air, a ten-inch two-by-four is sup-posed to hit me in the head. The take was difficult in that you had to coordinate explosions, stunt-men jumping out of windows, and debris being catapulted into the air with me coming out of the door at just the right time. The grip who was placed on the roof was sup-posed to hit me in the head with the two-by-four, but missed (take one). Missed again (take two). Wellman was pissed, "Get me a ladder, God damn it." Wellman got on a ten-foot ladder, and with the two-by-four in his hand, nailed me on the head at the perfect time. He seemed so pleased with him-self he didn't notice that, even with my leather helmet on, he almost knocked me down. Wellman's impatient reaction to me was to yell, " God damn it, do something."

My friend Tom Johnson. I helped him finish his qualifying swim and he later became Captain of the entire lifeguard service.

Hell, I could hardly stand up. But with a loaf of bread in my hand and still covered in flour, I simply took a bow, then walked off camera. Print!

On location I made three new friends, and these friendships would all come with a bit of irony. The first was David Janssen, and why we became friendly I really don't know. Perhaps it was because of our mutual friend Richard Lang, son of the famed film director Walter Lang. Janssen was the oldest and most sophisticated member of the cast, and I was the youngest and least sophisticated. Over the years we would run into each other at parties or restaurants, and our friendship would last until his premature passing. Years after the film ended, I was having lunch with a prominent banker, as I was in deep trouble getting financing for a big, complicated real estate project. Into the restaurant walked David. The banker said, "My god, there's David Janssen — *The Fugitive*. I casually mentioned that he was an old friend, but the banker in no way believed me. Before I saw him coming, David was in our booth with his arm around me, telling *Lafayette Escadrille* stories. Needless to say, at long last I got my project financed.

Lifeguard tower #15 which was one of the more challenging stations because of the pier and the Fun Zone. I worked there on and off all summer.

On another occasion I ran into David in Beverly Hills. He was with his friend, songwriter Carol Connors, who I casually knew. I had read where Carol had just been nominated for an Academy Award. I congratulated her, and in front of David then asked, "Carol, when you go to the Awards, could you please take David? He never gets to go." David again put his arm around me, tapped me on the head, and we all laughed. That was the last time I would ever see him. David died at age forty-eight, perhaps because he lived life a little too fully. At his funeral my childhood friend, and now a director in his own right, Richard Lang was his eulogist. He said, "David was a very good man, but a very bad boy." Irrespective, I liked David very much. I appreciated the kindness and friendship he showed me during that lonely, but exciting time on location.

The second person I became friends with was the man supplying the vintage aircraft for the film, Frank Tallman. He was the go-to guy when there was a need for airplanes or pilots for a film, and his credits were a mile long. When he first landed his vintage biplane in Santa Maria with the noise and the smoke and the smell of the castor oil it took my breath away. Seeing these airplanes firsthand, you could truly appreciate how delicate they were and how vulnerable were the men who flew them. Since childhood I've loved airplanes (I am a licensed pilot), and because of this I became friendly with Tallman.

Over the years I kept in touch with Frank and in the late sixties he formed Tallmantz Aviation with another flying legend, Paul Mantz. Their offices were in Orange County at the now John Wayne Airport. In the early seventies I dropped in to see Frank at his offices. We had a great time talking flying. I explained that I was visiting my parents who now lived in nearby Newport Beach. I mentioned I had a friend visiting from out of town and suggested we all have dinner at my parents' house where he could meet Dad. Frank was thrilled.

In the mid-sixties Frank was injured in a go-cart accident. An infection had set in and Frank's leg had to be amputated below the knee. It took some time to reinstate his FAA credentials, even in light of the fact that he was so famous. In addition to my parents, joining us for dinner was my skiing friend, Dr. Roger Neubeiser from Florida. Frank arrived and I introduced him to my parents. Both Frank and Dad were in awe of each other which made for a fun time. I then introduced Frank to my friend Roger. Without saying anything, they embraced each other. I asked, "Is there something I should know?" Frank looked at me and replied, "This is the guy who cut my damn leg off!" It was a memorable evening for everyone. Lots of Paul Mantz stories, lots of Ernie Gann stories, and lots of Bill Wellman stories. Sadly, Frank was killed a few years later near Orange County on a simple flight in bad weather.

The third was actor Jim Stacey. Jim's real name was Maurice Elias, and I knew his famous brother Louie who was a star football player at UCLA. Jim was a "James Dean" type, only more charming, tougher, and a better athlete. He had small parts in a number of films and then starred in his own television series *Lancer* for two years. Jim was married to and divorced from actresses Connie Stevens and Kim Darby (*True Grit*), and over the years I would see him around town. He had a real edge, but I liked him. Fifteen years after we did *Lafayette* together, I read that Jim had been sideswiped while on his motorcycle and his passenger had been killed, while he lost both his left arm and left leg.

When we started our construction and development company in the late sixties, one of our first employees was Marsha Siskind. She was a loyal employee and for many years asked for nothing. In late 1973 Marsha came to my partner and me and asked to borrow $5,000 because her boyfriend was in trouble. We lent her the money with no questions asked. Two weeks later I learned that the money went to Marsha's live-in boyfriend's attorney as a retainer, as her boyfriend was the drunk driver who sideswiped Stacey.

Location was over and we were now back at the studio doing interiors at Warner Bros. I was in a number of scenes and had my own mail call scene which was exciting. I did it in one take. When they didn't need me, I went home. I even suited up and played in a football game. I thought I'd get a lot of crap from my teammates, but they thought it commendable that I'd come back and play.

A humorous incident took place while we were shooting at the studio. The female star of the film was a very pretty French girl named Etchika Choureau. That wasn't her real name but her stage name (her first mistake- even the French can't pronounce it). She spoke absolutely no English (her second mistake). And she fell in love with a very gay Tab Hunter (her third mistake). While shooting at Warner Bros. she was living at the Beverly Hills Hotel. Not wanting to quit my "day job" I continued working on weekends at the hotel. Etchika had a woman companion and interpreter who stayed with her. At the hotel this woman came up to me, and in broken English, insisted I looked exactly like one of the young actors that was in the film.

The end of my participation in the film came rather unceremoniously. Although they were still filming, they didn't need me anymore. One morning an assistant director came up to me and said, "That's it, you can go home. Turn in your wardrobe." The loneliness I felt going up to location on the bus was nothing compared to the loneliness I felt walking out of the Warner Bros. gate. I wanted to thank Mr. Wellman, or say goodbye to my new friends, but all were busy so I just left. I enjoyed the studio, the people, and the pressure. I was proud that I had endured this on my own. I thought I would never come back to such an exciting place unless it was to see Dad. Little did I know that that choice would be mine in less than a year.

After *Lafayette* was released my parents never saw the film, and they never asked me what it was like making the film. Of course they never asked about my job parking cars or refurbishing bicycles either. I assumed they felt the making of the film was just another job. If anyone should have known it wasn't just another job, it was my parents. But I was philosophical about the fact that they were either busy or easily distracted. In any event there was little I could do about it. I simply returned to high school which wasn't a difficult adjustment. Thankfully it was like I'd never left. Gone in an instant were the studio, the costumes, the planes, and the friends I'd never known before.

Right after the film was released, I was asked to be a contestant on the Groucho Marx *You Bet Your Life* television program. First thing I did was meet with Groucho and two writers. The four of us sat down for thirty minutes so they could come up with any funny situations or stories. Groucho was a sarcastic hoot. All he did was give me a hard time. The show was very funny as I was teamed with this charming old Italian lady.

I played the last three football games, and we went undefeated and won the City Championship. In the final quarter of the final game Coach Tucker put me in at quarterback and I threw two completions. After always being on special teams (the goon platoon), it was a thrill to really get in there. However we never got to play the championship game in the L.A. Memorial Coliseum. I'd always thought it would be a thrill to stand on the Coliseum field and look up to the stands.

Swimming season was approaching and I was back to the old grind at Christensen's pool and Vince's gym. The time off to do the film was a good break, and I had renewed enthusiasm for my workouts. Although I'd only been training two plus years, my times were good enough that swimming in a major college program was becoming a possibility. Our swimming team was very good, and Coach Sias had become a better coach. We swept through our league championships and at the Memorial Coliseum pool won the L.A. City championship. I got a first and a second and our relay was second. Mom and Dad were in St. Louis and unable to see the meet.

The morning after our victory I sat for the SAT exams and didn't do well. I didn't know about prep courses, I just took the damn thing. I did great in math and the bottom of average in English. I just couldn't read fast enough. I wanted to go to Stanford like my brother and my grades were excellent, but because of my SAT English score, Stanford turned me down. I hadn't thought of or applied to any other school.

My football teammate and friend Bob Peters had gone to every school that I had ever attended, and he had just received a football scholarship to the University of Southern California. One day he came to my house with an application to USC and said why should we stop now. I filled out the application, and within a few weeks was accepted. I went to the university to speak with a counselor about my below-standard reading abilities. He was very understanding and reassuring. The counselor said, "You're a smart guy. Look at your grades, look at your math SATs, look at your activities. We'll help you with the reading. That's what we're here for." The counselor then asked me if I was ambidextrous, and I acknowledged that I was. He said that many people with reading issues were. In fact, Einstein had the same problem. I replied, "Yeah, but I think he was a bit better in math." That moment where the counselor was not judgmental about my reading skills and simply wanted to help endeared the university to me.

A week later I got a call from the Australian dual gold medal winner in the last Olympics, Murray Rose. Rose said he was going to USC and heard that I was going there as well. He said he looked forward to meeting me. I was speechless. Remember, I had only been swimming a short while and here is an Olympic champion calling me. I then learned that Rose's Olympic teammate and also a gold medal winner, Jon Hendricks, was also coming to USC. To top it off, I found out that the school had hired the former assistant swimming coach from Yale, Peter Daland. I remembered Daland as the polite and formal man I met a year before at the El Segundo swimming meet. Frankly, I was very excited about attending USC and thoughts of Stanford were quickly fading.

Dad was being considered for the lead in a New York show. So I thought it wise to sit down and explain that I was thinking about going to USC. Dad hit the ceiling; he hated USC. Why? Because his close friend's son went there as a star quarterback and didn't play. I was somewhat sympathetic to the issues as I was familiar with the situation. However, I looked Dad in the eye and told him he was wrong, dead wrong. "I've never caused you any trouble, and I've made you as proud as I could, and I think I've earned the right to go wherever I want to, irrespective of your feelings." Dad said he didn't care, I wasn't going to USC, and then he stormed out of my room.

A few minutes later the door opened. It was Dad and he was upset. He sat me down and said that even older people do and say stupid things. He sincerely apologized and said I could go wherever I wanted to and he would pay for it, and whatever I did I would have his full support. He had tears in his eyes and held me. I told him, "I'm proud of you, Dad, and love you very much." There was a pause. Then I said, " I know you're thinking about going to New York to do something you've never done before…and I'm thinking about going to college to do something I've never done before. I hope you're not as apprehensive as I am." Dad looked at me and replied, "Want to bet." We both laughed. It was moments like this that I cherished.

CHAPTER 25

Showboat
1957

Many things had changed for Mom and Dad. The *Wild Bill Hickok* television series had just ended after seven years. The show was still popular and was going into syndication. Because of Dad's ownership in the show, it appeared that Dad would soon be making more money than when he was actually shooting the series. The Van Nuys farm was sold, and a new home was purchased on the water in Newport Beach. John Wayne would soon follow, and their two homes would look upon each other across the bay.

Dad wanted to take it easy. Financially he was secure, and all he wanted was to enjoy this new house, his new friends, and golf. I don't think he was ever happier. Then came a call from Guy Lombardo in New York. Lombardo was a very popular society bandleader on the East Coast. However, he was really a businessman who had his hands into everything. He had obtained the rights to produce Jerome Kern's and Oscar Hammerstein's *Showboat*. He then optioned the waterfront theater at Jones Beach, New York.

The next thing Lombardo needed was an established actor to play Captain Andy. The theater was outdoors and sat eighteen thousand. The lead had to be played big and broad, and the director thought there was no New York actor who could handle it. Then Dad's name was suggested, and the director thought Dad would be perfect. What the director didn't know was that Dad, with all his radio, television, and film experience, had never appeared on the legitimate stage — ever! When Lombardo found this out he didn't care. He wanted Dad anyway. Lombardo had that kind of instinct and courage. Dad took the deal and flew to New York to rehearse for three weeks. He never worked harder but loved it, and the cast and director loved him back. Dad was very bright and truly had a gift. Because he had just obtained his actor's equity card (a requirement for stage work), his number was the highest of anyone in the company.

Dad hated to be alone, and the run of the play was for ten weeks. It was decided that Mom would take the first six weeks or so, then brother Tad would go, and I would fill in later. The production was lavish and had a huge cast. The Showboat actually floated and docked at center stage, with a larger stage behind. A symphony orchestra was stage right, led by Guy Lombardo's brother Carmen. The production was really something. It was like Disneyland, the Hollywood Bowl, and Broadway all rolled into one. Opening night was sold out and Dad held the New York audience of eighteen thousand in the palm of his hand. He received a standing ovation and glowing reviews from the New York papers. At fifty-two Andy Devine had found a new career.

CHAPTER 26

Decisions
1957

Previously Mom had left for New York to join Dad, who was finishing rehearsals. Now I was the only one at home. Upon graduation I was surprised and flattered to be elected into the Ephebian Society which is the highest honor a senior graduate from the Los Angeles City School system can receive. It was sad that neither Mom nor Dad could attend my graduation or, more importantly, see me receive my Ephebian conformation. However, work came first. It always did.

The USC thing seemed to be resolved and everything appeared to be set for college. I received a call from Coach Sias, who had formerly worked as a lifeguard. He wanted to know if I was interested in applying for a job with the Santa Monica (beach) Lifeguard Service. I asked, "Why me?" He said that I was the fastest swimmer he knew, and the Lifeguards were looking for fast swimmers for their inter-agency competition. Starting salary would be $320 per week (remember it was 1957), and I could still work nights at the hotel.

The day after Coach Sias called, I got a call from Wilt Melnick. He was the younger brother of Dad's agent Al Melnick. Wilt was different from his polished brother, a bit pugnacious, but I liked and trusted him. Wilt said he wanted to set up an interview. "Nothing serious, just a conversation." I had no idea what the hell he was talking about. Agents! Anyway, I was curious so I went to Wilt's office in Beverly Hills, and together we drove to 20th Century-Fox. Wilt and I met with one of the producers in his very large well-appointed office. We made small talk for about twenty minutes, and then the producer said to Wilt, "See what Sandy thinks."

At Fox they have the New York street, the sound stages and then there are little bungalows scattered here and there with extensive landscaping. It's very attractive and very impressive. We entered one of the bungalows and there sat this unpretentious middle-aged man. He was introduced to me only as Sandy, and I had no idea who he was or what he did. At first I was a little put off by him, because he seemed to be talking in riddles. It also became obvious that he was from New York, Jewish, and gay. But we just started to talk, and talk, and talk. In thirty minutes I was no longer put off and liked him; in an hour I loved him. Frankly, I didn't want to leave. I can't remember a time in my life when I related to someone so quickly or so thoroughly. When we said our goodbyes, I wanted to embrace him. Wilt asked me to step outside so he could speak privately with Sandy.

When Wilt and I walked to the car, Wilt said Sandy felt I was a natural and had real potential, and he wanted to work with me. By this time I assumed Sandy had something to do with drama or films. Wilt said he is Sanford Meisner, the preeminent drama coach in the country, with a staggering client list that includes Meryl Streep, Robert DeNiro, Paul Newman and numerous others. Wilt continued that Meisner sees many actors before he makes this kind of judgment. The next day Wilt called to tell me that because of Meisner, 20th Century-Fox was offering me a one-year contract at $300 per week. God, what do I do now? I wasn't sure if I wanted to be an actor, but remembered my sadness while walking out of the Warner Bros. gate. In addition, I knew I wanted to spend more time with this very wise, thoughtful, and sensitive man. To me the best thing about Meisner was that he made performing sound honorable, honest, and simple. I thought it would be amusing to tell Dad, "Don't worry, I'm not going to USC. I'm going to 20th Century-Fox!"

I drove to Santa Monica as I had originally planned to fill out papers for the Lifeguard Service. I went near the corner of Ocean Ave. and Wilshire Blvd. and sat there for hours looking at the ocean. I ran through all the pros and cons and still could not arrive at a decision. Finally, and I don't know why, it just came to me. My priorities became clear and the decision, although painful, was easy. I'm going to college. The next day I called Melnick and the producer and politely turned them down. The producer was surprised and Wilt was pissed. That same day I filled out papers for the Santa Monica Beach Lifeguard Service, and the next day I would be taking my open water swimming test. Things were swirling around me and I loved it.

The day after turning down the Fox contract I was in orientation at the headquarters of the Santa Monica Beach Lifeguard Service. After orientation they split us into twos for the swimming test. We were to go off the lower end of the Santa Monica pier, swim to a buoy and then back. It was a one thousand yard swim and it had to be completed in less than forty minutes. My partner in the swim was a rookie from Michigan named Tom Johnson. He was big, blond and very friendly. We started at the same time with one man on a paddleboard as our escort. I took off and told the escort to stay with Tom. I finished in twenty minutes (the fastest time that year) and Tom was still out there. I swam back out to get him as he wanted to quit. The escort and I kept encouraging Tom to keep going, and he finally made it with a minute to spare. Tom and I remained friends for years, and he eventually became Captain of the entire Santa Monica Lifeguard Service. It figures!

They hired me because I could swim fast; however, I also had to be a real lifeguard. Being a beach lifeguard is quite a large responsibility. There are people who get in trouble in the water, lost kids, drunks, fights, and cuts and bruises. It looks like you are just sitting there but you are always on edge. Yes, it got easier as I gained experience, but for the first month or so I was exhausted at the end of each day. Many of the other lifeguards were real characters. They were very good at their job, but most were beach boys who never wanted to grow up. They wanted to minimize life's responsibilities and had little thoughts of a traditional life. They lived in small apartments near the beach, and their main objective was having fun, and they were very good at it. They had names that lifeguards should have: Buzzy Trent, Tim Guard, Beans Keenert, Rudy Kroon, Tom Zahn and so forth.

At Santa Monica there were unofficial segmented beaches. There was "Gay" beach, "Black" beach, "Muscle" beach, etc. I was stationed near the Ocean Park pier as it didn't bother me to swim under the pier between the pilings. The early morning when no one was there was the best part of the day. I'd get there and open up my tower, check in, then sit down and have a cup of coffee from my thermos and look out at the ocean. It was beautiful. However, there was a subtle metamorphosis between that empty tranquil beach to the absolute bedlam it would become later on. If I needed help, which was often, communications were good and someone was there immediately. At my age it was fun being the master of my own little domain. I liked helping people get out of the water, or fixing a cut, or picking glass out of bare feet, or helping a mom find her lost kid. The drunks and the knife fights were another matter. I had a phone; I called the cops.

But my real value to them, aside from fixing cuts or stopping knife fights, was swimming. The inter-service competition was approaching. I had been swimming at least two miles a day in the ocean, and it was a wonderful diversion from the monotony of the pool. They called the event the "Tapplin" after Judge Tapplin who put up the first trophy. There were four lifeguard services competing. They were Santa Monica City, Los Angeles County (North), Los Angeles County (South) and the City of Los Angeles. The competition was a big deal, and even the radio and newspapers covered it. It was to be held in Manhattan Beach at night. The competition was a relay — a big relay. It started out with a four-man swimming relay, then paddle boards, then finishing with a two-man dory boat through the surf.

I was to lead off, but surfing great Ricky Grigg (who became a PhD in Oceanography) insisted. The problem was that Grigg was just an average swimmer and was blind as a bat. But because of who he was, they let him lead off, and in the ocean at night he got lost. When Grigg came in, our team was last. I swam second and picked up a position, but we ended up second overall.

The summer went by quickly and being a lifeguard was much more of an adventure and much more fulfilling than I had anticipated. On my last day as a guard, I left early because I had to pick up my airline tickets at the travel agent in Beverly Hills. From Santa Monica beach I drove east on Pico Blvd. right past 20th Century-Fox Studios. As I looked up at the billboards and the sound stages, I thought about Sandy and choices I had made and wondered what I'd be doing if I'd gone in a different direction. But right now just two things were before me — being with Dad and preparing for college.

CHAPTER 27

New York
1957

I flew first class and was wearing a new tan summer weight suit. We had great tailwinds, and it looked like we'd be in New York in six hours with no stop in Chicago for fuel. It was Tuesday so Dad could pick me up as the show was "dark." It was great to see him. He had lost weight from dancing almost every night and had a tan from daily golf. He had rented a house on Long Island adjacent to a golf course and near the water. We dropped off my things and went directly to dinner at a waterfront restaurant. The show was a big hit and autograph seekers were everywhere. I'd forgotten how famous Dad was or how wonderful he was with people.

Mom was not there as she had left for home that morning. She didn't want the house to be empty, and I think she was a little homesick. In addition, she wanted to start getting the new Newport Beach house in order. Dad and I had a wonderful conversation. I finally filled him in on the *Lafayette* filming, the meeting at 20th Century-Fox and the contract offer, plus my duties as a lifeguard. Dad was overwhelmed. Then I asked him why he didn't take interest in what I was doing before. He tried but couldn't answer, and I think for the first time he realized he had been pretty detached from my daily life. But I didn't make an issue of it as I wanted our time together to be as pleasant as possible.

Dad had been doing the show for eight weeks and now had established a ritual. He would play golf in the morning, have lunch, and then go to the theater at about five. The show started at seven-thirty and was really something. As the symphony orchestra played the well known and beautiful overture, from behind the island stage came the floating Showboat. On the levy to greet the Showboat were a hundred black singers and dancers. On the Showboat were the principal cast members with Dad on top near the wheelhouse. As I said about Guy Lombardo — I liked his style.

The first night I wanted to see the program from the seats, and then the following nights I would be backstage with Dad. The show was unbelievable; no wonder it was a hit. When I saw it, it had been playing for eight weeks, and there were fifteen thousand people in the audience. I was so proud of Dad, and he, deservedly, was proud of himself. After the show Dad and I would have a light supper, usually with a friend or a cast member, and then go home.

There were three vivid memories I have of that time. The first was Dad's many costume changes. One night I was stage right, and Dad went out during this big musical number with his fly unzipped. I motioned to him but he didn't understand. So he kind of danced off stage and asked me what was wrong. I told him his fly was unzipped and, without blinking an eye, he said, "Well, you never heard of a dead man falling out of an open window." He then zipped up his fly and kind of danced back on stage.

The second was Mary Wickes. Mary was a well-known and accomplished character actress who had done everything. She was playing Captain Andy's wife Parthy in the show. She was a sweetheart and Dad adored her. She was also a pro who rarely made mistakes. However, one night when Dad and Mary had a lot of back and forth dialogue, Mary went blank. Dad picked up the slack brilliantly. "I know you like to keep things to yourself, Parthy, but I know what you're thinking, and that is…" Then Dad spoke all her lines. After ten agonizing minutes of Dad speaking to himself, Mary finally woke up and responded, "Captain Andy, sometimes you just talk too much," and then she went back to doing her own lines. No one panicked and everyone's timing was perfect. It was a master class in improvisation, all performed before thousands of patrons.

My third memory was of Don Drysdale. He was from Van Nuys and knew all of us. His nickname was "Porky" and, believe it or not, he was our high school's second-string pitcher. He was in his second year with the Brooklyn Dodgers, and they were in their last year at Ebbets Field. Ebbets Field was a bandbox (it held only 25,000) and was right in the middle of a neighborhood. If you hit a foul ball, it would land on somebody's roof. Don came to see the show and Dad told him I was coming, so Don made arrangements for me to see him pitch. I had never seen a major league game and it was a thrill to be there. Don won, but Hank Aaron tapped him for a home run and a double. The next week I went to Yankee Stadium. Now there was a ball park!

The time with Dad was special. We should have done it years ago. It was so special because it was one-on-one. Ever since spending that time with Dad, I have made it a point to spend one-on-one time with my daughter and my grandchildren. I loved going into the city and returning to all the famous places — The Statue of Liberty, The Plaza, Rockefeller Center, Empire State Building. I even walked by my favorite place, "21" Club. I made arrangements to work out at the New York Athletic Club. It was right off Central Park; old but very nice. The Club had a pool and a gym, and as I said, I just love fancy places.

Our two unforgettable weeks were coming to an end, and I had to enroll in school. Dad's play ended three days before I was to enroll, and we were driving his new car back to Los Angeles. We decided that I would leave two days early and drive to St. Louis. Dad would fly to St. Louis, and then we would drive together to Denver. From Denver I would fly home and Dad would drive alone back to Los Angeles.

Dad's car was an 88 Oldsmobile station wagon with three carburetors. The car was fast. After I left, it took me two hours to drive from Long Island to the Pennsylvania Turnpike. At two in the morning I arrived in Columbus, Ohio and stayed at a pleasant motel. It was five hours to St. Louis so I could be there mid-day. Dad was coming in the late afternoon, so everything should work out.

The next day I picked Dad up at the airport in St. Louis, and we went directly to the estate of his close friend, Mahlon Wallace. The estate was called Amagraja. It was built in 1908 and was an architectural master-piece. Mahlon was chairman of his family business, The Wallace Pencil Company, which is the largest wooden pencil company in the world. (Have you ever heard of a Ticonderoga #2?) Mahlon's wife was Audrey Faust of the beer family that became part of Anheuser-Busch. They were friends of Dad's because of their mutual interest in bird hunting and train-ing Labrador Retrievers. For all their wealth they were unpretentious and pleasant. However, at Amagraja it was difficult to be unpretentious. Dad and I were their guests for a spectacular dinner that was full of laughs and stories. We went to bed early as we were driving to Lincoln, Nebraska the next morning, then on to North Platte where a group including the Wallaces was going antelope hunting.

In Lincoln we met with another hunting friend, Bill Harder. Bill and I flew his plane to North Platte and Dad drove to meet us. The Wallaces arrived in their plane late the same afternoon. The next day the hunt-ing was challenging and the landscape beautiful (remember *Dances with Wolves*). Everyone had a great time, and old friendships became stronger. That afternoon Dad and I drove to Denver, and I was on an evening flight to Los Angeles.

CHAPTER 28

The Five Freshman
1958

With all the things I'd done in my life, I thought adjusting to college would be easy, but it wasn't. I rented a large two-bedroom apartment off campus as the rents were cheaper if you were further away from school. It needed a lot of work, but had potential. My first roommate was a friend from high school. However, he fell in love with a Cuban girl and then ran off to fight for Castro. Then I found two more roommates. One was an Orthodox Jew who was now an atheist. The other was an Evangelical Christian from Texas. They were both nuts. After two months I kicked them both out and lived alone for the rest of the semester. During that time I started refurbishing the apartment.

My first year I studied architecture, which is a very difficult major. For example, when I enrolled in my first semester design class, there were sixty-five students. When I finished, there were sixteen. My design teacher was Emmet Wemple. He had an active practice downtown and would eventually become dean of the school. I finished my freshman year in architecture, and then changed my major to finance and accounting. But the things I learned from that first year would serve me well in my career. Dean Wemple would remain my friend and mentor for many years. Sometime later I was invited to Dean Wemple's wedding. At the wedding he introduced a few of us as his favorite students. As we were standing to applause, he humorously continued that we were far from his best students, just his favorites.

I contacted Coach Peter Daland about swimming. He was very organized and so dedicated. I said to myself, if ever I was going to have a chance at a national ranking, this is the guy. He told me the two Australian Olympic Champions had enrolled and two of the best swimmers from Southern California would also be on the team. Peter said dryly, "With some work, the five of you might do something." I was flattered

FABULOUS FROSH WIN AAU CHAMPIONSHIP

TROY'S FIVE-MAN SWIM TEAM
NIPS FAVORED NEW HAVEN, 55-54

SC's Fabulous Frosh—performing like the true champions they are—captured the National AAU indoor swimming championship held last month at Yale University.

To quote Frank Birmingham, Sports Editor of the NEW HAVEN JOURNAL-COURIER, "No swim expert can recall when a five-man team ever captured the National Championship before, especially when the favored entry registered 27 competitors with representation in virtually every competition but diving."

'Most Startling'

He continued: "The most startling of all performances was turned in by the University of Southern California freshmen coached by Peter Deland, once a member of the Yale Staff."

"With just five members on the team—Captain Dennis Devine, son of movie and TV star Andy Devine, Murray Rose, Jon Henricks, Don Redington and Tom Winters—Deland's young squad stunned Coach Bob Kiphuth's favored New Haven swim club to score a one-point victory in the race for team honors," Birmingham stated.

Stunning Performances

Rose and Henricks, the two great Australian Olympic champions, turned in stunning performances as they paced teammates to victory. Rose competed in nine events during the three-day competition, while Henricks swam in 10 events in two days. Redington and Winters each competed in seven events and Devine raced in three.

"They're all eager and hungry freshmen," Deland enthused after the final score was officially recorded.

Going into the final event, SC had to finish fourth or better in the 400-yard medley relay to outscore favorite New Haven which was tabbed to win that event (and did). The Trojan relay team, sparked by Henrick's sizzling performance, came through with the decisive fourth place finish. Talk about excitement!

Top Scorer

Recording 21 points, triple winner Murray Rose was awarded the individual high point medal. Rose captured the 1,500-meters, 220-yard freestyle and 440-yard freestyle (the same three events he won at the '56 Olympics) and established meet records in the latter two events.

TEAM SCORES:
USC FROSH, 55; NEW HAVEN S.C. 54; COCA COLA S.C., 22; CLEVELAND S.C. 20; NORTH CAROLINA S.C. 19; PORPOISE CLUB, NEW YORK CITY, 17; INDIANAPOLIS A.C., 10; DOLPIN S.C. LONG BEACH, 9; U.S. ARMY, 7; WALTER REED S.C. 4; WICHITA S.C. 2.

MEET RESULTS:

220-YARDS FREESTYLE—
1. Rose (SC Frosh) 2:02.5
2. Henricks (SC Frosh) 2:02.5
3. Hanley (Unat.) 2:03.5
4. Anderson, R. (New Haven S.C.) 2:05.6
5. Farrell (Wichita S.C.) 2:06.2
6. Follett (New Haven S.C.) ... 2:08.

220-YARDS BREASTSTROKE—
1. Munsch (Porpoise Club, N.Y.C.) 2:38.5
2. Collet (Unat.) 2:39.8
3. Griffin (Walter Reed S.C.) . 2:41.7
4. Hopkins (Unat.) 2:42.3
5. Sanguily (Unat.) 2:42.6
6. Padgen (No. Carolina A.C.) . 2:44.8

220-YARDS BUTTERFLY—
1. Yorzyk (Unat.) 2:18.0
2. Tashnick (Unat.) 2:18.4
3. Jecko (New Haven S.C.) 2:21.6
4. Barton (Unat.) 2:24.3
5. Nelson (No. Carolina A.C.) . 2:24.7
6. Harrison (Unat.—Stanford, Cal.) 2:36.7

220-YARDS BACKSTROKE—
1. McKinney (Unat.) 2:16.9
2. Bittick (Dolphin S.C., L.B.) 2:17.6
3. Beaver (Unat.) 2:24.0
4. Schaefer (Cleveland S.C.) .. 2:24.8
5. Dolbey (New Haven S.C.) 2:27.8
6. Dearstyne (Unat.) 2:30.1

100-YARDS FREESTYLE—
1. Larson (Unat.—Los Angeles) . 49.5
2. Anderson (New Haven S.C.) .. 49.6
3. Henricks (SC Frosh) 49.6
4. Aubrey (New Haven S.C.) 50.1
5. Van Horn (Unat.) 50.1

100-YARDS BREASTSTROKE—
1. Sanguily (Unat.) 1:04.2
2. Munsch (Porpoise Club, NYC) 1:04.9
3. Collet (Unat.) 1:05.1
4. Padgen (No. Carolina A.C.) . 1:06.2
5. Koletsky (New Haven S.C.) .. 1:06.2
6. Rumpel (New York A.C.) 1:07.6

100-YARDS BUTTERFLY—
1. Tashnick (Unat.) 54.3
2. Larson (Unat.—Los Angeles) . 54.3
3. Jerko (New Haven S.C.) 55.0
4. Fredericks (Unat.—Los Angeles) 56.2
5. Weldon (Unat.—Palos Verdes Est.) 56.4
6. Jastremski (Glass City Aquat. Club) 56.4

440-YARDS FREESTYLE—
1. Rose (SC Frosh) 4:21.6
2. Henricks (SC Frosh) 4:36.9
3. Heinrich (Unat.—Hayward, Cal.) 4:37.1
4. Gyorffy (New Haven S.C.) ... 4:37.5
5. Nordstrom (Coca Cola S.C.) . 4:37.6
Hopkins, G. (Unat.) 4:38.8

"Fabulous Frosh Win AAU Championship."

he included me in that group. He then informed me that he was also coaching at the Los Angeles Athletic Club downtown. I would become a member and would train there part time.

Dry land exercises and weight work would start the following Monday at the Athletic Club. The way Daland informed me he made it sound more like an order than a suggestion. Peter's workouts at the Club were

USC swim team at large.

very demanding and I was exhausted the whole first month. Lots of light weights with numerous repetitions concentrating on specific muscle groups. This training was done on a mat under Peter's careful supervision. In addition, we did wall-mounted pulley weights and ran on the indoor track. I would train at the Club every day for three months before I would get into the water and for six months before the season started.

The months of training and school flew by. Christmas vacation was approaching and Daland was having two-a-day workouts all through the holidays. I worked out every workout of every day as the season was about to start. The five freshman were the mainstay of the team. We came from different places, had different interests, had different abilities, and enjoyed different degrees of public attention. The five of us had separate and individual personalities, and we were not each other's best friend. However, we all got along great. There was no jealousy or competitiveness among us. As a team we had flexibility because we all could swim different events besides our specialty. I don't remember anyone ever having a bitch, but

FABULOUS FROSH—Troy's sensational f i v e - man swimming team, pictured above with Coach Peter Deland, gathers around scoreboard after winning Senior Men's National AAU Indoor Swim Championships at Yale University. Coach Deland, obviously quite pleased, points to 55 points SC Frosh tallied in nosing out the favored New Haven Swim Club, 55-54. Standing in front are Murray Rose and Jon Henricks (right). Left to right, in rear, are Tom Winters, Don Redington and Captain Dennis Devine. Devine is holding the team championship trophy. Story and meet results on page 2.

"Fabulous Frosh."

if we did, it was all brought out in the team meetings. Peter loved team meetings and these meetings would usually end up with a great deal of laughter. It seemed we all laughed a lot. And much of that laughter was aimed at the formal and buttoned-down Daland, who handled it all so well. Daland was my new Father Smith, a person I admired and loved.

Just before the season started I was elected team Captain, an honor I

The Five Freshmen and Coach Daland leaving for Yale, circa 1958.

cherish to this day. Our first dual meet was with our own varsity, and we beat them soundly. One of the members of that varsity team was a tall, unassuming, intelligent guy named Bill Lugosi. However his real name was Bella Lugosi, Jr. Yes, he really was the son of Dracula. He went on to become a prominent attorney, have a family, and do it all without much fanfare. What has always fascinated me was the number of celebrity children who go to school, have families, pay taxes, and nobody ever hears about 'em.

Our freshman team easily won all of our remaining dual meets. However, our mild appearing coach was far more ambitious than we had given him credit for. He was looking ahead and wanted us to compete in the National AAU championships at Yale University, his former employer.

In the late fifties, freshmen could not compete in NCAA events. Therefore, our only chance for national exposure was to compete in the

National AAUs. To compete, the other universities would combine their varsity with the freshmen and the alumni and enter as a club team. For example, Yale University competed as the New Haven Swim Club, and Indiana University competed as the Hoosier Athletic Club. Never before or since has a university freshman team, by itself, entered the National AAU Championships. Daland knew there were just five of us and his

1960 Olympic Trials, Detroit, Michigan. "Close, but no cigar."

goal was to have us make a good showing and gain some national experience. Because the finals were on national television, Daland thought the exposure would be helpful in future recruiting. Little did any of us know what magical thing would take place.

We won the National Championship, and we won it over The New Haven Swim Club (Yale) by just one point. Daland was thought of as the least likely to succeed when he left the Yale staff. And here he was, with his very first team, beating the naysayers in their own backyard. Most of us knew the Yale "back-story," and how much this meant to Peter. It was retribution of the highest order. The win catapulted the USC swimming program into national prominence, as evidenced by the bumper crop of freshmen that would enroll the following year. That new freshman team would be led by my old competitor Lance Larson.

In 2008 the five freshmen would be honored by the University in celebrating the fiftieth anniversary of their victory. It would be held at half-time on the floor of the Los Angeles Memorial Coliseum before ninety-four thousand people. As I was now approaching seventy, I finally had the opportunity to stand on Coliseum grass and look up into the stands filled with people. It was the dream I'd had since high school.

Dennis Devine.

CHAPTER 29

Embracing Success
1958

The *Hickok* money was coming in and Dad was taking it easy. Ten weeks of *Showboat* was physically exhausting for a fifty-three-year-old man who weighed two hundred and seventy-five pounds. Dad loved his new waterfront home, golf at his country club, and boating with his new Orange County friends. He was proud of my freshman accomplishments and had met Coach Daland and some of my professors. He now loved USC. He even acquired a red Stanford blanket with the white block 'S' in the middle. He had a seamstress put a gold U and C on each side of the Stanford S.

Dad was now able to spend more time with his friends at the Bohemian Club in San Francisco. The Bohemian Club was founded in 1872 by newspapermen who enjoyed each other's company. Over the years the membership of the Club expanded to include members beyond the Bay area while still focusing on art and entertainment. The Club has a wide variety of members from all types of backgrounds. In the early forties Bing Crosby introduced Dad to his attorney Jack O'Melveny. Jack asked Dad if he would be his guest at the Club's retreat which is located north of San Francisco and is called the Bohemian Grove. The Club has many events at the Grove, but the big one is the two-week summer encampment. Dad had the time of his life and wanted to join. Walter Bunker first met Dad on *The Jack Benny Show* and became Dad's sponsor for membership in the Club. At first he was rejected because the Membership Chairman said, "We have singers Laurence Melchior and John Charles Thomas, and we don't need any more fat entertainers or people from Hollywood." The next year Dad was accepted and over the years he participated in numerous Club events. He became a beloved member and would remain so for the rest of his life.

Dad also had the time to enjoy bird shooting. He belonged to two duck clubs, one north of Los Angeles and another in Utah. Once a year Dad would go pheasant hunting in Nebraska, and we always had the annual

September family dove hunt in lower California. He had a number of friends in the exclusive and expensive Venice Island Duck Club. It was started by Barron Hilton and was limited to ten members. Clark Gable was a member and Phil Harris had often attended as a guest. Dad was invited many times but replied, "I don't want to go because I can't afford it and I'm sure I'd like it too much. I can't even afford the cashmere long underwear all those rich guys wear." As an adult I have attended as the guest of William Tilley and Dana Martin. At the Club there are lots of birds, but more laughs. It would have been a dream to share this Shangri-La of duck hunting with Dad. The founder, Barron Hilton, who although well known, is truly a regular guy and one of the nicest men to grace this earth.

Dad and Mom were getting along well and both looked happy and rested. Mom was tall and athletic and always kept her figure. She was attractive and it was as though she would never age. Although Dad was big, he was strong and carried himself well. He had a wonderful tailor named Roberto DeChillis who dressed him very well. Actors Robert Cummings and James Coburn also were customers. I remember in the early sixties going with Dad to a fitting. Coburn showed up in his beautiful Ferrari with an additional clothing designer. With his toothy smile and thin build, there was pure joy on the actor's face as the three men created jackets, suits, and overcoats. Coburn was a man who truly embraced life.

It was 1958 and Dad would not make a film until 1960. He had worked so hard for so long, and I admired his ability to finally relax. Many compulsive workers are uncomfortable when they don't have a project or have too much time. Dad did not suffer from that problem. However, his summer of golf and boating was interrupted when he got a call from St. Louis. The famed St. Louis Muni Opera wanted Dad to reprise his role as Captain Andy in *Showboat*. It would be presented with a full symphony orchestra and would be showcased more like an operetta than a New York stage production. The presentation would be far more lavish than even New York. In the two-week run, there would only be eight performances. Although Dad's phrasing and timing were perfect, the contrast of Andy Devine singing with opera singers was humorously unforgettable. Dad made the most of it and enjoyed a standing ovation every night.

Coming home from the Yale Championship was an adjustment. I never had people pay much attention to me before. Many of our family friends knew of our success, and I even heard from old high school class-mates. At the swimming banquet our team was honored, and each of the five freshmen was presented with a gold wrist watch. For the summer I planned to stay at school and train with Daland. I would represent the Los Angeles Athletic Club, and they would pay my travel expenses. We would be training at the Coliseum pool, and for the first time in my life I wasn't going to work during the summer. My freshman year was coming to an end and for a brief period of time there were no workouts. Although my academic finals were looming, it was going to be fun living a normal life, if only for a few weeks.

I was living alone in the apartment which was now in great shape. I had refinished the old wooden floors, purchased furniture from swap meets, bought new appliances, and painted the entire place. That year I met Michael Wilkie who was a junior at Black-Foxe prep school. He was also training with Daland at the Los Angeles Athletic Club. Mike was a very good swimmer and came from a prominent family. He and I became good friends and, although he was going to be a senior in high school, he looked older than I did.

Over time I got to know his parents, who were very bright, interested in everything, and fun to be with. Mike asked if he could move into my apartment for his high school senior year. I thought it would be great as he had no money issues, was easy to be with, and seemed reasonable. He went to his parents and after some selling, they thoughtfully agreed. Mike was a wonderful companion and I didn't realize how lonely I had been being there alone. We would live together in that same apartment for three-plus years.

Mike would usually go home to Chicago for the summer and then take an extended trip. I would stay home and train. Summer training at an Olympic-sized (fifty meter) pool is where you really improve. It was three hours in the morning (starting at seven) and two hours in the afternoon (ending at five). I would be training with the best swimmers in the world. The work was repetitive and tedious and I had no outside life. After a week or so it was like being in a trance, and I only had time to eat and swim and sleep. Athletically I had a lot of catching up to do, and before me was the opportunity. I couldn't feel sorry for myself as this is what all the world class athletes do. The chance to work hard and try to really accomplish something was exciting.

In the early months of 1958, I went to a talk given by William Yorzick who had won the gold medal in the 200-meter butterfly in the 1956 Olympics. Afterward there was a question and answer period and then I was able to meet him. That summer there were no international events or dual meets like in college. There were only spot meets that were like glorified time-trials. What everyone was shooting for was the National

Outdoor Championships to be held in Michigan. I entered the 200-meter butterfly and the 200-meter freestyle. In the Nationals you swim heats in order to qualify for the finals. They take the eight fastest times for each final. So if you make the finals in an event, it means you're one of the top eight swimmers in the country. I didn't make it in the freestyle, but qualified seventh in the butterfly. When I stepped to my starting block for the finals, next to me was William Yorzick, the man whose lecture I attended some four months before. Yorzick came in second, I came in sixth; I was getting closer.

The summer swimming season and the National championships were over. I did better than I or anyone else expected. My sophomore year was about to commence and I was looking forward to my new finance courses. My major wasn't easy, but it was less demanding than architecture. Mike Wilkie was a great roommate. He was fun to be with. It was six weeks before dry land workouts would start at the Athletic Club, and I wanted to enjoy the fall season (even in California) with football games, parties, etc.

My first year of college I did not have a date, and I like girls. It was the start of my sophomore year and one of the larger fraternities was rushing me. They fixed me up with a date and invited me to a fraternity-sorority party. My very first college party was unforgettable. I was fixed up with a very attractive sorority girl, and the party was to be held at the home of one of the sorority parents. The home was large and beautiful and located in Beverly Hills. Believe me, I was clueless. My date rang the doorbell and Danny Thomas opened the door and greeted us. Margie Thomas (now Marlo) was the sorority sister hosting the party and it was far more sophisticated than any college party I'd ever heard of. I was under the impression that college parties were like *Animal House* and this looked more like *Mad Men* (remember it was November of 1958). Later I would find out that there were parties like *Animal House* — lots of 'em!

I had always thought Danny Thomas was Jewish. However, in the home were numerous crosses and religious artifacts, including a wooden carving of *The Last Supper* in the dining room. As the story goes, Hillcrest Country Club is the most prominent all-Jewish country club in the Los Angeles area. Its membership includes all of the Jewish show business stalwarts such as Jack Benny, Al Jolson, and Milton Berle. The Club finally decided to accept Danny Thomas, who would become the club's first Gentile member. George Burns quipped, "You'd think that when we finally took in a Gentile, we could have gotten a Gentile that looked like a Gentile."

As my roommate and I became better friends, I went to visit his parents in the Montecito area of Santa Barbara. In the thirties Michael's father Leighton started a machine tool company that turned into a giant. Leighton was smart and handsome and had insatiable interests. Michael's mother Adele was charismatic and enthusiastic about everything. It was great spending time with them in Santa Barbara. There were dinner parties at the Wilkie's home, debutante parties at Christmas and scuba diving off the nearby Channel Islands with Mike's Santa Barbara friends. Life was so good I could hardly believe it, but I did believe it, I truly did!

CHAPTER 30

Mortality
1959

Dad was now fifty-four and becoming more aware of his own mortality. Down deep he wanted to prove himself to his father but felt he was running out of time. Of course there was nothing he could do about it. That year alone Dad lost friends including Oliver "Babe" Hardy (Laurel and Hardy), Tyrone Power, Bud Abbott (Abbott and Costello), and Victor McLaglen. It was also during that time that the infamous Harry Cohn died. He was a big part of Dad's life as Dad had worked for Cohn off and on for nineteen years. Cohn was the autocratic head of Columbia pictures and a rude, penny-pinching bastard. He would often show up on a set just to berate anyone available. Just before he died, he ordered a screen test for New York actor Peter Falk (*Columbo*). Falk, who only had one eye, nailed the test and Cohn loved it. When Falk's agent quoted his price, Cohn replied, "Hell, for that much money I can get an actor with two eyes."

There was a very famous portrait painter whom Cohn had summoned in order to have his portrait painted. Cohn was immediately abrupt and rude to the artist. After a few minutes the painter, knowing Cohn's reputation, decided to decline the commission. Cohn really wanted this portrait and told the painter that he would double whatever he normally charged. The artist further declined. Cohn then asked, "What would it take for you to paint my portrait?" As the artist was exiting Cohn's office, he turned to Cohn and replied, "Perhaps a broom and a bucket of shit."

When Cohn died Dad went to his funeral. The word got out that everyone would be there, so now Dad really wanted to attend. The memorial was held at one of the sound stages at Columbia. Dad sat with Bill Wellman and the place was standing room only. The services were about to begin and a hush came over the room. Red Skelton then stood up and made his famous comment, "Harry Cohn always believed if you give the public something they really want to see, and at a fair price, you'll pack the house." The next year Ward Bond unexpectedly passed away in Texas. At his funeral, knowing that Bond was a Ford favorite, the press asked director John Ford to comment on Bond's passing. The irascible and plain spoken Ford simply replied, "Now Andy Devine is the biggest asshole I know."

Because of these deaths, Dad thought maybe it was time to do some of the things he had always wanted to do. He continued to turn down work as he had gotten into the rhythm of staying home, playing golf, and being with my mom. He always dreamed of having a van for personal travel, so he made the purchase and had it customized to accommodate his size and needs. I was worried it might be a passing fancy, but two days after he took delivery, he and Mom took off and they didn't come home for a month. Their first stop was Las Vegas where they had been married. Then to Dad's home town of Kingman, Arizona, where the main street now bore his name and there was a small museum which contained his memorabilia. Next was Denver, Aspen, Salt Lake, Reno, and The Bohemian Grove north of San Francisco. The final leg was his favorite, Highway 1 from San Francisco to Los Angeles.

He also became a licensed ham radio operator (WB6RER). While they were touring, Dad would be in contact with his friends all over the country. Their married life was far from perfect, but the trip in that van really did something. They got to know each other and became friends and lovers all over again. Throughout the years the two of them would continue to take trips. Years later, when Dad first got sick, Mom and I refurbished the van (including body work and a great paint job) and put the reconditioned vehicle outside his hospital room window. You never saw a man get well faster.

Although Dad said he didn't want to work, he did change his mind and accepted the role of Captain Andy in another production of *Showboat*. The show would be held in Clio, Michigan and was another lavish production with only eight performances. Best of all, the money was great.

CHAPTER 31

The Boys Club
1959

My sophomore year continued and I was enjoying a more active social life. Both Mike Wilkie and I joined the same fraternity. The apartment building Mike and I lived in evolved into kind of a club. The building had only eight units, and as vacancies came up, my friends (who weren't nuts) would move in. We would eventually call the place The 25th Street Boys Club. My classes were challenging as my reading, although improved, was still slow. I became a big fan of Dr. Frank Baxter and would often go to his readings. He was a PhD in literature who specialized in Shakespeare, but he should have been an actor. Dry land exercises had started and it was back to the old grind. The new freshman team was with us, and we were loaded with talent. Unfortunately our school was put on one-year athletic probation because of football recruiting violations. Some genius decided to recruit a bunch of coal miners from Pennsylvania. This would prevent us from competing in the NCAA national championships. However, we could compete, along with the new freshman, in the National AAU Championships.

Again I stayed at school during Christmas vacation to train with Daland. However, I did take three days off to visit the Wilkies in Santa Barbara and partake in the debutante season. The black-tie parties, the young girls, and the fabulous homes were all a wonder. Even after my time in Beverly Hills, I had no idea that anyone really lived like this. The rest of the semester was classes, football games, and working out. I'd gotten into a groove and life was fun and predictable. With the new freshmen and a few transfers, we easily won the National AAU Championships. It was again held at Yale in the spectacular Payne-Whitney Gymnasium, the most overwhelming athletic facility I had ever seen. I came in fifth in the nation in the 200-yard butterfly and scored in the relay.

Upon returning from Yale via a "red-eye" from New York, I immediately went to school. As I entered my first morning class I saw that they were having a mid-term exam. I was up on my reading, but had no idea they were having a mid-term. As they passed out the "blue books," this guy behind me tapped me on the shoulder and said, "I don't know anything, you gotta help me." I replied, "Not only are you ill prepared, but unlucky. I just got off of a plane from New York." But he looked like a good guy, so I said, "I'll try to help." Imagine someone wanting to cheat off of me! When the exam was finished, I left the room thinking I'd never see this guy again.

I went home, took a nap and that afternoon drove to Las Vegas as an old friend was getting married the next day Following the wedding at a Las Vegas hotel, I was exiting through the casino and stopped at a crap table. I rolled five straight passes which created a nice little nest egg. Just as I was about to leave, this guy from behind tapped me on the shoulder. "I'm broke, you gotta help me." I turned around and it was the same guy from the test. "How in the hell do I get rid of you?" He pleaded, "I need a hundred bucks." I gave him the hundred, and he rolled four straight passes. Now he had six hundred dollars and paid me back my hundred. He said he'd like to buy me a beer. "A beer!? I get you through your exam, I finance your crap game and you want to buy me a beer!" "Well, how about dinner?" " You're on." We have been friends ever since. His name is Mike Mandekic and we've shared many adventures. We've skied all over the Rockies, water-skied at Lake Powell, even raced a sailboat to Hawaii. We've endured numerous football games and tailgate parties and competed with vengeance on the tennis court. Our moms, wives, and kids became friends. Mike owned one of the most popular bars in L.A. and then became successful in real estate. Mike has more friends in Los Angeles than anyone I know. By the way, we both got a "C" on that mid-term.

During that time I also got to know Dad's publicity agent. Stanley Musgrove had a large and diverse client list. As a kid I hardly knew Stanley, but he loved Dad and had worked for him for years. He had graduated from USC with a major in film and television, and was an avid alumni. When I was Captain of the National Championship swimming team he was very involved and very proud. Stanley was clever, knew everybody, and was very gay. He had the greatest stories and lived in a section of West Hollywood known as Boy's Town. From time to time we would have lunch or dinner, but always kept in touch.

One night, Stanley invited me to have dinner with himself, Rock Hudson, and Cole Porter. In passing I mentioned this to Mom. She hit the roof. She said, "You're not going to dinner — you are the dinner!" I said Stanley is harmless, but if you want me to cancel dinner I'll simply call him. Mom said, "Bullshit, I'll call him." I never went to dinner, and I never met Rock Hudson or Cole Porter. Stanley would continue to work for Dad, and he would remain my close friend until his passing. When Cole Porter died in 1964, Stanley was the only one with him. Stanley was holding Porter's hand.

I often played racquetball at school with assistant football coaches Dave Levy and Marv Goux. Through them I met a new assistant football coach named John McKay. He had an aura about him that was authoritarian and a little scary. In many ways he reminded me of film director Bill Wellman. As the years went by he became head football coach and we remained friendly. A few years after graduation I got to know a man named Hulsey Lokey. Hulsey and his army buddy Hugh Culverhouse were trying to acquire the Tampa Bay NFL franchise. With Hulsey and Hugh I sweated through this process for over two years. I was with them the day they closed the deal. When everything was concluded, they hired John McKay as their first head coach. Because of my relationship with the owners, I got to know John and his wife Corky even better. McKay was very smart, very funny, and very moody. There was nobody quite like him.

During my junior year my roommate Mike Wilkie and I developed a new skill. It was crashing parties. Not just any parties, but really big parties. In those days they always had the post Academy Awards party at the Beverly Hilton. I knew how to go to the lower men's room, then up the elevator where you were right outside the entrance to the main ballroom. In the elevator I would pick someone really famous, introduce myself, then as we were exiting the elevator, put my arm around the famous person and walk in while you are speaking with him. It was very exciting. Mike and I must have done the Academy Awards three years in a row.

We also crashed movie premieres, big private parties and Hollywood charity events. We got thrown out a few times, but who bats a thousand? There was one party that was the party crashers' "Super Bowl." In the early sixties there were three prominent Hollywood restaurants. They were The Brown Derby (still hanging in there), Chasen's, and Romanoff's. Prince Michael Romanoff (he wasn't the prince of anything — except maybe bullshit) was a real Hollywood character, and he and his restaurant had been famous for years. The word on the street was that he was carrying so many IOUs from broke actors that he had to go out of business. So he decided to have one final party (I'm sure his wealthier patrons paid for it) and have it on New Year's Eve. And what a party it was. As I said, Tony Duquette's party (the one with Mike Todd) was the biggest party

Hollywood had seen in years. However this one was by far the best —
without question.

Now when you go to any Hollywood party there are about fifteen
percent famous people and eighty-five percent people who kind of look
famous, but you really have no idea as to who they really are. At this party
everyone was famous. Frank Sinatra, Dean Martin, Marlon Brando, James
Stewart, Gene Kelly, and on and on and on. It didn't look like names
were being checked at the door because everyone was so famous. I told
Mike Wilkie we should just barge in without a care in the world. Our
dates were really pretty, sexy, and beautifully dressed (not overdone). To
my amazement both girls thought this was really going to be fun, as we
hadn't told them our plans until we picked them up. We pulled up, got
out of the car and laughed all the way in — nobody laid a glove on us.
Once we were inside it was overwhelming. Les Brown was playing with
his fifty-piece orchestra. Champagne and caviar were everywhere, and
before us were one-hundred A list celebrities.

We went to the bar and there was actress Melina Mercouri, who had
just won an Oscar for *Never on Sunday*. My date knew a little Greek,
so they started talking and laughing and drinking right away. Then the
columnist James Bacon showed up and gave me a big hug and started to
introduce me around. For some reason Bacon wasn't surprised I was there.
He introduced me to Warren Beatty, who was with Natalie Wood. Of
course I knew Natalie, but Warren thought he knew me because without
his glasses he can't see anything. Wilkie and I were having the time of our
lives, and we wishfully started to believe we were really invited.

Our dates were really something and they both were handling this
whole thing with such cool sophistication. Then Bacon brought over our
host Mike Romanoff. My date also spoke some Russian and Romanoff
loved it. He was all over her. With Romanoff and Bacon on each side
of us at the bar, there was an endless parade of celebrities who came by
to wish us well. After an hour or so the dinner bell tastefully rang and
everyone commenced to be seated. Problem was all the seats had place
cards. We waited to see if there were any empty seats, but no luck. Time
to go, and our dates agreed. Wearing black tie, and with the girls looking
so beautiful, we went to a wonderful diner and reminisced and laughed
about our unforgettable New Year's Eve adventure. I didn't get home that
night so the next day, still in my tuxedo, I hitchhiked to the Rose Bowl
football game. Ah, youth!

Through my friendship with Michael Wilkie, I met an unforgettable
character who lived in Michael's hometown of Chicago. With very little

money, he bought an abandoned strip club on the North Side of Chicago and opened it up as a bar carrying his own name — Butch McGuire's. Butch was a loyal family man and kind of a resident philosopher. He just had that innate leadership quality and people were drawn to him. When I first met Butch, he and a group of friends were going to start a disco near Butch's bar. Observing the popularity fluctuations of these types of businesses, I talked the group out of entering into this venture, and that's when Butch and I became close friends. In later years Butch became a member of the Bohemian Club, and he regaled the other members with stories of owning a bar on the North Side of Chicago. When he died a few years ago, there were six thousand people paying tribute to Butch's memory. He was truly an unforgettable character.

CHAPTER 32

Rome
1960

The 1959 Pan American trials didn't go as hoped. Although I swam my best times, I came in fourth in the 200-butterfly (they took three) and seventh in the 200-freestyle (they took six). I missed, but came so close. Although I didn't make it, Coach Daland felt I still had a shot at making the Rome Olympics. The next real test would be the next NCAA indoor championships.

Because of the importance of the upcoming meets, I took a lighter academic schedule. Our team was loaded, but everyone was aware that Indiana and Yale had great teams. We easily won all of our dual meets. In fact, most of the leading swimmers trained through these meets. In our training Daland did two very unique things. First we trained in a long course 50-meter Olympic pool, but the indoor Nationals would be held in a short course 25-yard pool. Secondly, we worked and worked, as Daland was tearing us down. When we started tapering down and working on speed, I thought I was going to jump out of my skin.

My first event in the NCAA Championships was the 200-yard butterfly, and I broke the existing American record and came in a close second to Mike Troy of Indiana. My second event was the 100-yard butterfly, and I came in third behind Troy and Lance Larson. The only people to beat me in that meet would win gold medals in that year's Olympics. Everyone swam great, and we won the NCAA Championship. USC has had a proud heritage in athletics, but this was their very first NCAA Championship in swimming. Because of that team, many more NCAA Swimming Championships would come to USC.

The semester was over and now everyone was training for the National Outdoors and the Olympic trials. For an average swimmer, making the Olympic team is not only difficult, it is tricky and often requires a bit of luck. In the past they took three athletes in each event. That doesn't limit you to that event but gets you on the team. After you are on the team, you swim whatever event you're best at. In 1960 they decided to take two swimmers in each event instead of three. In addition, my best two events were scheduled thirty minutes apart in seven days of trials. That planning was thoughtless and inexcusable.

This meant I had to choose one event or the other, but not both. Also, in those days they had far fewer events than they do today. I pulled out of the 200-butterfly and entered the 200-freestyle because they were taking six for the relay. I narrowly missed. I played the odds and lost. David Gillanders from Michigan was a swimmer I swam against four times in National competition, and I beat him all four times. He came in second in the 200-butterfly trials and made the team. He then came in third in the Olympics and received a bronze medal. Good for him. As for myself, I guess there were certain things that weren't meant to be.

CHAPTER 33

Back to Work

1960

After two years of semi-retirement Dad sensed something missing from his life. It was just his nature to be working, and he realized that as a public figure you can be easily forgotten. In addition, Dad was aware that most overweight actors seemed to be interchangeable. This became evident one day at lunch. Dad was doing voiceovers in Hollywood and I met him for lunch at the The Brown Derby. Benny Massi was there and we had fun reminiscing. While we were there, this nice older woman came to our booth. She went on and on as to what a great actor Dad was. She then politely asked, "Could I have your autograph, Mr. Laughton?" (thinking Dad was Charles Laughton). Dad obliged her request by signing Charles Laughton and she was on her way.

A copy of the huge photo mural from the film How the West Was Won, *located in the reception foyer at MGM Studios. Dad is behind the camera in the Union Army uniform directing, of all people, director John Ford (in front of the camera). Also in the photograph are actress Carole Baker, standing near the camera, and actor George Peppard, sitting with the dog in his lap. Circa 1963.*

Dad's quest for work continued and he was cast in the film *Huckleberry Finn* at M-G-M. A humorous thing took place while they were shooting interiors at the studio. At USC, three weeks before Homecoming they choose five princesses. Then the night before Homecoming they choose one of the princesses as Homecoming Queen. During their reign they take the girls on tours of this and that, which this time included M-G-M

Andy in an ad for Kellogg's. This was in conjunction with the television series Wild Bill Hickok. *The show was sponsored by Kellogg's for 7 years.*

Studios. So all the girls were invited on the set of *Huckleberry Finn*, and there was Dad. Now I assure you I'm no lothario, but I happened to be dating two of the girls. However, neither girl was aware I was dating the other. "Hello, Mr. Devine, I'm Linda. I'm dating your son Dennis." "Oh, hello, Mr. Devine. I'm Jane. I'm also dating your son." Dad called and said it was a little awkward, but very funny, and the crew loved it. A few days later I visited Dad on the set, and Archie Moore, the fighter who was in the film, asked me with a wink, "Where are all your girlfriends?"

The next thing Dad would do was more summer theater. He did *Showboat* in Framingham, Massachusetts, *Anything Goes* in St. Louis, Missouri, and *Showboat* in Pittsburgh, Pennsylvania. The shows went great with sold-out performances and positive reviews. There was a rumor that *Showboat* was coming to Los Angeles for an eight-week run next year. The show was to feature the L A Philharmonic orchestra, plus big sets and a large supporting cast. Dad wanted to be in that show for a number of reasons and told his agents to chase it. Dad also contacted Stanley Musgrove to see if there were any political issues. Dad was wise enough to know that politics are involved in everything.

Left: Dad had his own comic book series that was part of his television series Andy's Gang *which ran for five years. Right: Dad was always working and would do anything, as evidenced by his hosting a travelogue.*

The year rolled around and Dad had campaigned mightily for the show. However, the job went to Joe E. Brown. Dad could hardly hide his disappointment about not appearing in the eight-week run. They wanted Dad (at least they said they did), but hired Joe E. Brown because of three things. First, Brown was in the 1951 film. Second, Brown started his career as a circus acrobat and the producers thought his tumbling on stage would be a great addition. However, they forgot Brown was seventy at the time. And finally, and most importantly, Brown would work for less money.

After making all those crappy films at Universal, Dad felt he could get more quality film roles if the Hollywood insiders could see him doing so well on stage. It's odd, but he had a better reputation in New York, Ohio,

Dad and Lon Chaney, Jr. the day Universal Studios tried to humiliate two of them by making both wear horse and bear costumes. The studio did this in an effort to break their existing contracts.

Dad's favorite friends on any film were the stuntmen. Here are three of the very best. The photo was taken on the film Two Rode Together *directed by John Ford.*

and Pennsylvania than in Hollywood. Being financially secure and not being under contract, Dad now didn't have to do just anything they threw at him. He did guest appearances, but had kept his calendar open.

The morning after the opening night Dad wanted to read the reviews. He was curious because he knew so many of the supporting cast members and was hoping Brown would be lousy. After all, Dad was that human. Dad had just finished reading the reviews when the phone rang. It was Edwin Lester, the powerful head of the L.A. Civic Light Opera Association. "Andy, last night Joe E. Brown was doing his tumbling routine, and in the final act he broke his arm. We want you to take over the show."

The differences between Dad and Brown were age and money. Dad was reluctant to lower his fee because that amount becomes your bench-mark and it is often difficult to raise it. Edwin Lester said he wanted Dad to do the show but for what they were paying Brown. Dad agreed, but stipulated that he wanted to do the show when it returned to the new Dorothy Chandler Pavilion. Lester agreed, but not in writing. Dad went on that night. Prior to the performance, Edwin Lester himself went before the audience to explain that Dad was taking Brown's place with just a few hours' notice.

Dad had a wonderful memory and, with many former cast members plus a script girl working between each scene, he didn't miss a line. The audience gave him a standing ovation. The show ran for eight weeks and Dad's reviews were wonderful. Five years later, *Showboat* would open at the new Dorothy Chandler Pavilion with Pat O'Brien as Captain Andy. Dad was extremely disappointed but not surprised. Even if that stipula-tion was in writing, there's not a lot you can do about it. After all, this is show business, and there will be other shows; there always are.

CHAPTER 34

Liberty Valance
1962

Dad got a call to be in John Ford's *Two Rode Together*. It was to star Jimmy Stewart, Richard Widmark, and Shirley Jones. Dad had made a number of films for John Ford and knew how difficult he could be. Ford was now getting older (sixty-seven) and his health was deteriorating because of his drinking. Ford really didn't like the script and only did the film for the money. He was unhappy the entire time he was making it. Ford's eyesight was failing and he wore a patch over one eye in addition to very dark glasses. Every time I saw him he would be sitting in a dark place on the set. The first time Dad introduced me to Ford, he simply grunted. In the future, like most people, I avoided him.

Dad got this job because his instincts were correct as to *Showboat*'s L.A. run. It reminded casting directors that Andy Devine was still a viable commodity. Another treat for Dad was my brother's participation in the film. He had just ended his Naval enlistment and had no immediate plans. Dad got him a part as a young cavalry officer (uncredited), and he and Dad roomed together for six weeks while on location in Texas. They had a wonderful time together. The picture did only fair at the box office and was received poorly by the critics. However, that picture would set the stage for Ford's next film. That film, one of his last, would employ nearly all of Ford's favorite actors and would become a classic.

I loved my new apartment and its location away from school. I was training with Daland and knew this would be my last year of competition. In the NCAAs at Ohio State University, I came in third and fifth in the nation. In the National AAUs at Bartlesville, Oklahoma, Daland asked me to anchor the freestyle relay. It was on Television's Wide World of Sports and this would be my very last competitive swim — I gave it my all. I "rolled" the start and took chances on every turn. I did a 48.6 in the 100-yard freestyle which was faster than the existing American record.

Even today (fifty-two years later) it's not a bad time…for high school. That was my final swim. I threw my suit in a bag, got dressed, and simply headed for home.

On coming home from Oklahoma, I entered my apartment and saw two suitcases sitting side by side. I looked into my bedroom and there was Dad asleep on my bed. I didn't even know he had a key. When he woke up, he told me he was making a film at Paramount with John Wayne and Jimmy Stewart. The film was to be directed by John Ford and called *The Man Who Shot Liberty Valance*. Dad said that my apartment was only ten minutes from the studio, so he thought he'd stay with me. I said, "That's fine, but who gets the bed?" He asked, "Aren't I paying the rent on this place?" I replied, "I'll take the couch."

The film *Liberty Valance* had so many issues and back stories a film historian could write a book solely on the making of this picture. Because of the cast alone, I realized how unique this film was going to be, and made a point of being on the set three or four times a week. Dad and I would live together, off and on, for six weeks. The main issue in making this film was everyone's age. Stewart's character was that of a young lawyer fresh out of college, but he was fifty-three at the time. They were originally going to cast a young leading man in the role. However, he would have made everyone else look so old that they cast Stewart instead. In the film they never disclosed any of the characters' ages.

Everyone on the set was well aware that time was marching on and knew this would probably be the last major film they would all do together. Ford seemed to be in a better mood as he loved the irony of the story, and he truly loved John Wayne. The cast was large and very accomplished and to appreciate their contribution to films, I have outlined their career highlights. I have also included their ages at the time the film was made.

JOHN FORD (66) 140 films, SIX OSCARS: *How Green was My Valley, Stagecoach*

JOHN WAYNE (54) 100 films, ONE OSCAR: *True Grit, Stagecoach, The Searchers*

JAMES STEWART (53) 92 films, TWO OSCARS: *The Philadelphia Story, Harvey*

LEE MARVIN (38) 60 films*, ONE OSCAR: *Cat Ballou, The Dirty Dozen, The Professionals*

* *An estimate as to the number of films.*

EDMOND O'BRIEN (47) 70 films*, ONE OSCAR: *The Barefoot Contessa, The Wild Bunch*

VERA MILES (32) 40 films: *Psycho, The Searchers, The Wrong Man*

ANDY DEVINE (57) 186 films: *Stagecoach, Romeo and Juliet, A Star is Born*

JOHN CARRADINE (56) 97 films: *The Grapes of Wrath, Stagecoach, The Ten Commandments*

STROTHER MARTIN (43) 50 films*: *Cool Hand Luke, Butch Cassidy and the Sundance Kid, The Wild Bunch*

LEE VAN CLEEF (37) 80 films*: *The Good, the Bad, and the Ugly, The Young Lions. High Noon*

WOODY STRODE (47) 40 films: *Spartacus, The Professionals, The Ten Commandments*

JOHN QUALEN (63) 100 films: *Casablanca, The High and the Mighty, The Searchers*

JEANETTE NOLAN (51) 60 films*: *Macbeth, Psycho, The Horse Whisperer, The Searchers*

ANNA LEE (49) 30 films*: *The Sound of Music, How Green was My Valley, What Ever Happened to Baby Jane*

DENVER PYLE (41) 35 films: Uncle Jesse on *The Dukes of Hazard*

KEN MURRAY (59) 5 films: Vaudeville Showman, Radio and Television Personality

MONTE MONTANA (52) 4 films credited, numerous uncredited, Popular parade performer.

Plus too many uncredited character actors to mention.

TRIVIA:

John Wayne's shirt in the film recently sold at auction for $47,500

Burt Bacharach and Hal David wrote a hit song that was recorded by Gene Pitney about the film, but the song was never in the film.

Five of the actors wore hairpieces. They were: John Wayne, James Stewart, Lee Marvin, Andy Devine, and Woody Strode.

When Jimmy Stewart saw Woody Strode with the white hairpiece, Stewart humorously said he looked like Uncle Remus. In front of the crew John Ford called out Stewart as a racist. Stewart went into his trailer and never came out unless it was to do a scene. He never spoke to Ford again.

There was controversy as to why the film was shot in black-and-white. Some say it was to make the film more dramatic; others say Paramount was trying to save money.

As the shooting progressed, the actors who had finished their assignment didn't want to leave. The sound stage was filled with these old character actors sitting around telling stories and enjoying each other's company. When the film was finished, most never saw each other ever again. The film was not critically embraced at first, but did great business. Over the years it slowly acquired classic status and is now considered one of the greatest western films ever made. For many of the performers it was the end of their careers.

Because of my visiting the *Liberty Valance* set so often, I had more exposure to John Wayne. As I said, Wayne and Dad lived near each other on the water in Newport Beach. Wayne's home was also next door to his friend, a man named Ken Reyfsnyder. Reyfsnyder's daughter was getting married, and they were having an evening reception on the front lawn of his home. They had chosen to only serve champagne and white wine. At the reception from behind me came an unmistakable voice, "Hey, kid, ya like tequila?" I nodded. "Well, then follow me." Wayne walked me to the hedge that separated their two homes, and in the hedge was a bottle of extraordinary tequila. "I hate drinking that cat piss (referring to the champagne and white wine) and I hate drinking alone, but don't tell anyone." During the evening the more tequila Wayne had, the more he sounded like John Wayne. At the reception he would put his index finger to his lips, confirming that I should keep my mouth shut.

Besides *Liberty Valance* Dad would always stay with me when working on other projects. The two biggest films Dad ever made were *How the West was Won*, and *It's a Mad, Mad, Mad, Mad World*. *How the West was Won* was an ensemble picture with hundreds of actors and four directors. It was shot in CinemaScope with a wide screen. Dad worked on the Civil War segment, again directed by John Ford. The film was presented with an intermission, and the opening of the second act showed Dad driving a wagon in a garish Union Army uniform. A wonderful treasure from that film was a photo I would receive. Many years after the film was released, a business associate was taking me on a tour of the new producers building at M-G-M. In hallway after hallway photos were displayed of every actor who had ever worked at the studio, but none of Dad.

We then entered the large, post-screening reception foyer. There was this massive photo mural of Dad from *How the West was Won*. He was behind the camera, in his garish uniform, directing (of all people) John Ford, who was now in front of the camera. Behind Ford were actors George Peppard and Carol Baker. This photo mural was a treasure, and I had to have it. I found a studio executive who got me the negative and I had it blown up to three feet by six feet. It was in my home office for many years, and then I felt it appropriate to donate it to Dad's museum in Arizona, where it resides today.

It's a Mad, Mad, Mad, Mad World was unforgettable for Dad because he would be working with Spencer Tracy for the first and only time. In the film Tracy played the Police Chief and Dad played his deputy. Dad knew Tracy through Gable, but had never worked with him. Tracy was a great guy, but was often melancholy, a loner, and a drinker. It was 1963 and Tracy was in poor health, but he and Dad reminisced about the deceased Gable (1960). Eight months after the film Tracy would be hospitalized and almost die due to a lung condition. Tracy would die in 1967, a few days after finishing the film *Guess Who's Coming to Dinner.*

Dad would stay with me once again. This time it was for an episode of *The Twilight Zone.* Dad was to star in a segment entitled "Hocus-Pocus Frisby." It was about a store and gas station owner who loved to tell tall tales. When some strangers came in for gas, Frisby told them about all his accomplishments. The strangers were aliens and thought Frisby was the smartest man in the world, so they abducted him and took him back to their flying saucer. Dad was great, and the show was very funny. Most of all, it meant a lot just having Dad around.

CHAPTER 35

The Military
1962

The fall semester was filled with football games and parties. My advanced classes were getting more interesting and some of my new professors were from eastern universities. I also attended an outside Real Estate school as I wanted to obtain my California Real Estate license. Real Estate school was so much different from college. They really taught you the "nuts and bolts." In college they seemed to teach you a lot of theory or exotic problems you would rarely encounter in day-to-day business. I became fascinated with real estate law and real estate contracts.

Vietnam was heating up and I was now twenty-three. I went to El Toro Marine base in Orange County to look into the PLC (Platoon Leader Class) program and then possibly progress into flying. The flying program was seven years and eleven months. Wow! I'd be thirty years old. If I didn't do anything I might be drafted. So I joined the California Air National Guard and was able to pick my time to go to boot camp. At the start of the spring semester I got very sick and was in bed for two weeks. Right after I got well, I severely injured my right toe. That was it. I was going to drop out of school for one semester, go to boot camp, and finish up everything later. Frankly, I was looking forward to the break.

When you go into the National Guard, you think you are taking the easy way out, and you are really not in the military, but you are. We went through the same basic training as everyone else. There was a rumor to stay clear of a drill instructor named Sgt. Christopher Owen, better known as the "Black Panther." When we arrived we were assigned Airman 1st Class Mays. He was a good ol' boy from the south and very easy to deal with. On the military plane ride down to Texas I ran into a college friend, an old high school football friend, and made a new friend from Orange County. The four of us got a room together at the end of the hall in the dormitory. For four weeks we had it made. Then Airman Mays broke his arm while he was having intercourse in a dumpster. The lid fell on it.

So we were assigned a new drill instructor. Guess who? The "Black Panther." After four weeks it was like starting all over again. He was a cruel son-of-a-bitch and rearranged everything. No more cushy room at the end of the hall. No more wise friends looking out for your backside. Midnight hikes, numerous drills at the obstacle course. Most of all, he hated "Hollywood" and anyone from Los Angeles was from Hollywood. When he found out my father was an actor, he singled me out.

He made me race him through the obstacle course without knowing what kind of shape I was in. I whipped his ass. He then ordered me to box in the inter-squad boxing matches, which I did twice and won. He then ordered me to fight at a "Smoker" they had for the officers. Airman Mays (with his arm in a cast) contacted me and said it was a setup. The Air Force has these really good fighters who they bring in and who beat the crap out of the National Guard boot camp trainees. Mays said you don't have to do it, and you'll probably get hurt if you do. I thanked Mays. He said he always was a fan of Andy Devine.

I finally escaped "The Panther" and finished boot camp. I was then assigned to a Marine base in Orange County. Our permanent facility was being built and they had nowhere else to put us. Also I was assigned to be a cook which was great because of the hours. We would come in one hour early but would leave four hours early. In addition, we had no inspections and never wore class B uniforms. It was such a good deal I encouraged two of my college friends to also become cooks. God, we had fun. My close friends in the Guard were far from slackers and all were successful in their civilian lives. For example: Ed Nelson (cook), Chairman and President of Nelson & Bauman, attorneys and CPAs specializing in re-insurance. They had offices in Los Angeles, New York and London. Larry Vaughn (motor pool), President of the Orange County Motor Speedway. Rick Poggi (cook), National Sales Manager, Champ Lift Trucks. George Argyros (motor pool), a successful real estate investor who became the Ambassador to Spain. Howard Poyer (radio relay), Coors Beer distributor, Seattle, Washington, and, last but not least, Mark Mandella (radio relay), President of ABC Television.

After boot camp I had four weeks before I had to be back to school. Dad asked if I wanted to join him in going to Mexico on his friend's boat. I jumped at the opportunity as it would be fun to be with Dad and I really liked his friend who owned the boat. Going down to the tip of Baja California in a fifty-foot boat is nothing to sneeze at. You are a long way from home and many things can happen in Mexico. It can be a dangerous place where there are few laws and even those are not enforced. But it was primitive and beautiful and truly an adventure.

The memorable moments on the trip were going to Magdalena Bay to see the whales. Then arriving at San Jose del Cabo. It was beautiful and a welcome sight after five days at sea. The final thrill was returning home. Rod Rodriguez was the developer of the area and a real hotshot. He was good looking, well connected, and loved to live the glamorous life. He was kind of a Mexican Bob Cobb. I had to return to California and Rod said I could go on his Aero Commander. I was alone with Rodriguez's pilot Lupe Amaya. While en-route we encountered higher than normal headwinds. I didn't know it, but we were running out of gas. We were going to clear customs in San Diego and then fly on to Van Nuys. Five miles out the engines stopped. We were at ten thousand feet and "dead stick" landed in San Diego. It all happened so fast that I wasn't scared until it was over. I didn't mention what happened to Dad because he was a friend of Rodriguez.

CHAPTER 36

Graduation and Work
1962

I wanted my college days to be over. I was chomping at the bit to graduate and get into business; any business. My degree and education were in demand as I took useful courses. At the start of my final semester, I received a call from Mike Wilkie's father, Leighton. He was an intelligent and wonderful man. He asked me to drive to Santa Barbara and meet him at the Miramar Hotel instead of his nearby vast estate. I had a feeling what was coming, but didn't want to be presumptuous. I met him at the hotel and we had a great talk. He then offered me a job with his firm. I politely turned him down, explaining that I cherished the friendship of his son and had great admiration for the entire family. I wanted to go my way as an equal and not as an employee. I told him it was my hope to be part of the family for many years. We embraced and I drove back to Los Angeles. I immediately wrote him a carefully crafted letter thanking him for the opportunity he had offered me. To this day I remain a close family friend. Jon Henricks (the Olympic champion and one of the five freshman) married Michael's sister Bonnie and we see each other often. Leighton Wilkie lived into his nineties, and I was honored to speak at his memorial.

At USC some senior undergraduate courses double as first year graduate school courses. During my last semester a professor announced that a New York advertising firm was looking for a person with a finance background who had writing skills. The professor then gave the phone number to call in New York. I immediately got up, left the room and called New York. This agency had just been retained by William Zeckendorf who was the Donald Trump of the sixties. He owned the Chrysler Building and the Astor Hotel and had developments scattered throughout Manhattan. The rumor in 1962 was that 20th Century-Fox, because of losses (*Cleopatra*), was going to sell off their back lot to Zeckendorf who was planning a large development to be called Century City.

The advertising man in New York was an alumnus of USC and knew of me from swimming. We made an appointment for the next week in Los Angeles. The meeting went great and he offered me the job, which I accepted. As I was just starting my final semester, there were electives I could take. He suggested I take advertising principles and copyrighting. During that semester I spoke with him about once a week. As graduation approached, I terminated the lease on my apartment which was immediately re-leased. I had one month to vacate. I then got a call from my mentor in New York, and he said the agency owner and president would be in Los Angeles and he wanted to meet me. The next day we all would meet at the Beverly Hills Hotel in one of the bungalows (very fancy.)

I arrived at the appointed time wearing a white shirt, dark tie, and dark blue suit. As I entered the bungalow I was greeted by this small man and my mentor. They asked me to sit down, and the small man asked me if I was looking forward to New York. I politely replied that I had been there a few times and thought it would be exciting. The whole conversation took less than a minute. I didn't talk too fast, or try to sell it. I simply answered his question. He didn't look at me, he stared at me, and then said, "I think you are one of the biggest assholes I've ever met."

I was dumbfounded and looked at my mentor, who now had a blank stare. Without having the presence of mind to give some "screw you" snappy reply, I simply said, "Well…I guess I'm not going to New York, am I? Have a nice day, gentlemen." I then exited the bungalow. As I went to get my car, all my parking buddies kidded me that after getting some big job, would I then begin to tip them? No. Hell, I was thinking about asking for my old parking job back.

Fifty years later, at an intimate black-tie dinner party at an ultra-exclusive New York private club, the riddle of the little man would be answered. I was sitting next to a very attractive older woman and we were having a great time. She mentioned that I should have made my career in New York, and I then told her the story. After I identified the little man and the agency, she howled with laughter. She said the little man was her father, and he was always intimidated by men who looked strong. She elaborated that her first husband was an athlete, and her father had fired him.

Anyway, I had sold all my furniture and my apartment would be gone in two weeks. I called Dad to see if I could stay in the apartment over the garage until I found something. Nope. "I said I'd cover you until you graduated. Have you graduated?" "Yes." "Goodbye." and the phone hung up. I moved into the guestroom of a married friend for about ten days. I went everywhere with my resume looking for jobs. I decided that money was secondary, and the important thing was learning and having responsibility.

The formal graduation ceremony was two days later, and it was exciting but a little anticlimactic. It was a long day and the best part was the attendance of my grandmother. She had six children and eleven grandchildren. My brother and I were the only two, out of all those people, to graduate from college. I loved my grandma very much and was so pleased to make her proud.

I got a call from a family friend named Ed Walsh. Ed worked for C.I.T. Corporation in their industrial division. I always liked Ed and he and I became friendly. C.I.T.'s primary business was consumer loans such as furniture, appliances, and cars. However, they were also into the business of financing heavy construction equipment and other high-end chattels. Ed was in the field and called on dealers or direct users such as heavy equipment operators. Ed wanted to know if I wanted to be his inside man. He explained what I'd be doing and I took the job knowing I'd be right on the firing-line.

My job was to analyze the credit, do a write-up, and then submit the packages to the credit department. During the submission process there was always a great deal of haggling between the credit department, the dealer, the customer and me. After the deal was approved, I would draw the documents and submit them to the legal department. It wasn't glamorous, but it would take five years or more before I would have that much responsibility working for a bank. In addition, Ed's dealers would call me directly, and relationships quickly took place.

One of my early dealers was a man named Murray Wilson. He was a Ford tractor dealer in the San Fernando Valley and was always struggling. I liked Murray and he and I would have coffee or lunch once a week. After we got to know each other, he told me about his family. He had three kids who were all hellions and were aspiring musicians. He said he was trying to help them out by getting them small jobs, sometimes for free. About a year after I got to know Murray, he came to me and said he had just sold his dealership. I asked him what he was going to do. He replied that he was going to manage his kids as they had just cut their first demo record, one of which he handed me. I think I should have kept it. Murray said, "I'm going to call 'em the Beach Boys. What do you think?"

On occasions we had walk-in customers at the office. Our office was very sparse. It was one big room with linoleum floors and metal desks. One day I got this walk-in, and I took him to our small, windowless conference room. The man's name was Bill Meyers and he presented his package which included his resume. Stanford, Harvard Business School — very impressive. Then I looked at the deal. I told him I didn't go to Stanford or Harvard, and I'd only been working here a short time, but this is the stupidest deal I'd ever seen. He asked, "What do you think I should do?" We sat back, looked at each other and just laughed. He then asked me if I would like to join his businessmen's group for breakfast. It was called the 20th Century Roundtable, and although I wasn't a founding member, I would attend their very first meeting. This year we will celebrate our fiftieth anniversary. Bill Meyers was a fearless entrepreneur and would go on to do many deals, including the ownership of a major airline.

I became more comfortable with my job and more familiar with the people. I heard a rumor that two prominent C.I.T. employees would be coming to our office. They were H. Anthony "Tony" Ittelson, the grandson of the founder of the company and Peter Sidlow, nephew of the Chairman. They were both college graduates and smart. Tony was wealthy and pleasant, but aloof. Behind his back, his nickname around the office was "Id the Yid." Peter understood the street better than Tony, but didn't have his money. Peter knew how to make deals in addition to being irreverently funny. I liked him right away.

The office was run by a man named Lee McGraw. He knew the value of equipment and was very adept at making odd-ball deals and saving screwed-up deals. However, McGraw was a terrible alcoholic. He would come to work around eight and work diligently until one-thirty and then go to lunch. He'd get drunk at lunch, and you hoped he wouldn't come back because if he did, he would usually fire someone. The credit head was an Ian Jamison. He was a good guy, smart and steady. The job was really lousy, but the experience was priceless. Soon I could take any financial statement apart in two minutes. Because we were dealing with borrowers on the edge, I learned more in a month than I had all through college.

Sidlow became my direct boss and we became friends. We started doing a lot of restaurant deals which can be very risky. However, we were able to create additional security through limited recourse situations which gave us tremendous leverage in case of default. We financed many restaurants including most of the Denny's coffee shops and all of the Hamburger Hamlet restaurants.

Working at C.I.T. I learned the finance business not taught to you in business school. For example, McGraw had made an equipment loan on a bar and restaurant he frequented near the office. The loan was delinquent, and the owner was in trouble. So McGraw advanced him the money to hire singer/guitar-player Trini Lopez, who alone brought in a good crowd, plus a stripper who was dressed like a secretary. On a Thursday afternoon Trini started to play and the secretary started to dance. She let her hair down, then took off her glasses, and then slowly almost everything else. The next Thursday you couldn't get in the place. McGraw put "keepers" on the cash registers, and asked me to be there every Thursday just to keep my eyes open. The loan was current in two weeks and in five it was paid off.

Soon it became evident to both Sidlow and me that our jobs were a road to nowhere. Most of the men who worked there were older retreads who were just biding time. They were very smart but afraid. It was time to move on. Sidlow and I decided that he would get a job as the controller for a real estate developer, and I would get a job with a real estate lender. Perhaps in the future we would become partners.

Within a month Sidlow took a job with Louis Neiman Development. In short order Sidlow realized that he had more money than Neiman, but he soldiered on. I was offered two jobs. The first was with the leviathan Home Savings in their Newport Beach office. It was at three times my salary at C.I.T. The second was for a little bit more money than C.I.T., but with a small savings and loan in the Granada Hills area of the San Fernando Valley. It was called Lifetime Savings. I took the Lifetime job because I would be a loan officer, sit on the loan committee, be the chief construction loan inspector, and be in charge of all foreclosed properties. The job was a real education because this lender was so small and was in real trouble. The bank was next door to Granada Hills High School. After work I would go to their team's football practice to see this tenth grade kid play quarterback. His name was John Elway.

One day Sidlow called me to ask if I would meet with him at an architect's office to review plans for a small apartment building. He was now partners with Neiman and wanted my advice. I made some suggestions which the architect agreed with as we had the same design teacher at USC. I took a real interest in the plans and made more suggestions. In a few weeks Sidlow and I bought out Neiman by putting more debt on the building. It's called buying out your partner with his own asset. At twenty-five, Sidlow and I now owned a small apartment building which hadn't been built yet! Soon the two of us would be in hock, not up to, but beyond our eyeballs. I wanted a shot at success and, although risky, it seemed the thing to do. I really wasn't afraid (what the hell can they do to me?), but I was glad the very smart Sidlow was involved.

CHAPTER 37

Marriage
1963

Of all the girls I had met in college, there was no one quite like Barbara Baumgartner. She was pretty, the daughter of a prominent Beverly Hills surgeon, and had attended the best schools. She had a great sense as to what was appropriate. We started dating in my junior year and it was a typical courtship. Lots of parties, lots of her friends. Everything was very polite and proper. Her parents were another story. They were both from the Midwest, but had spent a great deal of time in Rochester, Minnesota, where her father was training and practicing at the Mayo Clinic. Somehow her mother decided it was the thing to do to live in Beverly Hills.

Her father was a timid but very kind man. He had no more business being in Beverly Hills than the man in the moon. But his wife was the boss and insisted, so off they went. His surgery practice flourished because of his reputation and the Mayo Clinic connection. However, after living in Beverly Hills for years, they had made few friends. Looking back it was because he was so reserved and she was the ultimate snob, who thought no one was good enough. They lived in isolation in this Beverly Hills cocoon and rarely ventured outside the home. Throughout all the years I knew them, the few visitors they had were either doctor associates or relatives.

When I asked Barbara's father for her hand in marriage, he quietly said yes. I then asked him to join me in asking his wife for her approval. He quickly responded that he had to go to the hospital. I asked him who was there? He replied, "I don't know." When I asked the mother, she looked at me and responded with a simple and sarcastic "No." She continued, "If I had my way I'd throw you half way to Sunset (Boulevard). You're not a professional, you're irresponsible, and you're not good enough for my daughter." What always stuck with me was that Barbara, my hoped-for fiancée, said nothing during this whole encounter — for or against. I realized that she was taught to play it safe, but her passivity would put a strain on our marriage in years to come. As they say, "To risk nothing is to risk everything."

I should have "walked" right there because here I was, pumping uphill again. I had a future mother-in law who didn't think I was good enough and never would. I had a future father-in-law who was petrified of everything, especially his wife. I had a future wife who would never choose sides and would rarely voice an opinion. I wanted a partner, not a subordinate. I wanted someone who would give me a hand when I stumbled, or give me unsolicited praise at my accomplishments. Most importantly, a kick in the ass when I did something stupid, thoughtless, or inappropriate. At twenty-four years old, how dumb could I be? But she was decent and pretty and liked to laugh, and I cared for her very much. So I forged ahead, and that year we were married. Her mother was not happy, but she was never happy about much of anything.

Father Smith officiated along with the new young pastor of Beverly Hills Presbyterian Church. The young pastor was totally full of himself because of his new Beverly Hills affiliation. Father Smith handled him perfectly. The reception was at Barbara's parents' house, and we went to Hawaii for our honeymoon. The C.I.T. people arranged for a new Ford convertible as C.I.T. financed auto dealers. Through a swimming friend we stayed at a small private cottage behind Diamond Head which was perfect. We ran into many friends, created many adventures, and had a great time. Upon our return I went back to the bank, and Barbara started teaching grammar school. But soon things would change as I was about to start construction on my very first building.

CHAPTER 38

Taking the Plunge
1966

As I spent more time at Lifetime Savings, I came to realize that the president of the bank, although likeable, wasn't very bright. He was the epitome of a ne'er-do-well. He looked like a bank president, acted like a bank president, and had a great line of bull. He drove a big black Lincoln and was president of the Chamber of Commerce. At C.I.T. I had been dealing with some very smart finance guys, but now I was dealing with this empty suit. Fortunately the head loan officer was a young man about my age named Dave Pinsley. He was very capable and had been in the real estate lending business his entire life, having never gone to college. He and I got along great, he taught me a lot, and the two of us ran the loan department.

I knew that the apartment building Sidlow and I would be building would take some of my time. Because the bank president was pleased with my job performance, I asked him for permission to be involved in the construction of our building. He was very understanding and gave me the go ahead. Actually, I think he was impressed and a little envious. The building went up fast as we had a contractor, with Sidlow and me hovering over its completion. The finished building was beautiful and Sidlow and I moved in. We rented the remaining units immediately.

I was then looking for land deals. I ran across a well located but oddball property in Studio City. The lot was 50 X 500 and was seen as difficult. Therefore the price was cheap. I thought we could work out a design and we purchased the property for $50,000. We secured the property for a deposit of $5,000, with the balance due in one hundred and twenty days. We hired a much less expensive architect and with some creativity put twenty-one apartment units on the site. As to the design, a partial overhang over the long driveway did the trick. A wild spiral staircase in the front of the building would really get the renters' attention. The interiors featured beam ceilings and second floor catwalks going from the bedroom to the bathroom. For 1966 it was very avant-garde.

Apartment land in the area was selling for about ten-thousand per unit. I suggested to Sidlow that we have the land appraised using our twenty-one unit preliminary plan. We had our plan reviewed and stamped by Codes so the appraiser was sure we had the twenty-one units. We did and the appraised value came in at $180,000. We would syndicate the venture at $150,000 giving the investors a preferred return. That gave us a land profit of $100,000 which was disclosed to the investors. It would all be subject to our obtaining construction as well as long-term financing. With aggressive money raising efforts, we put the deal together in thirty days. Having one-hundred thousand in working capital, we both quit our jobs. The day I turned in my resignation to Lifetime Savings, Dave Pinsley, the other loan officer, coincidentally turned in his resignation. The bank president was fired within a month.

The new building was to be located on a street called Aqua Vista because it backed up to the L.A. River. When we started construction, we used every cost cutting method we could think of, yet build a solid first class structure. First we would build it ourselves without a general contractor. We purchased the fixtures from a hotel that was being refurbished. We did the grading ourselves. Then after all of the structural block work was installed, we personally did all the waterproofing. The inspector, Mr. Mayfield, seemed like a good guy, so we asked him if we could do the waterproofing over the weekend so we could finish the massive backfill and turn in our rented D-8 tractor. Mayfield said he would trust us. Sidlow and I and two laborers finished the job with the drain lines, gravel, tar, and plastic — all installed properly. We then backfilled, thereby covering up all our work. Temperatures were in the high nineties all weekend and it was hell. Without seeing our actual work, the inspector Mr. Mayfield signed off the following day. The finished building was a hit, and it filled up immediately. Our tenants were show business types and gays. They loved the location and the unique interiors and we started to develop a strong tenant following. Sidlow and I would then form a company which was named D & S.

CHAPTER 39

The New Broom
1967

It was the 22nd of November, 1934 and Mom and Dad were having a Mexican dinner with John Wayne and his then wife Josephine Sanez. Wayne was only twenty-seven and Dad was twenty-nine. Neither one was well known as they were mostly doing small parts in lousy films or big parts in really lousy films. At dinner both women were very pregnant. John bet Dad a dinner on which baby would come first. The next day, November 23rd, Michael Wayne was born and on the 26th brother Tad was born. The Duke won dinner.

Michael Wayne graduated from college and went through the grunt work young people do. Sure, it helped that his dad was John Wayne, but Michael Wayne earned everything he ever achieved. The first film he was involved with as a producer was *McClintock* in 1963. John Wayne loved to be around the people he liked and trusted. However, as a producer Michael was a bottom line-guy, and all things, including actors, had to work within the budget or no deal. As the producer of a new John Wayne film, Michael offered Dad less money than his normal fee and my mother hit the ceiling. "Michael Wayne is trying to screw your father. Who does he think he is?" Mother was angry and told the agents to turn the deal down. Fine, Michael just went out and hired another character actor at his price.

I got to know Michael in the late seventies and found him to be smart, tough, and fair. He had a great sense of humor and I really liked him. As to the situation with Dad, Michael was absolutely correct. To reprise a famous quote, "It isn't personal, it's simply business." As I got to know Michael better, I casually suggested *Stagecoach* could be a musical. All you would need was a large coach, a bar and a town. The libretto would be straightforward, simple, and have all the necessary ingredients. Michael jumped at it and said he could easily obtain the rights, and for very little money. But unfortunately we both got busy, and other more pressing business demands would consume both of our schedules. Over the years we would both laugh that we would now have the money to send our kids to college because we didn't produce *Stagecoach* the musical.

Because of Mom's screw-up with Michael Wayne, I wanted to get more involved in Dad's career. Mother had little sophistication as to business relationships or contractual dealings (she was raised with a bunch of conniving horse traders). Dad hadn't been working and wasn't looking. He did a few guest appearances, but in reality he had dropped out of sight. He was then offered a chance to be the actor in residence on Chapman College's "Campus Afloat." He would be at sea for four months and would go around the world. Dad decided to go, and both he and Mom loved the experience. However, this would make him even more out of touch with the public or potential employers. The *Hickok* syndication was now in its tenth year and payments were diminishing. Broidy, the producer, had sold his interest to Screen Gems, and their creative accounting had become an issue. Dad was sixty-two years old and, because of his absence, many people assumed he was dead. Al Melnick had been Dad's agent for over twenty years and was far more interested in his working clients such as Debbie Reynolds, Kim Novak, and Bob Hope. After all, agents do work on a percentage.

Some time had passed, then Dad asked me to come to Newport so we could talk. He had just been diagnosed with type II diabetes, but felt good. He was in good shape financially with money in the bank, his home paid for, no other debts, and no expensive hobbies. However, he had no job prospects. When we met I didn't convey any sense of urgency as to his inactivity, but Dad was scared to death. I tried to be positive and as matter of fact as possible because Dad hated pressure. I asked him what he wanted to do, and he simply replied, "I want to go back to work and make some money."

What struck me was how performers (insecure or otherwise) treasure their brief moments of triumph. I surmise that they covet this adulation because they are sure someone is going to come along and take it all away. Dad was a modest man, but you should have seen him on the stage in New York. He loved every minute of it, and when he received his standing ovation he seemed so fulfilled.

After a few days and much thought, I presented Dad our game plan in writing. It was as follows:

FIRST — Hire a well-known show business attorney and write Screen Gems a "Screw You" letter regarding the disposition of the *Hickok* royalties.

SECOND — Assemble a list of new, young, aggressive agents. They should be specialists in specific areas of representation (i.e., films, TV, commercials, legitimate stage, etc.). We'll get one agent for each specialty and I'll run all of 'em. I want to hire the commercial agent first.

THIRD — When the new agents are in place, fire Uncle Al.

FOURTH — After Uncle Al is fired, get as much national media exposure as possible. But not until we fire Uncle Al.

FIFTH — When we have national exposure, insist that our new commercial agent contacts Leo Burnett personally. Not just the agency.

SIXTH — Get your health issues in order, and let's get ready for work.

I never thought there would be such profound role reversals, but here I was speaking to my father and he was listening intensely to my every word. As the discussion continued, Dad asked me what I would charge for my services and I told him five percent of his gross earnings. In the next four weeks we accomplished things beyond Dad's or my comprehension. The following is a list of what we were able to achieve:

FIRST — We hired Dick Link, a former partner at O'Melveny and Myers, who now had his own small law firm. However, he was very familiar with the *Hickok* contracts. He was a little strange, but had the reputation of a "junk yard dog." He was our guy as I thought Screen Gems wouldn't want to mess with him. We wrote Screen Gems a strong letter and they responded with a check for $50,000 and a letter to shut up. I told Dad to cash the check, and we would shut up — for now.

SECOND — I interviewed a series of agents and came up with three right away. The first was Jack Wormser. He wasn't young, but he was a top flight commercial guy and a joy to work with. The second agent was in New York, and he would handle all of Dad's legitimate stage bookings. He had a good reputation and had already represented Dad, but through the Melnick Agency. For film representation I hired a young guy (and a real hustler) formerly from the William Morris Agency. Within a few days he had a deal working with producer Marty Melcher for a new Doris Day film. Melcher was Doris Day's husband and a supreme asshole. The new agent and I were on the speaker phone with Melcher for the negotiations. Melcher didn't know it, but I would have taken anything just to get Dad working. Melcher only wanted Dad for marquee value and thus offered him a third of his usual salary. I countered with half and we split the difference. Then it came to length of contract. Melcher offered three weeks, I countered at seven and we settled at five and a half. Because we hadn't fired Melnick yet, I explained to the new agent that he would get paid even if I had to pay two commissions.

THIRD — It was now time to fire Uncle Al. Dad and I drove to Al's office on Rodeo Drive in Beverly Hills. We pulled up and parked, and as I was getting out of the car, I said, " Okay, Dad, let's do it." Dad sat in the car and replied, "For five percent you fire him." I immediately, but reluctantly, went into Al's elegant office, and there he was behind his large desk. I got right to the point. "Al, both Dad and I think he should have new representation." Al looked at me like he wanted to kill me. "Who's going to represent him — You? You little prick." I said, "I'm sorry, Al, I really am." I left his office knowing his agency agreements had expired, so we were free to do as we pleased. When I returned to the car, I told Dad that Al was very gracious and wished him well. I never told Dad what really happened. The next day I filed the necessary papers with the Screen Actors Guild and formally hired the new agents.

FOURTH — Now national exposure was a priority. Walter Sande was a character actor who also had a woodworking shop in Van Nuys. There were three actors who loved to hang out at Walt's shop when they weren't working. They were Milburn Stone ("Doc" on *Gunsmoke*), Johnny Carson, and Dad. Johnny had initially come to Hollywood to be an actor, but then got into radio, then TV game shows, and finally *The Tonight Show*. At Walt's place Dad and Johnny became friends, and Johnny didn't make friends easily.

Because I was aware of their friendship, I took it upon myself to call one of *The Tonight Show* producers. Within an hour I got a call back asking, "Would he like to be on tonight?" I said tomorrow will be fine. The next day in the early afternoon I picked up Dad in Newport and drove him to Burbank. *The Tonight Show* was recorded around six in the afternoon and then shown later in the evening in the various time slots around the country. Dad was as nervous as a cat and seemed to have lost all his confidence. It was sad because I had never seen him like this before. In the past he wasn't afraid of anything, except for his agent, and I remembered it was just ten years ago he was confidently running around before eighteen thousand people with his fly unzipped.

Before the show Johnny came by Dad's dressing room. The meeting was brief as Johnny was still working on his monologue, and in person Carson is very shy and retiring. When Dad went on, his nervousness continued.

At first he spoke about his kid (me) now guiding his career. Carson, who was an absolute master, sensed Dad's state and slowly started to bring him around. They talked about the old days and Walt Sande's woodworking shop and what Dad had been doing. The whole tone changed and, thanks to Carson, Dad's metamorphosis was profound. Dad now had the audience in the palm of his hand and had returned to his charming and confident self. There was a different person in the car driving back to Newport. People speak about how remote and detached Johnny Carson was in private. I assure you that during the show his mind was going a hundred miles an hour trying to anticipate what his guest was going to do or say. For an hour or so Carson was walking on eggs, and when the show was over he was exhausted and didn't want to talk to anyone.

FIFTH — I asked Jack Wormser not to contact The Leo Burnett Agency, but Leo himself. I suggested Wormser use Dad's name and Leo would take the call. Wormser and Burnett spoke, and in one week Dad had a contract for $18,000 to do voiceovers for Kellogg's.

SIXTH — Dad got very serious about his health and started to take care of himself. As a result, his medical problems became very manageable.

Much work would come through the door and Dad was busier than ever. He was "back in harness" and loving it. This new spirit of being productive enveloped Dad. He took the time to contact old friends, because now he had an answer when asked, "What are you doing?" One person Dad really wanted to reconnect with was George Murphy. "Murph" was a song and dance man at M-G-M in the thirties, forties and fifties and a great friend of Dad's. George was also a camp mate of Dad's at the Bohemian Grove. George had retired in the mid-fifties and then became president of the Screen Actors Guild. He then was elected to the US Senate in 1964. We were all with George on election night. Joining us that evening was Cesar Romero, one of the greatest characters I've ever met. Cesar started out as a dancer and was in a number of musicals with George in the late thirties and forties. They were great friends. Cesar's nickname was "Butch" and that's how everyone addressed him (except me). Truth be known, George's success as a former actor in winning his senate seat was the real spark that got Ronald Reagan to run for governor of California two years later in 1966.

CHAPTER 40

D &S
1968

Dad was on his way and now I had my own career to think about. The Aqua Vista building was a big success and was providing a nice return to investors. Sidlow and I were still working out of the apartment building where we lived, using our dining room tables as desks. I wanted to build cash flow, so I went to all the large property management companies and made the proposal that we would take over any buildings they didn't want to manage. Did we inherit some nightmares! I saw things you can't imagine. I can still remember the address of those horrible places. To this day, I won't even drive near those buildings. But that unpleasant task brought in the needed cash flow to keep things going.

On the development front our investors were happy and had told others, so we started looking for a new property. We found a small corner lot in Studio City for a six-unit building. The building design with our new cheaper architect was unique in that we used all wood with heavy beams and lots of glass.

Our first tenant signed on even before the building was finished. It was a friend of Dad's from New York. She was an art director named Mary who worked on *Showboat* in 1957 and had stayed in touch with Dad. In 1959 she married a New York stage actor named Jack Dodson and continued her work as an art director. In 1969 she was hired by CBS for TV shows. She had learned from Dad that I was building near the studios and she was interested. I personally showed her the unfinished apartment and she loved its unique design. After she consulted with her husband, they decided to take the apartment and stayed in a motel until it was finished. Later Dad invited them to dinner in Newport, and Dad liked her husband Jack right away. Jack was looking for work and Dad volunteered to help. Dad called Bob Sweeney, a TV director who had worked everywhere. Sweeney met Jack and suggested him to Andy

Griffith, who had briefly seen Jack in New York. Jack Dodson was cast on *The Andy Griffith Show* as "Howard Sprague" and would be on the show for six years. Both Jack and Mary would become friends of mine and would live in the building for many years.

The second tenant in that small building was a young crippled man. One weekend I was sitting in front of the building studying for my Real Estate Brokers Exam (I had my salesman's license from college). I had a phone and a long extension cord (remember it was 1968) because we had a large ad running. I received a call from a man who asked if the unit with the spiral staircase was still available. He told me don't rent it, he'd take it, and he'd be there in a hour. In an hour I got a call, "Hi, I'm the crippled guy, are you still saving the apartment? I'm running late." I told him, "Relax, pal, life is too short. The unit is yours, and if someone wanted to pay me three times what I'm asking, I'm still saving it for you." Three times...Well, maybe.

When you are trying to sell anything, "tire kickers" will happily run you around. I think it somehow gives them a feeling of power. But I liked this guy and trusted him. I really think I would have saved it had someone actually wanted it. He arrived with the check and moved in immediately. I ask him what he did, and he told me he was a hair stylist. He went on to say that he was Herb Alpert's barber, and Herb was helping him get into the record business. His name was Tommy Li Puma, and we got along great. He did get into the record business and how. During the time he lived in the building, I watched his star ascend. Over the years he produced for Barbra Streisand, Miles Davis, Natalie Cole, and many, many others. He was nominated for thirty Grammies and won three. Through his being a tenant, our next building across the street would be filled with many record people.

CHAPTER 41

The Candidate
1968

Our new property was across the street and right in the middle of town. However, it still had the original old barn on it. So after we closed escrow, we thought it would be fun to have a hoedown for our friends and business associates. Everyone would wear western clothes and we would have bartenders, a barbeque, and a cowboy band. But the night before our party there was a national tragedy that completely changed the tone of our gathering.

In early 1968 I gave a speech to the 20th Century Roundtable, the group I joined in 1963, regarding the bureaucracy surrounding real estate and the political shenanigans therein. One of the members brought a guest who was working for Senator Tom Kuchel (minority whip of the U.S. Senate). After my speech this man came up to me and wanted to talk. We sat down and he asked if I wanted to be on Senator Tom Kuchel's speaking committee. Our job was to go around the state and speak on behalf of the Senator. Senator Kuchel, a moderate, was in a tough battle in the primary with State School Superintendent Max Rafferty, who was extremely conservative.

The whole thing was really a setup by the Democrats and a smart play. Liberal California would rarely elect a conservative to anything, with Reagan being the exception. Kuchel had great standing in the Senate in addition to being Minority Whip. Because he was so moderate, he could easily beat any of the Democratic frontrunners, including Alan Cranston. So the Democrats quietly started funding the campaign of Rafferty. What were the Republicans thinking? When I was debating for Kuchel, I was going up against paid professional Democratic operatives secretly acting on behalf of Rafferty. Did Rafferty really think he would win? He always was self righteous and arrogant, but I thought he had more common sense. Tom Kuchel was smart, thoughtful and humble.

Francis Rafferty was an actress who had been under contract to M-G-M and then had her own television series called *September Bride*. She was a close family friend and also Max Rafferty's younger sister. The night of the primaries, Max was winning big. When I knew it was over for Kuchel, I went to Rafferty's headquarters to congratulate Max and say hello to Francis. His headquarters were located at the Ambassador Hotel across the street from Kuchel's headquarters.

After I said my hellos and congratulations, I wanted to hear Bobby Kennedy's victory speech as he was in the same hotel. To save time and get closer, I went through the kitchen. It sounded like his speech was coming to an end because of the applause, but I just wanted to take a look. At the door from the kitchen into the ballroom there were secret service men everywhere. I could now see Kennedy's entourage, and it was coming straight toward me. Time to go. As I was exiting the kitchen into the hotel lobby, shots rang out. I had no idea what had happened, but knew that I didn't want to be there. I quickly returned to Kuchel's headquarters where I heard the news. The next day at the hoedown people were affected in different ways by the previous night's event. The party was quite subdued. In the general election Democrat Alan Cranston beat Max Rafferty in a landslide.

CHAPTER 42

Palos Verdes
1969

Success was at our doorstep and, frankly, it was a little frightening. We now had three projects underway, and I was building a new home in the foothills of Sherman Oaks. As it evolved, I was good at doing deals and Sidlow was good at running the business. We had moved into a small building in the Valley and we now had a secretary. About this time Sidlow met an unemployed guy from New Orleans who had recently graduated from Tulane University. He was a real character and hung around the office all the time, often playing gin with Sidlow. He was very funny, very charming, and very smart. He wanted to get into the movie business and thought it was just a matter of time. However, he didn't know anybody. He finally got a job reading scripts and within three years he had produced his first major film (only in Hollywood). He subsequently produced *Die Hard, 48 Hrs.*, *Field of Dreams*, and many others. In the mid-eighties he became president of 20th Century-Fox. His name is Larry Gordon, and I don't know why, but I always called him "The Doctor." He now runs with all the big dogs, but I do see him occasionally and we reminisce about his unemployment, the gin rummy days, and the man with the bump (a story that's much too long).

Our existing architect was competent and inexpensive. But there was a problem. He was an Orthodox Jew and went to Temple every day. As the jobs got bigger, he could not perform. We decided to go back to our original architects for our next project. While with our new architects, they proposed we build an office building that we could share together in West Los Angeles. We would both take space in this new building, and they had a Fortune 500 company that would take the remainder. I found a lot, we got it financed and started construction 120 days after the initial meeting. We built the building in record time as we had the help of our architect partners. The building was beautiful and won many awards, including the most beautiful small office building in Los Angeles.

There I was at the age of thirty, sitting in my new beautiful corner office for the first time. As I sat there I also couldn't believe the phone call I received. It was my wife Barbara informing me she was pregnant. Many things would change as Barbara would quit teaching, and we would move into our new home, which I was trying to finish. I was excited about this new little person who would be entering our lives. I also wanted to keep a level head as to all the business things which were swirling about me. Little did I anticipate the enormous opportunities and challenges which would present themselves in the very near future.

My wife Barbara had attended Marlborough, the exclusive Los Angeles girls school. One of her close friends at Marlborough was Debbie Daves. Debbie was the daughter of film writer and director Delmer Daves. Delmer was an intellectual who wrote numerous schmaltzy screenplays such as *An Affair to Remember*, *A Summer Place*, *Parrish*, and others. He also wrote and directed many exciting dramas such as *Destination Tokyo* and the film noir *Dark Passage*. Delmer was a sentimentalist who always depicted some good in everyone. I liked him because he was so kind, enthusiastic, and positive about everything.

Debbie Daves and my wife Barbara remained friends through their college years. When Debbie married, both she and her new husband Bill Richards became our friends. His family was in the military with no distinguishing achievements. However, Bill had attended Stanford and then Harvard Business School. When we met he was working for a large, prestigious consulting firm. The moment I met Bill I liked him, although I was probably more impressed with his diplomas than his true intellect. However, I did think enough of Bill to sponsor him in the Roundtable group that I had joined years before. Debbie was not particularly active socially, but she knew everyone and was very well liked. Bill, who was modest in appearance and demeanor, was a social climber par-excellence. Although I was unaware of this at the time, he was using Debbie's contacts to further his own ambitious agenda. After a year or so of friendship, Bill called me and asked if I knew Z. Wayne Griffin, Jr. I replied that I had met him, but only knew him casually, other than what I read in the society pages. Bill said he and Wayne were very close friends (that was bullshit) and he had suggested my name to Wayne, who was looking at a new piece of land for development. I really didn't think much of it at the time as I couldn't imagine someone like Wayne calling me about anything.

In a couple of days I did receive a call from Z. Wayne. On the phone he was charming and extremely open. When I met him he seemed carefree and friendly and forthright. I can imagine that to some, Wayne's laissez fair demeanor would mask his intelligence. Wayne was in business with Michael Niven and was married to Niven's sister. Wayne's father, Z. Wayne, Sr., was a well-met man who knew everybody. He dabbled in everything from show business to real estate and had made a fortune. Michael Niven's mother was the eldest of the Doheny children and she had been married to VanCott Niven, the senior partner of Gibson, Dunn & Crutcher, the second largest law firm on the west coast. These two young men had spotless reputations and their connections were endless.

When Wayne called me, he said he wanted to show me a piece of property he was interested in. He drove me to Palos Verdes, and on the one-hour trip we got to know each other and got along great. Wayne was easy to like. When I stepped out of his car and onto the property, I couldn't believe my eyes. It was an elevated, gently sloping piece of land overlooking a golf course with the entire Pacific Ocean in the background. It was spectacular! I had never seen anything like it. Supposedly the property was zoned for apartments, but it was surrounded by expensive homes. Wayne asked if I liked it, and I could hardly respond. He said it was owned by Great Lakes Carbon and, because he knew the Skakel family (Ethel Kennedy was a Skakel), he thought we could buy it.

He then suggested the possibility of a joint venture where we would split everything fifty-fifty. Just being affiliated with these two young men was a tremendous endorsement. But first I wanted to get my bearing and try to comprehend all that was taking place. The next day I went to the title company to check easements, deed restrictions, etc., then the County Department of Building and Safety (to check zoning, height limits, sewer access, etc.). Then I had a long meeting with a highly regarded civil engineer who confirmed all my findings. By the afternoon of the second day, I knew everything necessary about the property, and to my amazement, it all checked out as represented. I wrote a three-page memorandum to Wayne which summed up everything.

The following week we met with the Great Lakes Carbon people and by that afternoon we were in contract. With what I knew about the property, I estimated it was worth at least four million dollars and we were buying it for two. Our plan was to syndicate 2.5 million so that we would have immediate working capital of $500,000, and those funds would stay in the deal. I estimated the improvements would cost 18 million, which was cheap considering the rents we were going to receive. Sidlow was in Europe on vacation with his family (his father had taken everyone to Israel), but we spoke every other day. He really couldn't believe all of this was happening so fast, and neither could I.

Raising the capital was a story unto itself. Peter Sidlow and I had created a lot of good will with our investors because our other deals had worked out so well. But now we were in rarefied air as we had never come close to raising this kind of money. We called all of our investors plus anyone else we knew or anyone else our past investors knew. Mike and Wayne brought out the real firepower. It looked like a convention of heavy-hitters. I told them the way to sell the deal was to take the investors to the site and show them the property. We put together an investor package with all the trimmings, i.e., floor plans, plot plans, renderings, profit and loss statements, and partnership agreements. I wanted to provide everything except pictures of the property. I wanted this spectacular piece of land to be as big a surprise to the investors, as it was to me.

We all met at Wayne Griffin's home in Bel Air and took an ultra-fancy bus to the property. During the one-hour bus trip I used a microphone to explain the venture, the building concept, the financing, the risks, etc. While on the bus, I encouraged the other partners to answer questions as I felt we should all be involved. The entire ride went quickly, as the potential investors were all engaged in learning about our proposal. When we arrived at the property, it was a cool, clear, beautiful day. As everyone departed the bus, they were speechless. It was just like the first time I saw the site. On the way home we had wine, cocktails and very nice hors d'oeuvres. In that one day we privately raised the entire capital requirement, two and one-half million dollars! As to the money-raising efforts, Sidlow and I raised about one-third of the capital and Niven and Griffin raised about two-thirds.

No matter what business or activity you are in, "The knife always has two edges." As success became evident to others, the opportunists would emerge from the depths like the cicadas in summer. I got a call from Bill Richards who casually said he'd like to talk to me. I went downtown to his office, and there he was, posturing behind his desk. He started out by saying, "Okay, I did you a big favor. Now what's in it for me? After all, I'm the one who put this deal together." I was taken aback by his tone, but then replied, "You didn't put any deal together, you simply asked Wayne to call me. If you are so good at putting deals together, why the hell didn't you do the deal yourself? What did you need me for?" However, in the interest of placating his demands, I suggested that I would speak with Mike and Wayne, and see if the venture would pay him a fee. I said it would be okay with me. Then Richards replied, "No, they are my friends. This is just between you and me." I now felt betrayed and knew I was being used. I told Richards, "This has nothing to do with friendship, this has to do with your trying to extort money from me because you think you have the leverage to do so. It also has to do with your kissing the ass of your new rich friends, who you are afraid of pissing off." Richards paused, then replied, "You know I can ruin you socially in this town." I replied, "I'm sure I can do that without your help." That was the last time I would ever speak to him — thankfully! I did miss his wife Debbie, as she was outgoing, smart, and fun to be with. I was just sorry she had an opportunist for a husband.

We planned to build the project in three phases of approximately 130 units each. We did this for absorption purposes, because we wanted to handle our debt service coverage and didn't want too many vacant apartments at one time. When we were at seventy percent occupied in phase one, we would start phase two and so on. The design process went very quickly because of our concept. In architecture you draw a box, then try to make it interesting. In reality, the interior space is far more important than the exterior appearance because you spend more time inside than outside. However, the outside must be attractive; otherwise no one will want to go inside. With the architects I designed a two-story, eight-unit building which had two entrances serving four units each. Utilizing the views, we placed these buildings over the entire site, expanding the size to accommodate the topography. Because of this we finished the plans in just sixty days.

We started construction and everything went as planned. There are always problems when building anything, especially when it is something as large as this. We ran into a tremendous amount of rocks, which slowed our sewer completion, and we had the typical disputes with subcontractors. But all in all we finished the first phase on time and on budget. We had two field superintendents who both became ill during the final weeks of construction (heart attack and gallstones). I took over and was at the site fourteen hours a day, seven days a week, for a month. We got it finished.

We started our rental program and the units didn't rent as quickly as we had anticipated. But the rent-up was steady and the quality of occupants was excellent. We wanted to start our second phase but only had thirty percent occupancy. The worst thing you can have in a building is vacancies, because that is money you'll never see again. Nearby was a large development called High Ridge. They were advertising aggressively and had tremendous traffic, but they had a small disclaimer forbidding pets. At the entrance and exit of their project, I put a man in a gorilla suit wearing a sandwich sign saying, "We love pets, and we're only two blocks away."

That weekend we rented sixty units. Yes, we had problems with pets, but we could easily weed those out later. The main thing was that we were filling up the building. We did phase two and then phase three, and the building became very stable because people loved living there.

What frightened me most were the moral obligations that were being imposed upon Sidlow and myself. We were now both looked upon as real movers in the real estate world and very adept at doing big deals. However we were both young (thirty and thirty-one) and we knew there were two big problems. First, we really didn't have that much experience as these large deals had sort of landed in our laps. Secondly, although we had been prudent, we still didn't have the kind of capital that went with our reputations. We didn't want to walk away from opportunities nor did we want to overreach. Both Sidlow and I wanted to be very careful as we knew we were walking on land mines.

CHAPTER 43

The Sunset Years
1971

Dad was busy as ever, and voiceovers had turned into a gold mine. I was involved in my own business so I turned over the management to Mom. The agents were doing a great job, and if there was a real problem, they would call me. Dad's health seemed good as he had lost thirty pounds and was exercising and watching his diet. His diabetes was now under control, and he had gone from shots to pills. However, Dad seemed more tired than usual, and went for a checkup. The doctors discovered Dad had leukemia. He was now sixty-six and the news came as quite a shock. Dad had given much of his time to the large, local hospital and knew most of the doctors. Dad, to his credit, immediately met with all the doctors to map out his care. He was very personally involved in his treatment and the staff loved him. The first year was light chemotherapy. He didn't experience any hair loss and his energy level improved. Actually he felt great.

What was most interesting was Dad's outlook on his life and his mortality. He didn't want to change anything and felt he hadn't missed much. In the long run, he knew the leukemia would be terminal, but he thought he would stretch out his treatment and do the best he could. Dad loved the house and his pleasant, simple life. He had his golf, his fishing trips, his hunting trips and his grandchildren. He was very happy, and it showed.

One day I received an interesting call from Dad's agent, Jack Wormser. He was the one I had hired for commercials. Jack said that he had received a call from a representative of Alaska Airlines. Jack said that their request was a little out of his field so he wanted me to handle it. I called the airline and they wanted to do a commercial for the airline promoting hunting and fishing in Alaska. They said they couldn't pay much, but could offer Dad a great trip. I said he would do it providing his manager could come along, and the airline quickly agreed.

Now I had to sell it. When I explained the situation to Dad, and told him that I would be going with him, he jumped at the chance. We had a wonderful week together. Dad was far more complicated than he appeared and there must have been something very profound that drove him. I would never find this out, as perhaps Dad didn't even know it himself. However, when you are living in the middle of nowhere in a log cabin, you get to know a person pretty well. Dad and I really became friends.

As for future work, Dad's doctors advised him to do whatever he felt like doing, but not to get too tired. In late 1971 Dad was cast in the final film of his career. He was to be the voice of Friar Tuck in the Disney animation of *Robin Hood*. The recording was fun because Dad was working with old friends Phil Harris, Pat Buttrum, George Lindsey, and Ken Curtis. Also that year Dad did his final television program. It was called *Tail of a Whale* for National General. Dad felt up to appearing on stage and starred in *Never too Late* in Monroe, Louisiana. The next year Dad would appear in *Showboat* for two weeks. He then took on *Music in the Air* for two weeks each in four Midwestern cities. This eight-week schedule really took its toll, and Dad got dangerously tired. He would never appear on the stage again.

Although Dad would do occasional appearances, he was now well aware that he was semi-retired. Financially he was in good shape. Although he wasn't a wealthy man, his home was paid for and he had cash in the bank. He also had various pensions, social security, and income from the boat docks in front of the house. Mom used to joke that they were better off now than when Dad was working. In a way it was now everyone's responsibility to help Dad maintain his health and promote an enjoyable way of life. It was advantageous that my brother lived a mile away and I lived an hour away. We would all rally round and would enjoy those final years as much as possible; but it was sad. Dad was a good guy, but vulnerable in many ways. He really needed all of us, and we all knew what was coming would be difficult.

During that time I started to enjoy my life with outside activities. Through my college roommate Mike Wilkie I joined the exclusive Rancheros Visitadores. It is a horseback riding group headquartered in Santa Barbara. Once a year they have a one-week ride through the hills of the Santa Ynez Valley. Dad came as my overnight guest a few times to entertain the members. It became kind of a ritual as all the Rancheros enjoyed meeting Dad and enjoyed his stories. The summer following Dad's death, I asked entertainer Phil Harris to be my guest and fill in for Dad. It was emotional for Phil to be standing in for Dad, but he did a great job, and there was applause all around.

That year I also made application to the Bohemian Club. The Club's waiting list is about eighteen years, so becoming a member would take a while. However, as a guest I participated in as many Club activities as possible. Finally I purchased a large off-shore power boat to keep at Lake Powell which is one of the most beautiful places on earth. My four favorite places in the world are not far away. They are: Highway One, Lake Powell, Aspen Mountain, and The Bohemian Grove.

CHAPTER 44

Studio Village
1972

Opportunity was about to knock again, and this time in spades. However, we didn't even see it coming and I couldn't believe what was about to take place. Herbert J. Yates was the head of Republic Pictures where most of the Roy Rogers and other "B" pictures had been filmed. Dad had worked there for years and for a period of time was under contract. After Yates' death the studio was sold to CBS, and many popular television shows would be produced and filmed there. The back lot was untouched as in the old days it was used for filming close-up exteriors. Now, in the early seventies it was one of the most desirable pieces of raw land in the Los Angeles basin. The word got out that the property was going to be sold, and all the major developers were after this rare and valuable property. Sidlow and I had no business whatsoever trying to acquire the property, but ignorance is bliss, and we decided to go after it.

I remembered that Robert Wood was the President of CBS and a graduate of USC. He was an active alumnus and on the board of trustees. Nick Pappas was a former USC quarterback and was now Associate Athletic Director of the University. He was sort of "Mr. Fix-it" for the athletes. If an athlete had money problems or grades problems or whatever, Nick would try to help. He knew me through swimming, but our friendship became closer through the football players, especially Craig Fertig. I went to see Nick to ask him if he would write a letter to Bob Wood to tell him that I was interested in purchasing the back lot of CBS. Nick replied, "No, I'm not going to do that! Hell, let's give him a call." In two days I was in contract on the biggest and most valuable piece of residential land in the City of Los Angeles. I really had the tiger by the tail. I first went to the councilman for that district who was a good friend. I explained what I wanted to develop and wanted to get his concurrence. We both knew he would catch heat from the neighbors because the property was so large.

Both the Councilman and I had to trust each other. Trust a politician; surely you jest. But I had no choice. With some prodding and occasional threats, he kept his word.

Construction started and this large deal was in all the papers. Our reputation became very well known and D & S was thought of as a real powerhouse in the local real estate market. Even after we got the purchase and the financing in order, there were always heartaches when building a major development. The unions were powerful and relentless during those days. I had to fly to New York on the "red-eye" to meet with some thug and beg him to get strikers off the job. But it was very exciting, and Sidlow and I were creating something and having lots of fun. However, there was a problem. It seems there always is. Like many new businesses which achieve success quickly, we were undercapitalized for our new larger size. We had to slow down so we didn't go broke amidst all of our success.

We called the new development Studio Village. We did this because it was in the middle of Studio City and of course backed up to CBS Studios. We obtained the financing through my friend Anthony M. Frank's bank. It was a big success, as sales were good and profits were substantial. But the bank was sold during construction and the new owners had fresh accounting ideas as to how profits should be distributed. We were getting screwed and there was nothing we could do about it.

Our new, inherited partners were very rich, very ruthless, and frankly a little scary. We made a living, and we had to just go on our way. The irony of this whole experience was that the Bank Chairman (the guy who screwed us) asked me to lunch at the Beverly Wilshire Hotel (remember *Pretty Woman*). The Chairman wanted to know if we wanted to do another joint venture together. At lunch he was unnecessarily rude as he was continually distracted. He was trying to buy a Picasso painting in New York and was screaming over the telephone. Remember he called the lunch. As he hung up the telephone, he said in a pushy yet condescending manner as he was rubbing his hands together, "What do you think, do you boys want to do some business together?" I said, "What do I think? I think that you and Picasso can kiss my Irish ass."

CHAPTER 45

Almost Famous
1973

After doing Studio Village and Palos Verdes, our reputation for doing big deals was well known in Los Angeles. As a result, big deals were coming our way and we made substantial profits just "flipping" land. We had three land deals which we bought and sold in less than a year which gave us needed cash. We were then chosen by the City of Pasadena to head their redevelopment efforts. We built two projects in Pasadena which, after some heartache, made money and won numerous architectural awards. The redevelopment people were thrilled and our reputation grew. I was then contacted by William Lund.

Bill Lund was an academic who was associated with Harrison "Buzz" Price. Price, who attended MIT and then Stanford, started a company called Stanford Research Associates. Price was infatuated by leisure time and how people spent it. In the fifties Price was approached by Walt Disney who wanted to put a small amusement park that would serve adults as well as children adjacent to his Burbank studio. Price advised Disney it wouldn't work because there were only eight acres. Walt Disney then asked how big should it be and where should it be located. Price responded that it would take time to study the parameters. Because of Price's reputation and the fact that Disney trusted him, a study was ordered. The conclusion was 150 acres, and the best place to acquire that much land close to Los Angeles was in the city of Anaheim. That was the beginning of Disneyland.

Price became famous and started a new company called Economic Research Associates. Bill Lund came aboard and in the ensuing years he married Walt Disney's daughter Sharon. ERA had numerous high profile projects and their reputation was impeccable. When Lund called me to do a joint venture with Economic Research Associates, I was overwhelmed. I thought now our company could achieve national prominence.

The property in question was twenty plus acres on the beach in Santa Monica. The whole project would have a value of about 100 million. The buy-in was eight million and was the same for all selected bidders. The City chose four firms, and after their individual presentations, the City would select a winner.

I had made many presentations as had Lund. Our combined proposal was a knockout and we won the bid. We were formally notified by the City and then heard nothing. Another firm upped the price to ten million and they were chosen. That wasn't the way it was presented and we could have sued. However, two famous quotes come to mind: "Don't sue City Hall" and "Litigation is a rich man's game." It was sad as our little company could have really been something.

It was also during that time that I got involved with the Barnes brothers. Their father was an executive with Firestone Tire, and thus the oldest son Chuck became involved with the company's racing division. Chuck's involvement then expanded into the management of well known race drivers. This included but was not limited to such drivers as Roger Ward, Mario Andretti, Al Unser and Bobby Unser. Chuck's brother Bruce became involved and they expanded their operation to include professional football players. This included Johnny Unitas, Calvin Hill, Bob Chandler, Al Cowlings and O.J. Simpson. Of course I already knew O.J. and Al from USC and my friendship with John McKay and the other football coaches.

Chuck Barnes was handling many aspects of the athletes' lives. This included their contracts, endorsements, and how to invest their money. My job was to get them into sound real estate deals without screwing them. These guys could be so vulnerable and I really felt an obligation to watch out for them. Every one of our deals with these celebrities made money, and I continued to represent them in real estate until Chuck's premature death from drowning.

Chuck's company was called Sports Headliners, and it was the trailblazer as it pertained to sports management. I was asked by Andretti to be his guest at the Indianapolis 500 race and be in his pit. The day before the race there was a cocktail party preceding the parade honoring the celebrities in attendance. At the bar there was a group of race drivers and all forms of film and television actors. The drinking and stories and laughter were abundant. Now Mario Andretti is not a demonstrative person, but there was a pause in the revelry, and O.J. Simpson asked Mario why there weren't any black race drivers. Mario simply replied, "They turn white at 150."

Through the Sports Headliners association I also met one of the smartest and most unforgettable gentleman I've ever met. His name was Mark McCormick and he was the man who took sports management into the stratosphere. At the same time he was a regular guy. One evening in Los Angeles Mark invited me to have dinner with his client Arnold Palmer and himself. We went to a small restaurant in Santa Monica frequented by the locals called The Galley. No one in the restaurant paid any attention to Palmer. The three of us had a great time with lots of wine, lots of stories and more laughs. What I didn't realized was that Palmer had a 7:30 tee-off time for the L.A. Open. The next day Arnold shot an eighty-three.

CHAPTER 46

Trips, Trauma, Tributes
1975

Dad was enjoying his leisure time as much as anyone could. He was still doing occasional voiceovers and financially everything was fine. His leukemia was starting to be a problem, but Dad was still able to do what he wanted and he had a great attitude. In October of that year he was honored on his seventieth birthday with a huge affair hosted by John Wayne in the main ballroom of the Disneyland Hotel. There must have been two thousand in attendance. After all the speeches and acknowledgments a large cake was wheeled out. One of the wheels got stuck and the cake fell on the stage. It was all handled with great humor.

Everyone knew that Dad's time on this earth was coming to an end. As a result, many awards and tributes came his way. However, Dad lived his life as he always had, although he moved a little slower and had a bit less energy. But a series of wonderful adventures were about to come his way. They would not only involve his family and the friends he cherished, but the United States of America as well.

Early the next year (1976) Donald Tennant asked Mom and Dad to plan for an extended summer trip. As I mentioned earlier, Don was the marketing genius who created all those successful campaigns for the Leo Burnett Agency (The Marlboro Man, The Pillsbury Doughboy, The Jolly Green Giant, and so on). Don had become fascinated with a sailing yacht named the *Juanita*. Apparently the boat had a long and checkered past as a gunrunner, a coastal watch vessel in World War II, and a smuggler of contraband. He purchased and then restored the vessel to pristine condition, as he was preparing to give the ultimate gift to Dad. It was to be a six-week sailing trip throughout the Greek Islands. Don and his captain mapped out the most interesting destinations and scheduled the trip with numerous stops in port so Dad could get his rest.

Mom and Dad flew from Los Angeles to New York. I was in New York on business so I met them at Kennedy airport. Dad was as excited as a little kid and was so appreciative of Don's efforts. As has been said, "The candle burns brightest at the end," and this was the case with Dad.

The day Mother and I skied through the trees to a small clearing and had the wonderful wine and pheasant lunch.

He looked wonderful and had more energy than in recent months. I said goodbye at the airport, and their next stop was Athens. The trip was a revelation as they had abundant time to go everywhere and do everything they dreamed of. It was a wonderful tonic for both Dad and Mom. Upon their return they looked twenty years younger.

However, soon after their return Dad's health started to deteriorate. He got a call from his agent regarding the State Department. The State Department! It was now 1976 and the government was planning numerous events surrounding the Bicentennial, and they wanted Dad to participate. The premier event and centerpiece of the Bicentennial was to be held on the evening of July 4th. It would be a black-tie event at Kennedy Center which would include the House, the Senate, the Supreme Court, the Cabinet and the President. Part of the program was

My graduation day from the University of Southern California. A special memory of that day was sharing it with my grandmother.

Gaviota Beach where we spent the night on our last trip up the coast, circa 1976.

to have three actors read to the audience. James Stewart was chosen to read "The Government," John Wayne was chosen to read "The People," and Andy Devine was chosen to read "The Land."

Behind the actors was a philharmonic orchestra playing an Aaron Copeland composition. I don't care who you are, or what you have accomplished in your life, this was a very big deal, and Dad knew it! But bad luck

The last Thanksgiving at the Grill Room of the Bohemian Grove, circa 1976. In the photograph is the entire Devine family. Dad would be gone in a few months.

was lurking, and his poor health was becoming a factor. After much deliberation he bowed out as he just didn't want to screw things up because he wasn't positive as to how he might feel. It broke his heart to turn it down. He would have been with his old friends Wayne and Stewart besides having the honor of participating in this career-capping event. I know in my heart that Dad thought a great deal about his ambitious and judgmental father and how proud that tough Irishman, Thomas Devine, would have been of the accomplishments of the son he had worried so much about.

In the early part of the summer Dad felt pretty good, so my brother and I accompanied him to the Bohemian Grove for a special weekend. Dad wanted to visit this place he loved so much. While there Dad got very sick and was hospitalized. He went into a coma and was in a northern California hospital for almost a month. We thought we were going to lose him. I stayed with him much of the time and worked as an orderly in the hospital when they were short-handed. I got to know the staff very well and promised that if Dad got through this I would throw a party for everyone. It became a running gag that as Dad got worse, I would up the ante as to what I would be serving. It started out with hot dogs and beer and worked its way into steak, lobster and Chardonnay. The entire staff was equally concerned about Dad, and this ever-evolving menu brought some needed levity to a grim situation.

I had been with Dad for over three weeks and Mom had been there for about ten days. Dad was still in a coma, but his vital signs were improving. Before he got sick, I had planned to visit my college friend Craig Fertig in Oregon, as he was now head football coach at Oregon State. After Oregon my wife and I were going to continue north to join another friend, Walter Clark, on his yacht for a cruise through the San Juan Islands. I don't know much about the subconscious, but on July 4th Dad partially came out of his coma. That was the day he was to have been at Kennedy Center in Washington. Because of this, and knowing Mom was there, I went north to visit my friends as planned.

Remember, Dad had been in a coma for about a month. I visited Oregon and it was now three days since I had left him. We were out to sea on Walter Clark's yacht, and I called Dad's room on the marine phone, hoping to speak with Mom. The phone rang and a man answered, "Ah, Y E L L O W. It was Dad. "Welcome back." "Hi, I guess I was out for a while." "No kidding" "And I think I lost some weight." "No kidding, how do you feel?" "Good, a little weak and I haven't stood up yet, but I want to go home." "No kidding. Well, welcome back, Dad, I knew you'd make it (that was a lie) and let's get you home soon."

Dad recovered quickly and my brother flew him home in his friend's private plane. I told Dad that I was on the hook for a big party honoring the staff that pulled him through. Dad had a great laugh as to my commitment toward the ever-increasing cost of the menu. He assured me, "Son, whatever it takes, I'll be there, especially if you're buying." Dad came home in mid-July, and we planned the trip to visit the hospital staff the following November. I was keeping my fingers crossed that he could make it. An interesting aspect of all of this was the way Dad was handling what was before him. Here was a man who was afraid of many things, but he was facing his future head on and with little apparent fear. In addition, he was living his life as fully as he could. Mom was wonderful during this time. She was so devoted to Dad and had a way about her that made things seem so fresh and fun.

CHAPTER 47

Up the Coast
1976

Thanksgiving was approaching, along with our commitment to see
the hospital staff. As I said, Dad loved the California coast, especially
Highway One between Los Angeles and San Francisco. He also loved
being in his van, and with Mom's help he felt well enough to make this
long and beautiful journey. I had also purchased a van so we decided to
take the two vans up the coast together. Mom and Dad would go in their
van and my wife Barbara, our six year old daughter Tricia, and I would
go in ours. After the trip up the coast, we would visit the hospital staff
and then the next day go to the Bohemian Grove for Thanksgiving. All
Dad's Bohemian friends knew that he had been ill, so there would be a
mob of well-wishers at the Grove.

We started out on Monday around noon and our first stop was lunch
in Santa Barbara. It was one of those crystal clear winter days and Dad
was feeling great. The next stop was a cookout and overnight at Gaviota
beach, just north of Santa Barbara. We parked our vans adjacent to the
beach, right below the old train trestle. It was sunset and we could see
the sun go down over the ocean. Because it was winter, no one else was
there. I built a big fire and Mom and Barbara made dinner. I knew that
Dad now liked to drink a little wine (why not), so I brought the three
best bottles I had from my cellar. The *Monday Night Football* game was
on, and I brought a color TV and set it up in Dad's van. Dad could only
eat liquids and Mom had made a wonderful creamed soup. There he was
on the bed in the van, covered up with his favorite cashmere blanket.
While listening to the waves crashing, the fire crackling, and enjoying
the exciting football game, he lifted his wine glass, then farted, and said,
"You know, life is pretty good, isn't it!"

In the morning we drove through the Santa Ynez Valley (the film
Sideways) and then past San Simeon Castle. At lunch Dad recalled

how memorable it was to go there for a dinner party in the late thirties. William Randolph Hearst did not like drinking, and the powder rooms had more action than most bars in Hollywood. About an hour later we stopped for a snack at Dad's all-time favorite place, Nepenthe, the restaurant that sits on the cliffs of Big Sur. He had a nice glass of wine and just sat there capturing the view. For a brief moment he was in heaven. After our stop Dad was a little tired, so we stayed at a nice motel in nearby Carmel. The next morning (Wednesday) we slept in and then drove to Santa Rosa and the promised party with the medical staff. We had the party at the home of our dear friends Tom and Mary-Bell Blackstone. It was a poignant reunion as Dad looked rested and was so happy to see everyone. Frankly, the doctors were amazed. It became evident that I knew the medical staff much better than Dad did because he had been in a coma for much of the time. But they sure knew him, and he was so gracious with everyone.

The next day we again slept in and then drove on to the Grove in the early afternoon for Thanksgiving. The Bohemian Grove is one of the most beautiful places on earth because it contains some of the largest redwood trees in the world. Why? Well, when the Southern Pacific Railroad was being built in the late 1800s, redwood was needed for railroad ties because redwood is impervious to termites. However, there was a landowner named Meeker who would not sell his land or his trees. Years later, the membership prevailed and the Club was able to buy a portion of Meeker's land. Along with the giant trees, a club-inspired lake and statuary make the Grove breathtaking. When Dad first saw the place he commented, "Just think what God could have done if he'd had enough money."

Thanksgiving was memorable because many of Dad's old friends made the effort to be there. Brother Tad flew up with his wife and children. Dad knew this would be his last visit, so he wanted to make the most of it. We had Thanksgiving dinner in the large Grill Room, which is covered in moss, has a large fireplace, and looks like a primeval log cabin. After dinner there were singers, musicians, magic acts, and Dad telling some of his favorite Club stories. The day was shared by everyone with great love and laughter. During an earlier part of the day, Dad took me aside and said he wanted to talk. He and I walked past the beautiful lake and lawn area and sat down on the Old Guards Bench. Dad explained that when he died he wanted to be cremated and have his ashes spread outside the Grove in a place he particularly loved. He then said he wanted an azalea bush symbolically planted near the Old Guards Bench. "Presidents and kings and university scholars have all sat on this bench and discussed many interesting and important things."

The next day we drove home using the faster central route. Dad slept most of the way on the bed in the back of the van as he was tired from all the travel and emotional activity. For a portion of the trip I drove his van to help Mom. Sitting next to me she said nothing, but occasionally held my hand. I knew she was frightened as to what was to come, and so was I. But what a meaningful and unforgettable trip! It wasn't just for Dad; it was for all of us.

CHAPTER 48

Hitting the Jackpot
1976

In 1975 our company was chosen to be the prime developer for the redevelopment agency of Pasadena. It was a large piece of property with a great location. The deal had been structured much the same way as the Santa Monica development we lost with Bill Lund. As a matter of fact, I think it was our presentation in Santa Monica that got the attention of the Pasadena people. We designed an entirely new product which we thought would fit the needs of the local buyers. The development was beautiful and won many awards. However, there was a problem — nobody was buying. We couldn't give them away.

It has been said that "Pasadena is the place where old folks go to visit their parents." There is some truth in that saying. Pasadena people are very conservative and take their time making decisions. I assumed that is why we had only sold a handful of units. November through February (the holidays) is the worst time to sell anything in real estate. It was November, and there I was with Dad and Mom in northern California. Frankly, I was scared stiff. When we stopped for gas, Barbara, who was driving my van, said an important call had come in from the office. Honestly, I didn't want to call back. When I did, our sales manager Ellis Sylvester told me that we had sold forty units in the first two days of the Thanksgiving weekend. He then speculated that we would be sold out by Sunday. The next phase of the project sold out over a weekend and we did very, very well.

Following the Pasadena project we did a twenty-million-dollar development in Woodland Hills. We went back to our old design which had served us so well. We had received a lot of good press and a good feedback from the early buyers. We finished the project in record time and were now applying for the final certificate of occupancy. Because of the size of the project, we had all three of our field superintendents at the site

My friends at Ranchero Vistadores. Left to Right: Businessman and NFL owner Hulsey Lokey, entertainer Phil Harris, business executive Lauro Neri, the author, and Ronald Reagan.

Success would provide Dad the opportunity to own a half interest in a twin Cessna.

plus two sales personnel. When the City inspectors arrived, they were accompanied by the new head of Building and Safety for the City of Los Angeles, none other than Mr. Mayfield, the inspector who let us backfill our wall years before. He was surprised to see Sidlow and me standing in front of this large development with our staff, and over one hundred families wanting to buy units.

My grandfather (far right) and his three sons (my uncles) representing my grandfather's horse facility, "Glendale Riding Academy." This is the only nationally ranked all family polo team in America. My grandfather made his money providing horses and wranglers for the studios.

As Mayfield entered the field construction and sales office, he stopped and addressed our employees. He said, "I'd like to tell all of you a little story. It was some years ago, and two young fellows came to me and asked if they could waterproof and then backfill a retaining wall over the weekend. It was really hot that summer weekend, but I let them go ahead. What they didn't know was that each day I went to the site with binoculars to see if they were doing the work correctly. The work was perfect, and there they were with that really old D-8 tractor in all that heat. Then Mayfield said, "Please give me the sign-off sheet. As far as I'm concerned, this project is complete. If these two men are involved, a field inspection is unnecessary." As Mayfield said this all my superintendents blew a sigh of relief. As he left the field office, all of our employees thought Sidlow and I needed a dose of humility, so in unison, gave us the finger. We had substantially raised the prices and sold out the project in four hours. Our company was now on very solid ground financially, and we finally had the resources and excess liquidity that everyone thought we had in the first place.

CHAPTER 49

Odd Jobs
1976

In addition to our development success, a new career was evolving. I was in California with a group of men having lunch. There was one man who stood out, not just because he was so tall, but because he was so interesting. After lunch we both stayed and spoke for almost an hour. I liked him, but other than his first name, I didn't know who he was or what he did.

Ten days later I was in New York, and ran into him in a restaurant. He asked me if I could meet with him the next morning. The next morning I met him at his beautiful apartment at the Pierre Hotel on Fifth Avenue. He explained that he was the Vice-Chairman of the Board of Rockwell International. He went on to explain that as Rockwell merged with other companies, they also acquired their pension assets. Within these newly melded portfolios were "cats and dogs" that had to be defined and perhaps disposed of. He asked if I wanted to do that job. I agreed, and it was the start of a demanding and exciting business adventure. The Rockwell people were fair and extremely competent. However, in dealing outside of Rockwell, I dealt with some of the most important financial people in the country. I became involved with incompetence, fraud, and social prejudice. I was being exposed to the profound arrogance that comes with dealing in high places. It became evident that because of family contacts, and the right schools, a person can be thrust into positions of tremendous responsibility which are far beyond their abilities. The irony is that they are so naive they are totally unaware of their shortcomings.

For over two years I identified those "cats and dogs" for Rockwell and sold many of their odd and underperforming assets. A marketing tool I used was to raise the price and then carry back the "paper." I would then sell the discounted "paper" to an investor with everything closing at the same time. It was a wonderful business relationship and my client became a trusted friend. Sadly, he would die at a young age and I would never do business with that firm again.

I liked this financial trouble shooting because it was lucrative, interesting, and always different. I did it for years and still do. My most memorable client was Robert Evans, the charismatic head of Paramount

The day we closed the repurchase of producer Robert Evans' home. Part of my fee agreement was that he would take me to lunch in the sidecar of my motorcycle at the Beverly Hills Hotel. My friend Susan Cox joined us. It was quite a sight driving up to the front door of the hotel.

Studios. He was the "boy wizard" and former actor who fought to "green light" both *The Godfather* and *Love Story* which saved the studio from financial ruin.

After that, he personally produced *Chinatown, Urban Cowboy,* and *Rosemary's Baby.* Then, after all his success, his world collapsed. He made some poor personal choices and then got involved in trying to make *The Cotton Club.* While writing the script there were numerous confrontations with Francis Ford Coppola. The studio was becoming reluctant as to financing and distribution issues. Then the icing on the cake, *The Cotton Club* murders. Bob's playboy reputation didn't help matters and everything started falling apart. At this time Bob thought he needed money so he sold his beloved house, with a leaseback, but not a buyback provision.

After a year or so the murders were solved, the movie was made and Bob was getting back on his feet. He had a new two-picture deal with Paramount and wanted to buy his house back. Although I had read about him, I'd never met him. It was Saturday and I was working at my office in the Valley. I received a call from Susan Cox, a girl I knew quite well. She was a friend of Bob's and asked if I would go to his house and speak with him about how to get his house back.

Because it was a weekend, I had ridden one of my motorcycles, the one with a sidecar, to the office. I then rode the motorcycle to Evans' house for the meeting. After he explained his situation, I said the problem is simple. First you've got to get the owner to sell you the house back, then get the money to pay for it. After much conversation I found out that the seller owed Jack Nicholson a favor. I knew that Nicholson was a close friend of Evans. So I suggested that Nicholson cancel out his favor and I would get the money. Now you'll owe Nicholson a favor, but you'll have your house back.

As we were leaving the house Evans asked me what I would charge, and I quoted him a flat fee and said if the deal didn't close he would owe me nothing. At his front door, as I was getting on my motorcycle, I said also you are going to take me to lunch at the Beverly Hills Hotel — on this motorcycle. Evans reluctantly agreed. The deal closed and Bob got his beloved house back. On the way to lunch with Evans in the sidecar, he grabbed my arm and said, "I'm scared to death. Now you know how much this Jew wanted his house back!"

CHAPTER 50

The Great Escape
1976

I built a new house and I must say it was spectacular. I spent six months on the plans with the architects and over a year personally supervising the construction. It was very modern, yet wasn't stark because it was all done with straight-grain redwood. It was voted House of the Year by *Builder Magazine* and was featured on its national cover. I had it photographed by the famed architectural photographer Julius Shulman, who subsequently had the house featured in many periodicals. When I originally bought the lot, I tore down the existing house and used its location for a tennis court. I built the new house on a sloping hill adjacent to the court, with a bridge for the entrance which went through the trees and over a stream. It was very dramatic.

In those days everybody was playing tennis, and having my own court was a luxury I could hardly comprehend. Because of the court, I made new tennis friends, one of whom was my neighbor named Gene. Through Gene I became thoroughly involved in an unforgettable adventure. The whole story is very involved and complicated, but I have distilled it into the following highlights.

Gene was a nice guy, a good athlete and was easy to be with. He was involved in a unique business where he rebuilt large airplane propeller hubs, which are the things that enable a pilot to change propeller pitch. As airliners become obsolete, they are often sold to foreign carriers as freight haulers. The problem is that, for these planes to enter the United States, they must have full USA certifications, and one of those certifications is for the propeller hubs. These big bulky hubs that weigh two hundred and fifty pounds must be rebuilt every ten thousand flight hours and could only be built in the USA for inspection purposes. Gene's shop was located at the Burbank Airport and was only one of three in the United States.

It was now 1979 and cocaine was everywhere. Gene always seemed to have a little, if anyone was interested. I realized his biggest airplane clients were located in Columbia, and I'm sure that there was more than grease and oil in those two-hundred-and-fifty pound propeller hubs. However, I can honestly say that the recreational use of cocaine by my friends was minor at best, and this included Gene. We were more the martini and margarita crowd. As I got to know Gene better, I became aware that the aircraft repair business was both lucrative and cutthroat. Gene did not get along with or trust his competitors; he actually feared them.

Gene was returning to Los Angeles from Columbia via Mexico City. His luggage had been checked as he was clearing customs into Mexico City because he was going to stay there for a few days. The customs people found two pounds of cocaine in each of his bags and Gene was immediately arrested. I assure you Gene was not a drug dealer, and the cocaine had to be a plant from one of his competitors who wanted to take over his business. Why would a man who ships two-hundred-and-fifty pound airplane parts put cocaine in his luggage?

I received a call from Gene's secretary and she explained what had happened. I asked, "Why me?" as Gene had other much closer friends. She explained that Gene felt I was resourceful, dependable, and would keep my mouth shut. Gene hired a top Mexican attorney and his trial was set quickly. He really had little defense and was found guilty and sentenced to nine and a half years in prison with no chance for parole.

Through Gene's secretary I was asked to come to Mexico City with three of his friends. The three were a successful businessman, an extremely wealthy property owner, and a world-renowned physician. All of them I knew or had met through Gene. The four of us flew to Mexico City together. I found these men to be "stand-up" guys who I grew to like the more I was with them.

We got to Mexico City and immediately went to the penitentiary. The penitentiary was built in a series of circles so that if you got over one fence, you had to go over three more to escape. No one had ever escaped from that penitentiary. You entered and exited from one large master tunnel which was highly secured. After thorough identity checks, we all entered the prison. To my amazement the inside of the prison looked like a park. We all sat down on the grass and had lunch. Gene, who had now been incarcerated for three months, had grown a beard and purposely lost twenty-five pounds.

Gene immediately took over the meeting, "Guys, when I get out of here, I'll be in my mid-fifties. This was a setup and the only way I'm coming home is to escape. Here is what I want to do." Gene then carefully went over his detailed plan and after an hour asked us what we thought. At first I was speechless and thought Gene to be crazy, but the more I thought about it, it was brilliant. If we were in, we would each be given assignments and then return to Mexico in two months. The main thing was to keep our mouths shut. The plan was very detailed and complicated, but we were helped by Gene's very knowledgeable girlfriend. Not only was she beautiful, but she was extremely cool under pressure. She had moved to Mexico City and was coordinating everything from her new offices which were rented under an assumed name.

Here is how the whole thing took place. The girlfriend's new offices were set up on the Reforma, the most prestigious boulevard in Mexico City. These offices contained a fictitious booking agency. Through this bogus agency she booked a well known Mexican "boy band" to perform one night within the prison. We paid a legitimate and unknowing recording company to record the performance, and this recording would later be used for a new album. This album was to be dedicated to the prison's warden. The recording equipment was to be trucked into the prison and then trucked out after the performance. Gene got a job as a trustee working backstage handling the equipment. There was one piece of equipment the (uninvolved) sound engineers didn't understand but never questioned. At the end of the performance Gene would then climb into the piece of equipment, and hopefully at the end of the concert it would be wheeled onto the truck and out of the prison. The escape piece had to be totally encapsulated (sniffing dogs) and Gene had a one-hour oxygen tank for breathing. My first assignment was overseeing the building of the escape device.

Because of my knowledge of aviation, my second job was to arrange for Gene's departure. I hired a disreputable pilot I knew from flying who would do anything for money. He chose a Lear 35 jet, but would fly it alone. We figured the least of our problems was being cited for not having a co-pilot. On the Lear's final approach into Mexico City, the pilot saw that military exercises were taking place. Thinking that it had to do with the escape, he aborted the landing and flew back to El Paso. As a backup I had a single engine 206 Cessna based at the Mexico City airport because I didn't completely trust the Lear pilot. Gene and the 206 pilot flew all night in order to land in Tijuana. Gene showered, shaved off his beard, put on clean unassuming clothes, and simply walked across the border with no luggage.

That day he was home in Los Angeles. This whole procedure took over five months and was very complex on many levels. Most of all, luck was on our side. As I said, I'm only giving you the highlights. However, we were happy for Gene and proud of what we all were able to accomplish, although it was slightly illegal. After this traumatic event was over, none of us went back to Mexico and we spent little time together. We never spoke about the ordeal with others or even amongst ourselves. I think we reexamined our lives and put things in a little better perspective. Frankly, I believe we grew up a little. Sadly, Gene would die from a malignant brain tumor a year and a half after his great escape.

CHAPTER 51

Reagan for President
1976

It all started in 1976, when I was a member of the Rancheros Vistadores riding group. There I had the chance to meet Ronald Reagan, who was also a member. We were far from friends, but I was often around him and discovered what a kind and decent man he was with a wonderful Irish humor. However, I did become friends with some of Reagan's closest advisers who were also in the same equestrian group. They included Justice William Clark, who would become National Security Advisor, and William Wilson, who would become Ambassador to the Vatican.

In late 1976 Wilson quietly advised me that Reagan was thinking about the White House. He said that nothing would happen for a while, but if he ran, would I come aboard? My answer was an enthusiastic yes. Well, the time went by, and Reagan entered the race in 1980. My contact was a bundle of energy named Charles Wick. He was an attorney who dabbled in everything from real estate to movies. When we met, I acknowledged that I was sure he was dealing with a hundred guys like me, so I suggested we get to the point. "How much money do you expect me to raise?" Wick suggested an amount which seemed reasonable, and I agreed. So that amount would be my goal.

Now when there is no specific need from a politician, and there is not an implied quid-pro-quo, it's often difficult to raise money. This was something I had never done before on such a high level, and it was a real challenge. I didn't call 'em, I went to see each and every person personally. In seven weeks there was going to be a reception and buffet held at Henry Singleton's spectacular Bel-Air home. Singleton was the genius who co-founded Teledyne and was one of Reagan's closest advisers. Reagan would be there and would personally meet each of my contributors.

I had a cocktail party at my home after which we would all go to Singleton's. It was a lot of work, but it was well worth it simply because of the people I would get to know. My favorite among these extremely talented men was Charles B."Tex"Thornton, who was the founder of Litton Industries. Like the other men who were surrounding Reagan, Thornton was wise and unpretentious. At the Singleton reception I handed Charlie (that's what he now asked me to call him) Wick an envelope containing checks which added up to my goal amount. He was thrilled because I didn't call him or bother him, I just did my job. Charlie Wick was an unforgettable character and would go on to become the Co-chair of the Presidential Inaugural Committee and then head of the U.S. Information Agency. Imagine, only a few months ago I was busting some guy out of a Mexican prison!

After the Singleton party my goal, in a sense, was complete, and now I participated in other minor fundraisers and luncheons. During that time I got to know more of Reagan's close associates. They were called his "Kitchen Cabinet." One of these members was a charismatic businessman named Jack Wrather. Wrather was the consummate salesman who was involved in oil, television (he owned *Lassie* and *The Lone Ranger*) and hotels (he owned the Disneyland Hotel). In the future, and by a twist of fate, Wrather would play a big part in my business life.

It was exciting as election night approached. However, with the early returns coming in, it became rather anticlimactic. My original motivation for the campaign was because Reagan was so likeable. In addition, I got to know Jimmy Carter's former secretary from when he was Governor of Georgia, She shared with me how totally incompetent he was. I had also attended a lecture by Professor Arthur Laffer, who subscribed to Reagan's economic policies, which I agreed with.

The Inauguration was unforgettable. Washington D.C. is a very special place, and during the Inauguration it was all shined up and looked spectacular. The night before the Inauguration we attended the Candlelight Dinner at the Kennedy Center in the private dining room. It was a black-tie sit down dinner for only one hundred people, and dignitaries were everywhere. The entertainment for the evening turned out to be the couple sitting at our table. It was evangelist Jim Baker and his wife Tammy Faye. They kept talking and making fools of themselves which made this elegant but reserved dinner party more fun. The next day the Inauguration itself was a mob scene. There were so many people you couldn't move or see anything.

There were five inaugural balls, and I attended the one with all my California horseback riding friends. It was fun seeing a bunch of cowboys all dressed up in white tie and tails. Reagan showed up for about fifteen minutes. There was a cocktail party at our hotel prior to the Ball. At the party was my friend Tom Barrett of the Barrett-Jackson auto auction fame. Tom is the kind of guy who knows everybody. He lived in Phoenix and was flown to the Inauguration in a Gulf Stream Jet owned by an important looking Mexican businessman.

Tom introduced me to the Mexican who quickly asked me to join him in a private conversation. As we sat down, he said he would like to tell me an interesting story. He said that Tom Barrett had asked for his help in getting my friend out of jail in Mexico City. He had many friends in Mexico, so he took it upon himself to personally see President Lopez-Portillo. After explaining the situation to the President, he said he would see what he could do. As he was still in the President's office, he called the prison authorities to check on the status of my friend. The President was informed that my friend escaped that morning. "Senor, you made me look like a *culero grande* in front of the President. Frankly, I hope I never see you again." The Mexican then abruptly got up and walked away. Later that evening I apologized to Tom Barrett about upsetting his friend. Barrett replied, "Don't worry about it. He's probably angry he wasn't in on it." Then Tom looked at me and asked, "Did you really bust that guy out of jail?"

Lauro Neri, my good friend and fellow member of Rancheros Vistadores, was also a man who was adored by President Reagan. Ten days after the Presidential Inauguration, Reagan returned to Los Angeles for the first time since he had taken office. Among the various functions he was attending was a large reception hosted by the Hispanic community. Because Lauro was an important member of this community, President Reagan asked him to join him at this reception. Lauro met the President in West Los Angeles at a hotel located at the 405 freeway and Sunset Boulevard. The two men got into the Presidential limousine and both felt rather uncomfortable as Reagan had only been President for ten days, and Lauro had never been with alone with a President. The motorcade got on the freeway which is usually filled with traffic. However, the local highway patrol had blocked all of the on-ramps, and the freeway was clear. So now President Reagan and Lauro Nero are on the freeway going ninety miles an hour with a half a dozen SUVs and twenty motorcycles and a helicopter overhead. There was silence in the limo for the first two minutes, then Reagan nudged Neri with his elbow and said, "Can you believe this?"

After Reagan took office I was invited to various affairs at the White House. It was a thrill to be there and Reagan always made everyone feel so comfortable. He was so natural and seemed to be having as much fun as his guests. What a guy, I'll never forget those moments, or my President.

CHAPTER 52

The Final Curtain
1977

Dad was going downhill fast. His tumors were growing and the leukemia was becoming difficult. When someone is as sick as Dad, the treatments just to keep him alive become a real juggling act for the doctors. Everyone gathered at Newport for Christmas and New Year's. They were somewhat somber affairs, but everyone kept their "game faces" on, including Dad.

Dad was to be honored by the Pacific Pioneer Broadcasters and really wanted to attend. Brother Tad drove him up to Los Angeles from Newport, and although he felt lousy, he looked great. When he received his award he gave a little speech and then took some questions and answers. After some "powder-puff" questions to evoke laughter and good will, some bozo from Associated Press asked Dad to comment on his health. Dad quickly replied, " Well, I've got just about everything but crabs. However, there is a bright side to it. I haven't been called by a life insurance salesman in months." With great laughter and applause from the large audience, Andy Devine walked off a stage for the very last time in his life.

It was now January of 1977 and Barbara, daughter Tricia and I went to Newport for my 38th birthday. Surprisingly, Dad had a great attitude, and we all had a wonderful dinner. I mentioned that I had had a business lunch at the Brown Derby and Benny Massi had waited on us. We all reminisced about my crazy birth night. Dad went to bed early as he now tired easily. In February things got worse, and Dad was admitted to the hospital. Mom called me on the afternoon of the seventeenth and said I had better get down to Newport. The problem was he had changed hospitals and Mom didn't tell me. I had no idea where he was and couldn't find Mom. However, by that evening I found the correct hospital and we were now there all together.

The next day Dad was somewhat awake and stable. He had beaten the "Grim Reaper" so many times in the past, why not once more? Mom and Tad were exhausted and hadn't taken a bath in almost two days. Mom said she and Tad were going home to take a shower and a short nap. If anyone needed or deserved it, they did. After being in hospital rooms for so long, I could read the monitors fairly well. I was there alone with Dad, and it appeared he was going into cardiac arrest. I was holding Dad's hand and his final words were "This is really the shits," and then his eyes closed. I summoned the nurse and she called for a "Code Blue." Dad's doctor, Dr. Armintrout, was right there with the paddles, morphine, and such. I took the doctor's hand and said, "It's your call, but Dad has been through a lot and let's have no heroics—please." I then left Dad's bedside to make room for the other doctors. In the blink of an eye, Dr. Armintrout came to tell me Dad was gone.

I couldn't reach Mom because she was in transit back to the hospital. When she arrived, I was in the waiting room to meet her and tell her. She instantly replied, "You're full of crap, Andy is not dead." She literally ran to find Dr. Armintrout. After she spoke with the doctor, she just sat down and wept. I had never seen a woman, especially my mother, cry like that. After all her dedicated support during his illness, it was now finally over. I think the infidelities, the negative feelings, and the distrust welled up inside her all at once, and she came to the realization that Dad was gone. Because of his intellect, his kindness, and the way he was with people, she knew she had just lost a truly great man who had been her devoted husband and companion for forty-three years.

CHAPTER 53

The Great Sendoff
1977

I love funerals. I believe in them. Funerals bring closure and provide a time for old friends to be together. It's a time to tell stories and reminisce about the newly departed. What I don't like is some distant and disinterested minister spouting the standard church dialogue. I believe funerals should be personal and performed by the friends of the deceased. To quote Carole Lombard on the day of my birth, "Let's make it a party, god damn it." And that's exactly what we did for Dad.

The funeral was held at a small church in Newport Beach. Fortunately the church had a very large parking lot because so many people attended. The eulogists were three very close friends: (Judge) Robert Gardner, (Actor) Guy Madison, and (TV Producer) Charles Lyon. Both John Wayne and Jimmy Stewart were in attendance, but did not speak. After the service I had a group of cowboy musicians led by Ken Curtis ("Festus" on *Gunsmoke*) playing Dad's favorite songs in the parking lot. In addition to the musicians, waiters were passing around bottles of good bourbon with green ribbons (for the Irish) tied to the necks. No loving cups — it was straight out of the bottle; and drink they all did. There were society matrons, actors, and guys who worked around the boat yards, all drinking from the same bottles. That's the way Dad would have liked it. I'm sure he was sorry he couldn't join in.

After the service there were two nearby receptions held at the same time. One was held at my brother's home, which was for the younger crowd. His party was full of music, great food, and lots of drinks, all enjoyed by Dad's younger friends. The other was an equally festive affair held at Mom's house, which was for her family and older friends. I went directly to Mom's house to be with her. It was bedlam at her house because her entire family was there. They were always a noisy and undisciplined bunch with in-laws, little kids, and so forth.

However, of all of Mom's brothers and sisters, there was no one like her older brother, my Uncle Newt. I have managed thousands of apartment units in my life and have been forced to deal with the absolute dregs of society. But the worst person I have ever known in my life is Uncle Newt. He was an insecure "blowhard" who was a bully, a liar, a cheat, and made enough money to be a pain in the ass. He was the guy with the big belt buckle, a new Cadillac, and a big diamond ring. Even as a little kid I didn't like him (I didn't know why), but as I got older, I grew to despise him more and more. On top of that, he was one of the most physically unattractive men I'd ever met. Mother was truly a beautiful woman and he surely didn't look like her brother.

I got to Mom's house and there was Uncle Newt. That week my picture and a prominent feature article were on the front page of *The Los Angeles Times* real estate section. Uncle Newt couldn't get over it. He had been drinking and was stalking me from the moment I arrived. With a drink in one hand and poking his index finger into my chest, he said to me on the day of my father's funeral, "I saw your picture in the paper, and you wouldn't be anything if your father wasn't so famous. What's it like to continually ride on someone's coattails?" I acknowledged that fact and tried to move on, but he followed me. I politely ask him to leave me alone as I wanted to be with Mom. She was busy and handling things well, but Newt kept pressing me. I finally told Mother that I had to leave or this might be the day that I finally kicked the living shit out of Uncle Newt. Honestly, I wanted to kill him. I think that if I had started on him, I might have. I don't think I have ever been madder or hated anyone more in my entire life. Mom understood and I reluctantly left.

I was stone sober, but was so upset I forgot about my brother's reception where my wife and daughter were located. All I could think of was Mom, Uncle Newt, and having to leave. I was driving home to the San Fernando Valley for little reason. It was now late afternoon and a truly beautiful day. I was driving a convertible and thought if I put the top down, I might feel better. As I was driving to town, the more I thought, the madder I got, and the madder I got, the faster I drove. It was now dark and I was on the 405 freeway near Los Angeles International Airport.

I was pulled over by the Highway Patrol who had clocked me going 95 miles an hour. There I was with the top down, in my suit, when the officer asked for my driver's license. I handed it to him, and he studied it very carefully. He then looked at me and said, "I've read the papers, and I imagine you've had a hell of a day. Your dad was a great guy and everyone loved him. He really brought me and my family a lot of happiness."

As the officer handed me back my driver's license he said, "Slow down and get home safe." The patrol car departed and there I was with the top down at night, sitting by the side of the freeway. I looked up at the stars and said to Dad, "Well, you're not even here, and you're still getting my ass out of trouble."

CHAPTER 54

Wishes Granted
1977

Remember, Dad wanted to be cremated and have his ashes spread outside the Grove in a place that he particularly loved. He then wanted an azalea bush planted near the Old Guards Bench in the Bohemian Grove. Tad and I had gone to the crematorium and picked up the box containing Dad's ashes. The box was much larger than I had thought it would be as Dad was still a large man, even in death. Tad put the box in a bag and off to the airport we went for our flight to San Francisco.

For a long time I had a driver in San Francisco named Harold Butler. I met him years before at the airport when I had left my wallet at home and had no money or credit cards. I asked him if I had an honest face and, if so, would he drive me for about three hours and then return me to the airport. I said I would send him a check immediately upon arriving home. Harold said, "Let's go," and that was the start of a beautiful friendship. He owned this old beat-up Cadillac limousine, but he was such a character that nobody cared. All my friends, including Dad, used him. Sadly, Harold died two weeks before Dad. Harold's wife used to send me copies of her instructions to Harold for pick-ups and deliveries. When Mrs. Butler heard of Dad's passing, she sent me a copy of an order instructing Harold (while in heaven) to pick up Mr. Devine and take him to wherever he needed to go. I responded to Mrs. Butler with a copy of a letter to Dad telling him that it was Harold's turn to ride in the back, and that Dad should have his fat ass up front. She passed away a few months later. They had been married for many years. The things you never forget about a person are good will, humor, and kindness. God bless you, Harold, I'll never forget you.

Because of Harold's passing, I hired a new driver for our journey. Tad and I were met at the airport by Patrick O'Melveny, a man Dad truly loved. Pat was the son of Dad's former attorney Jack O'Melveny. Our new driver was a young hotshot from Brooklyn who was unfamiliar with the area and had no idea where we were going or what we were up to. When we all got into the limo, Pat revealed a bottle of very good scotch. Tad in turn put the box containing Dad's ashes on the right rear seat. It was a big silver aluminum thing that looked rather mysterious.

To add to the drama, it started to mist and rain. We planned to stop along the way at the exclusive area of Tiburon. My friend Shawn Mcgreevy had offered to help by providing a post-hole digger and an azalea bush which was Dad's favorite plant. We pulled the limo off the freeway onto a shopping center parking lot. Through the gray sky and the mist, a black Rolls Royce drove up to meet us. Shawn and I embraced, and then I took the items out of the trunk of the Rolls and placed them in the trunk of the limo. All of this was being carefully observed by our neophyte chauffeur.

We then got back on the freeway for our trip towards the Bohemian Grove. As we got closer, we turned off the freeway and were now driving on a two-lane road through beautiful wine vineyards. The rain and mist continued as we entered the giant redwoods. Because of the height of the trees, it became very dark and even more mysterious. With the scotch, much laughter and storytelling was taking place. It also became necessary to pull over to the side of the road so all of us could take a leak. While out of the car, the driver approached me and asked, "Who are you guys?" I explained we had just come to spread an old friend's ashes. The driver said, "Thank god, I thought you guys were a bunch of incompetent drug dealers." As we got closer to the Grove, we spread Dad's ashes. When we arrived at the Grove, the entrance was abandoned. There was only one guard at a place that was usually teeming with security. There to meet us was Dick Sands who was also a favorite of Dad's. He was not only kind and entertaining, but was a person who could do anything. He was a former Navy carrier pilot, an accomplished musician, and a mesmerizing and hilarious storyteller who wrote and performed many shows for the club.

We entered the Grove like a bunch of hooligans. Brother Tad had the post-hole digger, Dick Sands had the azalea bush, and Pat O'Melveny had the scotch. Stories about Dad and laughter continued as we found our spot. The hole was difficult to dig because there were a lot of rocks and we wanted to plant the bush firmly. So we all put our things down and took turns digging. When the hole was finally ready, we, of course, discovered we had now misplaced the bush. After a little anguish and lots of laughter, the plant was recovered. Now the bush was where Dad wanted it. Symbolically it was close enough to the Old Guards bench to hear what was being said, but not so close it could be ripped out.

All of us departed the Grove for the long drive and the flight back home. Going through an ordeal like this makes one think about a lot of things. I hoped I could learn from Dad's mistakes as well as my own. If possible, it would be nice to come out of all of this a better person. Oddly, I didn't worry about Mom. Although she never finished high school, she was resourceful, fearless and the ultimate survivor. I also think she took comfort in the affection that everyone had shown Dad. Hopefully this affection would fill the void that his death had created.

But somehow I always held the feeling that Dad had never left. Perhaps it was because he was often on television, or maybe it was because he hadn't been around that much in the first place. But he would come alive when someone would tell me a personal story or when I would meet someone who knew him well. This immortality would stay with me forever. My favorite encounters were with the strangers who knew Dad primarily as a performer. These people were devoted fans who loved Dad and knew so much about him. They would tell me things that even I didn't know. We would sit and talk and laugh. These strangers would inquire about my life and then tell me all about themselves. Most seemed to have such interesting lives. This was the best part because these fans of Dad's and I were now becoming friends, and making friends was what Andy Devine was all about.

Epilogue

What happens to a family when a famous patriarch dies? Brother Tad was the steady one. After graduating from Stanford and completing his military obligation as a Navy SEAL officer, he married in 1963 and started a small but prosperous property management and landscape business. In 1965 he purchased a home in the Newport Beach area which he still lives in today. He and his wife of forty-nine years raised two great kids and now have three grand-children.

Mom's story is a little more complicated. After Dad died she stayed in the Newport house and was living a comfortable life. Being in good physical shape, she enjoyed many activities such as hunting, golf, horseback riding, and boating. However, while attending her high school reunion, she met an old boyfriend and they started dating. They married a few years later, but unfortunately he turned out to be a devious and lying opportunist. She was about to leave him when she had a massive stroke. My brother and I finally got rid of him, and he didn't cause us any trouble because we had obtained documentation on some of his shady dealings. Mom could not walk, but she had a wonderful attitude and made the most of her situation. A few years later she died peacefully at the age of eighty-five. Her memorial was memorable because many friends of all ages came from far and wide just to honor her. The group went as far back as my friends from grammar school and as current as Tad's Navy SEAL team. Everyone was there.

In the early forties actor Lew Ayres gave Mom a copy of the book *The Prophet* by Khalil Gibran. Because of his writings Mom believed that one's soul never dies, and when death occurs your soul goes into the heavens and attaches to a star. Because of her beliefs, I wrote the following poem which I presented at her memorial:

MEMORIAL POEM

I came to this earth from a star rather faint
My dad was a cowboy, my mom was a saint

Had five brothers and sisters, all very different, none very
meek
And who was my favorite among them, it really depends on
the day of the week

I fell in love with a simple man, whose devotion would never
shift
He was big and active and honest, and oh my god, did he
have a gift

We had two sons who were just alike, yet different as night
and day
And I wanted to do it all for them, but was always afraid I'd
get in the way

The grandchildren are my greatest achievement, to their tri-
umphs I join in the toast
And whenever I'm scared sad or lonely, they are the ones I
think about most

In time my husband departed, he went on to his own little star
But his memory moves all about me, like fireflies caught in
a jar

Now I see my vessel is cracking, and sand is all over the ground
What is that bittersweet music, what is that come-hither sound

My god it's my star and it's calling, boy this ride will be fun
Going back to that place of beginnings, knowing my job is
all done

In time you will come here to visit, because you have your
very own star
There are no game wardens, taxes, or lift lines, and everyone
here seems to shoot par

My personal issues were the most complicated. My wife Barbara and I separated in 1981 and divorced in 1982. At the same time D&S was sold to Wrather Corporation. The new buyers were enamored with my partner Sidlow as I only knew them socially. The sale came with the proviso that I would be terminated from the new company, but paid more money to leave. I quietly took the deal and could hardly hide my enthusiasm. Right after the deal closed, Wrather was folded into Disney Corporation. I thought it was a bad deal for all. We ran our business by the seat of our pants and now the impatient and arrogant Sidlow would be answering to accountants, attorneys and Disney vice presidents. And who was going to make and sell the deals? Sidlow and I were involved with our company for nineteen years and had the time of our lives. The Disney deal with Sidlow ended in a year. The breakup and sale of our company to Wrather was stupid for all parties involved. Only Sidlow and I could really take the blame for that debacle.

I formed my own company and started a big project in the north San Fernando Valley that was a big deal; too big. Although I'm not a great manager of things, we got the project up and going and finished. It was very attractive and sales were brisk. Then the roof fell in. My lender, The Bank of Beverly Hills, was deemed insolvent and the Resolution Trust took over the bank and my project. In addition, they took all my deposits in the bank. They said that they had the right because it was a joint venture and not a loan. It was clearly only a loan, and the trust was simply grabbing whatever assets they could get their hands on. I sued the Resolution Trust, Good luck! I sold my house and paid off all my creditors. Now I was homeless, broke, and almost fifty.

I took all kinds of odd jobs from mortgage deals to remodels. I rented a little apartment in Santa Monica and started all over again. I lost touch with my family, including my daughter, for a few years because I was embarrassed as to my state of affairs, as were they. But things started to slowly pick up and I started to make a good living. It was 1996 and I was 57 years old. Going through what I endured, you learn many things and become afraid of nothing. I had been single for almost fourteen years and met a wonderful woman. We were married in 1997 and moved to Nashville, Tennessee, but we keep an apartment in Los Angeles. I got back into being active in real estate development and built a beautiful and exciting new building in Nashville and I am about to start another. I have also continued my mortgage and real estate consulting business in both California and Tennessee. I reconnected with my family, including my brother, my daughter and even my ex-wife. My daughter has a wonderful husband and

The day Dad was inducted into the Cowboy Hall of Fame in Oklahoma City, Oklahoma. It was a black-tie affair attended by 3,000 people. Patrick Wayne presented my brother and me the statue. Patrick Wayne, Tad Devine, Dennis Devine and the museum curator.

Four of the Five Freshmen with Coach Daland being honored on the floor of the Los Angeles Memorial Coliseum before 94,000 spectators.

two great kids who are a big part of my life. Not wanting to let go of past memories, brother Tad and I still own our parents' Newport Beach home.

When I was honored on the field of the Coliseum before all those people, I remember walking back to my seat. While walking I reached into the pocket of my windbreaker and stuck my finger on the corner of a card. When I took out the card I found it was a note announcing that Dad was going to be inducted into the Cowboy Hall of Fame. It was a clear night and while still on the Coliseum floor I looked up at the stars and said to Dad, "Well, you didn't win any Academy Awards, and I never received any Olympic medals, but I think we both did okay."

My favorite picture of Mom, which we had printed for her memorial. She is holding her beloved Parker 12 gauge shotgun and what I would call at least "a gaggle of geese."

Andy Devine Days poster

Dad has two "stars" on Hollywood Boulevard. One is for films and the other is for television. The above "star" is well worn, as it was part of the initial installation of stars on Hollywood Boulevard. Presently it is located in front of a strip club, although a fancy one. Perhaps this is where Dad wanted to be all along.

Credits

FILM APPEARANCES

1926: Athlete extra, *The Collegians* .... UNIVERSAL
1928: Soldier, *We Americans* .... UNIVERSAL
1928: Joe Cassidy, *Naughty Baby* .... FIRST NATIONAL PICTURES
1928: Student, *Lonesome* .... UNIVERSAL
1928: Professor Fountain, *Red Lips* .... UNIVERSAL
1929: Bob, *Hot Stuff* .... WARNER BROS.
1931: Truck McCall, *The Spirit of Notre Dame* .... UNIVERSAL
1931: Cluck, *The Criminal Code* .... COLUMBIA
1931: Briney, *Danger Island* .... UNIVERSAL
1932: Pete Wiley, *Radio Patrol* .... UNIVERSAL
1932: Andy Wiley, *Man Wanted* .... WARNER BROS.
1932: Steve Hand, *The Man from Yesterday* .... PARAMOUNT
1932: Johnny Kinsman, *Law and Order* .... UNIVERSAL
1932: Clarence Howe, *The Impatient Maiden* .... UNIVERSAL
1932: Cowboy, *Destry Rides Again* .... UNIVERSAL
1932: Andy Moran, *The All-American* .... UNIVERSAL
1932: Chauffer, *Three Wise Girls* .... COLUMBIA
1932: Information Kid, *Fast Champions* .... UNIVERSAL
1932: Mac the call boy, *Tom Brown of Culver* .... UNIVERSAL
1933: Mud, *Song of the Eagle* .... PARAMOUNT
1933: Sam Travers, *Midnight Mary* .... M-G-M
1933: Larry Ward, *Doctor Bull* .... TWENTIETH CENTURY FOX
1933: Al, *Chance at Heaven* .... RKO RADIO PICTURES
1933: Andy Anderson, *The Cohens & Kellys in Trouble* .... UNIVERSAL
1933: Scoops, *The Big Cage* .... UNIVERSAL
1933: Andy, *Horseplay* .... UNIVERSAL
1933: Andy Jones, *Saturday's Millions* .... UNIVERSAL
1934: Egghead, *Wake Up and Dream* .... UNIVERSAL

1934: Oscar the chauffeur, *Upperworld*.......................... WARNER BROS.
1934: Val Orcott, *The President Vanishes*......................... PARAMOUNT
1934: Young Man, *The Poor Rich*................................. UNIVERSAL
1934: Gravel, *Let's Talk It Over*.. UNIVERSAL
1934: Sergeant Ham Davis, *Hell in the Heavens* ....
TWENTIETH CENTURY FOX
1934: McDougal, *Gift of Gab* .... UNIVERSAL
1934: Howie, *Stingaree* .... RKO RADIO PICTURES
1934: Careful, *Million Dollar Ransom*............................ UNIVERSAL
1935: Hi Holler, *Way Down East* .... TWENTIETH CENTURY FOX
1935: Edwards, *Straight from the Heart*............................ UNIVERSAL
1935: Liverlips, *Hold 'Em Yale*............................ PARAMOUNT
1935: Cy Kipp, *Fighting Youth*............................ UNIVERSAL
1935: Elmer Otway, *The Farmer Takes a Wife*............................
TWENTIETH CENTURY FOX
1935: George Mason, *Chinatown Squad* .... UNIVERSAL
1935: Pinky Falls, *Coronado*............................ PARAMOUNT
1935: Himself, *La Fiesta de Santa Barbara* .... M-G-M
1936: Pay Day, *Yellowstone* .... UNIVERSAL
1936: George, *Small Town Girl*............................ M-G-M
1936: Peter, *Romeo and Juliet* .... M-G-M
1936: Pop Andrews, *The Big Game* .... RKO RADIO PICTURES
1936: Joe Williams, *Flying Hostess* .... UNIVERSAL
1937: Daisy Day, *You're a Sweetheart*............................ UNIVERSAL
1937: Danny McGuire, *A Star is Born* .... UNITED ARTISTS
1937: Willy, *The Road Back*............................ UNIVERSAL
1937: Carolina, *Mysterious Crossing*............................ UNIVERSAL
1937: Pickle Bixby, *In Old Chicago* .... TWENTIETH CENTURY FOX
1937: Half Pint, *Double or Nothing*............................ PARAMOUNT
1938: Charlie Spuill, *Yellow Jack* .... M-G-M
1938: Hobbs, *Strange Faces*............................ UNIVERSAL
1938: Hansen, *The Storm*............................ UNIVERSAL
1938: "Snoop" Lewis, *Personal Secretary*............................ UNIVERSAL
1938: Joe Gibbs, *Men with Wings* .... PARAMOUNT
1938: Policeman Lawrence O'Roon, *Doctor Rhythm* .... PARAMOUNT
1938: Doc Saunders, *Swing That Cheer*............................ UNIVERSAL
1939: "Tiny" Andrews, *Tropic Fury* .... UNIVERSAL
1939: Tubby, *The Spirit of Culver*............................ UNIVERSAL
1939: Henry Munch, *Never Say Die*............................ PARAMOUNT
1939: Slim Collins, *Mutiny on the Blackhawk* .... UNIVERSAL

1939 "Beef" Brumley, *Legion of the Lost Flyers* .... UNIVERSAL
1939: Sneezer, *Geronimo* .... PARAMOUNT
1939: Buck Rickabaugh, *Stagecoach* .... UNITED ARTISTS
1940: Ozark Jones, *When the Daltons Rode* .... UNIVERSAL
1940: Meadows, *Trail of the Vigilantes* .... UNIVERSAL
1940: Wally Davis, *Torrid Zone* .... WARNER BROS.
1940: Unbilled guest star, *Margie* .... UNIVERSAL
1940: Constable Bones Blair, *The Man from Montreal* .... UNIVERSAL
1940: Commodore, *Little Old New York* ....TWENTIETH CENTURY FOX
1940: Andy Grogan, *The Leather Pushers* .... UNIVERSAL
1940: Matt Morrison, *Hot Steel* .... UNIVERSAL
1940: "Guppy" Wexel, *Danger on Wheels* .... UNIVERSAL
1940: Barney Tolliver, *Black Diamonds* .... UNIVERSAL
1940: Andy, *Buck Benny Rides Again* .... PARAMOUNT
1940: Andy, *The Devil's Pipeline* .... UNIVERSAL
1941: Moose, *South of Tahiti* .... UNIVERSAL
1941: Andy McCoy, *Raiders of the Desert* .... UNIVERSAL
1941: Andy Adams, *Mutiny in the Arctic* .... UNIVERSAL
1941: Lumberjack, *Men of the Timberland* .... UNIVERSAL
1941: Andy, *Lucky Devils* .... UNIVERSAL
1941: Joe, *The Kid from Kansas* .... UNIVERSAL
1941: Andy, *A Dangerous Game* .... UNIVERSAL
1941: Spear Fish, *Badlands of Dakota* .... UNIVERSAL
1941: First Sailor, *The Flame of New Orleans* .... UNIVERSAL
1941: Andy, *Road Agent* .... UNIVERSAL
1942: Sam, *Unseen Enemy* .... UNIVERSAL
1942: Andy Jarrett, *Top Sergeant* .... UNIVERSAL
1942: Arizona, *Timber* .... UNIVERSAL
1942: Judge Eustace Vale, *Sin Town* .... UNIVERSAL
1942: Klondike, *North to the Klondike* .... UNIVERSAL
1942: Himself, *Keeping Fit* (documentary) .... U.S. GOVERNMENT
1942: Blimp, *Escape from Hong Kong* .... UNIVERSAL
1942: Andy Parker, *Danger in the Pacific* .... UNIVERSAL
1942: Mike Kilinsky, *Between Us Girls* .... UNIVERSAL
1943: Eddie Dolan, *Rhythm of the Islands* .... UNIVERSAL
1943: Cowboy, *Crazy Horse* .... UNIVERSAL
1943: Walsh, *Corvette K-225* .... UNIVERSAL
1943: Slim, *Frontier Badmen* .... UNIVERSAL
1944: Horsehead, *The Ghost Catchers* .... UNIVERSAL
1944: Father Kelley, *Bowery to Broadway* .... UNIVERSAL

1944: Joe Costello, *Babes on Swing Street*............................ UNIVERSAL
1944: Abdullah, *Ali Baba & the Forty Thieves*...................... UNIVERSAL
1944: Himself, *Follow the Boys*... UNIVERSAL
1945: Martin, *That's the Spirit*.. UNIVERSAL
1945: Nebka, *Sudan*.. UNIVERSAL
1945: Big Ben, *Frontier Gal*... UNIVERSAL
1945: Bunny, *Frisco Sal*.. UNIVERSAL
1946: Ben Dance, *Canyon Passage*..................................... UNIVERSAL
1947: Andy, *The Vigilantes Return*..................................... UNIVERSAL
1947: Cookie Bullfincher, *Springtime in the Sierras*............... REPUBLIC
1947: Ben, *Slave Girl*.. UNIVERSAL
1947: Cookie Bullfincher, *On the Old Spanish Trail*............... REPUBLIC
1947: Buster, *The Michigan Kid*... UNIVERSAL
1947: Bill, *The Marauders* .... UNITED ARTISTS
1947: Cookie, *Bells of San Angelo* .... REPUBLIC
1947: Elihu, *The Fabulous Texan*....................................... REPUBLIC
1948: Sam Bowie, *Old Los Angeles* .... REPUBLIC
1948: Cookie Bullfincher, *Night Time in Nevada*.................... REPUBLIC
1948: Cookie Bullfincher, *Grand Canyon Trail*...................... REPUBLIC
1948: Cookie Bullfincher, *The Gay Ranchero*......................... REPUBLIC
1948: Windy Hornblower, *The Gallant Legion*........................ REPUBLIC
1948: Cookie Bullfincher, *Eyes of Texas*.............................. REPUBLIC
1948: Cookie Bullfincher, *Under California Stars* .... REPUBLIC
1949: Casey Brown, *The Last Bandit*................................... REPUBLIC
1949: Judge Cookie Bullfincher *The Far Frontier,*.................. REPUBLIC
1950: Waldo, *Traveling Saleswoman* .... COLUMBIA
1950: Orvie, *Never a Dull Moment*................. RKO RADIO PICTURES
1951: Sergeant McIntosh, *Slaughter Trail*........... RKO RADIO PICTURES
1951: Fat soldier, *The Red Badge of Courage*......................... M-G-M
1951: Sergeant Garrity, *New Mexico*........................... UNITED ARTISTS
1952: Jingles P. Jones, *The Yellow-Haired Kid*.................... MONOGRAM
1952: Jingles, *Trail of the Arrow* .... MONOGRAM
1952: Pete Bivens, *Montana Belle*................... RKO RADIO PICTURES
1952: Jingles, *The Ghost of Crossbones Canyon*..................... MONOGRAM
1952: Jingles, *Behind Southern Lines*................................ MONOGRAM
1953: Jingles P. Jones, *Secret of Outlaw Flats* .... ALLIED ARTISTS
1953: Jingles, *Border City Rustlers* .... ALLIED ARTISTS
1953: Jingles P. Jones, *The Six-Gun Decision* .... ALLIED ARTISTS
1953: Moon, *Island in the Sky*........................... WARNER BROS.
1954: Jingles, *The Two Gun Teacher* .... ALLIED ARTISTS

1954: Jingles, *Trouble on the Trail*...............................ALLIED ARTISTS

1954: Harry, *Thunder Pass*...LIPPERT

1954: Jingles, *Outlaw's Son* ....ALLIED ARTISTS

1954: Jingles P. Jones, *Marshals in Disguise*.................ALLIED ARTISTS

1955: Jingles P. Jones, *The Titled Tenderfoot*.................ALLIED ARTISTS

1955: Jingles, *Timber Country Trouble*..........................ALLIED ARTISTS

1955: Jingles P. Jones, *Phantom Trails* ....ALLIED ARTISTS

1955: George Tenell, *Pete Kelley's Blues* .... WARNER BROS.

1955: Jingles P. Jones, *The Matchmaking Marshal*.........ALLIED ARTISTS

1956: First Mate, *Around the World in Eighty Days*.....UNITED ARTISTS

1960: Mr. Carmody, *Huckleberry Finn* .... M-G-M

1961: Sgt. Darius P. Posey, *Two Rode Together*..................... COLUMBIA

1962: Link Appleyard, *The Man Who Shot Liberty Valence*.... PARAMOUNT

1963: Corporal Peterson, *How The West Was Won*................. CINERAMA

1963: Sheriff, *It's a Mad, Mad, Mad, Mad World*.........UNITED ARTISTS

1965: Branch Hawksbill, *Zebra in the Kitchen*............................ M-G-M

1967: Judge Tatum, *The Ballad of Josie Wales* .... UNIVERSAL

1968: Sheriff Estep, *The Road Hustlers* ....

AMERICAN INTERNATIONAL PICTURES

1969: Andy, *Ride a Northbound Horse*.............. WALT DISNEY PICTURES

1970: Coyote Bill, *Myra Breckinridge*.........TWENTIETH CENTURY FOX

1970: Mr. Stone, *Smoke* .... WALT DISNEY PICTURES

1970: Cameo, *The Phynx* .... WARNER BROS.

1973: Voice of Friar Tuck, *Robin Hood* (animated) ....BUENA VISTA

1976: Priest in a dog pound, *Won Ton Ton*........................ PARAMOUNT

1976: Captain Andy, *A Whale of a Tale*.................................... LUCKERIS

TELEVISION APPEARANCES: SERIES

1951-1958: Jingles P. Jones, *Wild Bill Hickok* (118 episodes) ....

SYNDICATED

1955-1960: Host, *Andy's Gang* (52 episodes) ....NBC

1964-1965: Hap Gorman, *Flipper* (5 episodes)..............................NBC

TELEVISION APPEARANCES: MOVIES

1969: Amos Polk, *The Over the Hill Gang*.... ABC MOVIE OF THE WEEK

1969: Andy, *Smoke*..DISNEY

1970: Amos Polk. *The Over the Hill Gang Rides Again*...........................

ABC MOVIE OF THE WEEK

1970: Andy, *North Bound Horse*..DISNEY
1971: Gramps, *Tale of a Whale* .... NATIONAL GENERAL

TELEVISION APPEARANCES: EPISODIC

1959: Jess MacAbbee, "The Jess MacAbbee Story,"...............................
Wagon Train, NBC
1962: Frisbee, "Hocus-Pocus and Frisbee,"......... *The Twilight Zone*, CBS
1966: Amos Tyke, "Yesterday's Timepiece,".............. *The Virginian*, NBC
1966: Santa, "The Duo is Slumming," ....*Batman*, ABC
1972: Sheriff Bintell, "The Men That Corrupted Hadleyburg,".............
Alias Smith and Jones, ABC

STAGE APPEARANCES

1957: Cap'n Andy, *Showboat*.............Jones Beach, NY *(77 performances)*
1958: Cap'n Andy, *Showboat*..
St. Louis Muni Opera *(10 performances)*
1959: Cap'n Andy, *Showboat*...........................Clio, MI *(8 performances)*
1960: Cap'n Andy, *Showboat*.............Farmingham, MA *(8 performances)*
1960: Priest, *Anything Goes* ....
St. Louis Muni Opera *(8 performances)*
1960: Cap'n Andy, *Showboat*..................Pittsburgh, PA *(8 performances)*
1961: Cap'n Andy, *Showboat*.............Los Angeles, CA *(48 performances)*
1961: Cap'n Andy, *Showboat*.......... San Francisco, CA *(16 performances)*
1962: Cap'n Andy, *Showboat*...............San Diego, CA *(16 performances)*
1963: Gramps, *On Borrowed Time*........Ann Arbor, MI *(8 performances)*
1963: Cap'n Andy, *Showboat*....................Andover, MD *(8 performances)*
1963: Cap'n Andy, *Showboat*..............Washington, DC *(8 performances)*
1963: Cap'n Andy, *Showboat*................. Baltimore, MD *(8 performances)*
1963: Cap'n Andy, *Showboat*...................Lawndale, NJ *(8 performances)*
1963: Cap'n Andy, *Showboat*.............. Valley Forge, PA *(8 performances)*
1963: Cap'n Andy, *Showboat*.............. Long Island, NY *(8 performances)*
1963: Cap'n Andy, *Showboat*...............Springfield, MA *(8 performances)*
1963: The Priest, *Anything Goes* .... Rochester, NY *(8 performances)*
1963: The Priest, *Anything Goes* .... Dalton, IL *(16 performances)*
1964: Cap'n Andy, *Showboat*..
St. Louis Muni Opera *(8 performances)*
1964: Cap'n Andy, *Showboat*..................Anaheim, CA *(16 performances)*
1965: The Father, *Never Too Late* ....Lakewood, CA *(8 performances)*

1965: The Father, *Never Too Late* ....Detroit, MI *(8 performances)*
1965: Gramps, *On Borrowed Time* ....
                              Houghton Lake, MI *(8 performances)*
1965: Gramps, *On Borrowed Time* ...... Indianapolis, IN *(8 performances)*
1965: Gramps, *On Borrowed Time* .... Louisville, KY *(8 performances)*
1966: The Father, *Never Too Late* .... San Carlos, CA *(8 performances)*
1966: The Father, *Never Too Late* ....Anaheim, CA *(8 performances)*
1966: The Father, *Never Too Late* ....
                              Woodland Hills, CA *(8 performances)*
1966: The Father, *Never Too Late* ....Sullivan, IL *(8 performances)*
1966: Gramps, *On Borrowed Time* .... Joliet, IL *(8 performances)*
1966: Cap'n Andy, *Showboat* ....Pittsburgh, PA *(16 performances)*
1967: The Father, *Never Too Late* .... San Diego, CA *(8 performances)*
1967: Cap'n Andy, *Showboat* .... Houston, TX *(16 performances)*
1967: The Convict, *My Three Angels* ....
                              Traverse City, MI *(8 performances)*
1967: The Convict, *My Three Angels* ....
                              Canal Fulton, OH *(8 performances)*
1967: The Convict, *My Three Angels* .... Sullivan, IL *(8 performances)*
1968: Andy Devine, *Knots Berry Farm* ....
                    Anaheim, CA *(4 weeks — personal appearance)*
1970: Cap'n Andy, *Showboat* .... Warren, OH *(8 performances)*
1970: Cap'n Andy, *Showboat* .... Dayton, OH *(8 performances)*
1970: Cap'n Andy, *Showboat* .... Columbus, OH *(8 performances)*
1971: The Father, *Never Too Late* .... Monroe, LA *(16 performances)*
1972: Cap'n Andy, *Showboat* ....Flint, MI *(8 performances)*
1972: Andy Devine Music in the Air .... Warren, OH *(8 performances)*
1972: Andy Devine Music in the Air .... Dayton, OH *(8 performances)*
1972: Andy Devine Music in the Air ....
                              Columbus, OH *(8 performances)*

RADIO APPEARANCES

1935-1940: Andy Devine, *Jack Benny Show* ....
                              (6 years, 30 performances) NBC
1938-1939: Andy Devine, *Al Pierce Show* .... *(26 weeks)* ABC
1939-1942: Andy Devine, *Lum & Abner* .... *(5 years)* NBC
1940: Andy Devine, *Melody Roundup* .... *(26 weeks)* CBS
1942: Andy Devine, *The Fitch Band Wagon* .... *(26 weeks)* NBC
1951-1956: Jingles P. Jones, *Wild Bill Hickok* .... *(150 episodes)* NBC

Index

20th Century Fox 54, 118, 121, 122
20th Century Roundtable 162, 175
21 Club 74, 84, 124
25th Street Boys Club 139
48 Hours 177
A Star is Born 62, 64, 69
A Summer Place 178
Abbott & Costello Meet Frankenstein 32
Abbott, Bud 137
Academy Awards 98
Adventures of Robin Hood, The 72
Al Melnick Agency 70, 170
Alaska Airlines 183
Ali Baba and the 40 Thieves 25
All Quiet on the Western Front 47, 64
Allen, Fred 54
Alpert, Herb 174
Amagraja 124
Ameche, Don 65
American Graffiti 89
An Affair to Remember 178
Andretti, Mario 189
Andrews, Dana 29, 30, 32
Andy Griffith Show, The 174
Andy's Gang 13, 103, 104
Angel and the Bad Man, The 76
Animal House 135
Anything Goes 147
Arizona State Teacher's College 38
Arlen, Richard 70
Around the World in 80 Days 80
Arquette, Cliff 59
Arrouge, Marty 63, 86
Aspen Mountain 185

Astor, Mary 54
Auer, Mischa 68
Autry, Gene 54, 71
Ayres, Lew 47, 50, 221
Bacharach, Burt 153
Bacon, James 98, 99, 142
Badlands of Dakota, The 69
Baker, Carol 155
Baker, Diane 89
Baker, Jim 211
Baker, Tammy Faye 211
Bakewell, William 47
Bank of Beverly Hills 223
Bardot, Bridget 108
Barnes, Bruce 189
Barnes, Chuck 189
Barrett, Tom 212
Barrett-Jackson Auto Auctions 212
Barron Hilton 133
Barrymore, John 63
Baumgartner Devine, Barbara 164, 165, 178,
    196, 199, 213, 223
Baxter, Dr. Frank 139
Beach Boys, The 161
Beatty, Warren 142
Benny, Jack 54, 56, 57, 98, 132, 135
Berle, Milton 83, 84, 135
Best Years of Our Lives, The 32
Beverly Hills Hotel, The 97, 113, 160, 205
Beverly Wilshire Hotel 187
Bey, Turhan 25
Big Trail, The 66
Blackstone, Tom and Mary Bell 197
Blane, Sally 47

Bond, Ward 25, 29, 42, 66, 138
Bong, Richard 26
Boyd, Jimmy 89
Boyer, Charles 50
Brando, Marlon 142
Brennan, Walter 63, 102
Bride of Frankenstein, The 32
Bridges, Lloyd 29
Broidy, William 75
Brooklyn Dodgers 123
Brooks, Ralph 23
Brown, Joe E. 148, 150
Buck Benny Rides Again 57, 68
Burbank Airport 207
Burnett, Leo 59, 75, 76, 170, 172
Burns, George 135
Butler, Harold 218
Buttrum, Pat 184
Cagney, James 68
Canyon Passage 29, 70
Carmichael, Hoagy 29, 32
Carradine, John 153
Carson, Johnny 171, 172
Carson, Robert 64
Carter, Jimmy 211
Casablanca 105
Castro, Fidel 125
CBS 186
Chandler, Bob 189
Chaney, Jr., Lon 71
Chapman College 169
Chasen's 141
Chinatown 204
Choureau, Etchika 113
CIT Corporation 161, 163
Clark, Justice William 210
Clark, Walter "Waddy" 195
Cleopatra 159
Cobb, Bob 17, 18, 158
Cobb, Sally 18
Cohn, Harry 137
Colbert, Claudette 50
Colburn, James 133
Cole, Natalie 174
Collegians 42
Colona, Jerry 64
Columbia Pictures 137
Cooper, Gary 42, 66
Copeland, Aaron 194

Coppola, Francis Ford 204
Corrigan Ranch 67
Cotton Club, The 204
Councilman, "Doc" 92
Cowlings, Al 189
Cox, Susan 205
Cranston, Alan 175
Criminal Code 47
Crosby, Bing 21, 25, 54, 55, 56, 62
Crosby, Dixie 62, 63
Culverhouse, Hugh 141
Cummings, Robert 133
Curtis, Ken 184, 215
D&S Company 167, 223
Daland, Peter 95, 115, 125, 127, 129, 130, 132, 134, 139, 144, 151
Dances with Wolves 124
Danger on Wheels 68
Darby, Kim 112
Dark Passage 178
Daves, Debbie 178
Daves, Delmer 178
David, Hal 153
Davis, Joan 75
Davis, Miles 174
Dawn Patrol 45
Day, Doris 170
de Havilland, Olivia 72
De Wilde, Brandon 102
Dean, James 108
DeNiro, Robert 119
Destination Tokyo 178
Devine, Andy 11, 13, 17, 18, 38, 40, 42, 43, 45, 46, 47, 53, 57, 62, 65, 67, 90, 101, 117, 138, 146, 147, 151, 152, 153, 154, 155, 160, 168, 169, 172, 183, 191, 192, 194, 195, 196, 198, 213, 215, 219, 220
Devine, Dennis 11, 21, 90, 99
Devine, Dorothy 17, 18, 52, 53, 54, 62, 213, 216, 221
Devine, Jr., Tom 37
Devine, Sr. Tom 37, 38, 40
Devine, Tad 21, 54, 62, 85, 151, 221, 225
Devine, Timothy (see Tad Devine)
Devine, Trisha 196, 213
Die Hard 177
Dietrich, Marlene 68, 69
Disney Corporation 223
Disney, Sharon 188

Disneyland 117, 188, 191
Disneyland Hotel, The 211
Dix, Richard 70
Dodson, Jack 173, 174
Dodson, Mary 174
Donlevy, Brian 29, 65
Dorothy Chandler Pavilion 150
Double or Nothing 64
Dr. Bull 52, 66
Dr. Rhythm 65
Dragnet 79, 80
Drysdale, Don 123
Dunne, Irene 54, 75
Duquette, Tony 80, 141
Eastwood, Clint 106
Ebbets Field 123
Economic Research Associates 188
Edwards, Ralph 83
Elliott "Wild", Bill 72, 74
Elway, John 163
Empire State Building 124
Evans, Robert 204, 205
Falk, Peter 137
Farmer Takes a Wife 62
Farmer, Francis 70
Farnsworth, Dick 76
Fat Jones 72
Father Smith 165
Faye, Alice 64, 65
Fellows, Robert 101
Fertig, Craig 186
Fibber McGee and Molly 54
Field of Dreams 177
Finders Keepers 43
Fitch Bandwagon, The 59
Fitzgerald, Ella 79, 80
Flagstaff, Arizona 37
Flame of New Orleans, The 69
Flying Tigers 23, 26
Fonda, Henry 62
Ford, John 52, 66, 67, 138, 151, 154, 155
Frank, Anthony M. 187
Frankenstein 25
Froggy the Gremlin 103, 104
Fugitive, The 110
Gable, Clark 17, 18, 24, 25, 67, 68, 90, 133,
   155
Gann, Ernest 69, 79
Gardner, Judge Robert 215

Garland, Judy 98
Garner, James 106
Gaynor, Janet 62, 63, 64
Gibson, Dunn & Crutcher 179
Giles, General Barney 23
Gillanders, David 145
Gleason, Jackie 84
Godfather 204
Goff, Norris 23, 24, 57, 68
Golden Cloud 72
Gone With the Wind 17, 65
Goodbye, My Lady 102
Gordon, Larry 177
Goux, Marv 141
Grauman's Chinese Theater 64
Gray, Virginia 24, 25
Grease 89
Great Lakes Carbon 179
Griffin, Jr., Z. Wayne 178, 179, 180
Grigg, Ricky 121
Guard, Tim 120
Guess Who's Coming to Dinner 155
Hall, Jon 25, 72
Hamburger Hamlet Restaurants 162
Hammerstein, Oscar 116
Hard Rock Land Company 24
Hardy, Olivier "Babe" 137
Harris, Dr. Joe 18
Harris, Phil 23, 24, 56, 57, 59, 102, 133, 184
Harvard Business School 162, 178
Harvard Military School 38
Hawks, Howard 25, 45
Hayes, George "Gabby" 45
Hayward, Susan 29
Hearst, William Randolph 197
Hell's Angels 93, 94
Henricks, Jon 115, 159
High and the Mighty, The 69, 79
Highway 1 185
Hill, Calvin 189
Hillcrest Country Club 135
Hocus-Pocus Frisby 155
Hollywood Blvd. 41
Hollywood Bowl, The 43, 117
Hollywood Brown Derby 17, 67, 141, 146, 213
Hollywood Squares 42
Holt, Jack 74
Honeymooners, The 84
Hooper, Mike 87, 97, 109

Hope, Bob 54, 70, 169
Horton, Edward Everett 34
Hot Steel 68
House, Jack 52
Huston, Celeste "Ce Ce" 78
Huston, John 50, 78
Huston, Walter 50
How the West Was Won 154
Howard Hughes Flying Boat 33
Howard, Leslie 63
Huckleberry Finn 147
Hudson, Rock 140, 141
Hughes, Howard 33, 99
Hunter, Tab 106, 109
Hussong's 52
Hutchens, Will 106, 107
Impatient Maiden 50
In Old Chicago 65
Island in the Sky 79
It's a Mad, Mad World 154, 55
Ittelson, H. Anthony "Tony" 162
Ives, Burl 75
Janssen, David 106, 110, 111
Jazz Singer, The 44
Jell-O 56, 59
Johnson, Tom 120
Jolson, Al 135
Jones, Shirley 151
Jungle Book 58
Keach, Stacy 89
Keenert, Beans 120
Kellogg's Cereals 75, 77
Kelly, Gene 142
Kennedy Center 192
Kennedy, Bobby 176
Kennedy, Ethel 179
Kern, Jerome 116
King, Larry 11
Kinmont, Jill 85
Kroan, Dan 90
Kroan, Dr. Red 18, 90
Kroon, Rudy 120
Kuchel, Senator Tom 175
LA Civic Light Opera 150
LA Memorial Coliseum 114
Lafayette Escadrille 105, 108, 113, 122
Laffer, Professor Arthur 211
Lake Powell, Utah 140, 185
Lang, Richard 110

Larson, Lance 95, 130, 144
Lassie 211
Last Bandit, The 74
Laughlin, Tom 106
Laughton, Charles 146
Law and Order 50, 78
Lazar, Irving "Swifty" 73, 74
Lee, Anna 153
Lee, Peggy 79, 80
Leigh, Janet 80
Lester, Edwin 150
Levy, Dave 141
Lilac Time 42
Lindsey, George 184
Link, Dick 170
Lipuma, Tommy 174
Lokey, Hulsey 141
Lollypop Kids 104
Lombard, Carole 17, 24, 90
Lombardo, Carmen 117
Lombardo, Guy 116, 117, 122
Lone Ranger, The 211
Lopez, Trini 163
Lopez-Portillo, President 212
Los Angeles Athletic Club 135
Los Angeles International Airport 216
Los Angeles Wildcats 42
Love Story 204
Lucky Devils 70
Lugosi, Jr., Bella 129
Lum and Abner 24, 57, 59
Lund, William 188, 189, 199
Lyon, Charles 215
M*A*S*H 25
MacDonald, J. Ferrell 47
Madison Square Garden 52
Madison, Guy 75, 76, 215
Man from Yesterday, The 50
Man Who Laughs, The 42
Man Who Shot Liberty Valance, The 11, 152, 154
Mandekic, Mike 140
Mandella, Mark 157
Mansfield, Jane 80
Mantz, Paul 112
March, Frederic 64
Maren, Jerry 104
Martin, Dana 133
Martin, Dean 142
Martin, Strother 153

Marvin, Lee 80, 152
Marx Brothers, The 54
Marx, Groucho 114
Massi, Benny 18, 146, 213
Maverick 105
Mayo Clinic 164
McClintock 168
McConnell, Ed 103
McCormick, Mark 190
McCoy, Dave 85
McCrea, Jody 106
Mcgreevy, Shawn 219
McGuire, Butch 143
McKay, Corky 141
McKay, John 141, 189
McLaglen, Victor 80, 137
McLaine, Shirley 80
McMurray, Fred 68, 75
Meisner, Sanford 119
Melcher, Marty 170
Melchior, Laurence 132
Melnick, Al 118, 169, 170, 171
Melnick, Wilt 118, 119
Melody Roundup 59
Menjou, Adolphe 64
Mercer, Johnny 64
Mercouri, Melina 142
Meyers, Bill 162
Midnight the Cat 103, 104
Miles, Vera 153
Milton Berle Texaco Hour 83
Monday Night Football 196
Montana, Monte 153
Montez, Maria 25, 70
Moore, Archie 147
Moraga Spit and Polish Club 25
Munchkins, The 54
Murphy, George 64, 172
Murray, Ken 153
Musgrove, Stanley 140, 141, 148
Music in the Air 184
National Velvet 25
Navy SEALS 221
Nelson, Ed 157
Neri, Lauro 212
Never a Dull Moment 75
Never On Sunday 142
Never Too Late 184
Newman, Paul 108, 109, 119

Nicholson, Jack 205
Niven, David 80
Niven, Michael 179, 180
Niven, Van Cott 179
Nixon, Richard 74
Noah's Ark 11, 44
Nolan, Jeanette 153
Nolan, Lloyd 66
Noland, Bob 71
Novak, Kim 70, 169
O'Brien, Edmond 80, 153
O'Brien, Pat 68, 150
O'Hara, Maureen 11
O'Keefe, Dennis 21
O'Melveny, Jack 132, 218
O'Melveny, Patrick 218, 219
Oakie, Jack 80
Ohio State University 151
Oliver, Edna May 63
Olson, Arvid 23
Pacific Pioneer Broadcasters 213
Palmer, Arnold 190
Pan American Games 144
Pappas, Nick 186
Paramount 54
Parker, Dorothy 64
Payne-Whitney Gymnasium 139
Peppard, George 155
Parrish 178
Pete Kelly's Blues 79
Peters, Bob 114
Pitney, Gene 153
Plaza Hotel 124
Poggi, Rick 157
Poitier, Sidney 102
Porter, Cole 140, 141
Postman Always Rings Twice, The 25
Power, Tyrone 64, 65, 137
Poyer, Howard 157
Presidential Inaugural Committee, The 211
Pretty Woman 187
Price, Harrison "Buzz" 188
Pride of the Marines 105
Prophet, The 221
Pyle, Denver 153
Qualen, John 153
Radio City Music Hall 64
Rafferty, Francis 176
Rafferty, Max 175, 176

Rancheros Visitadores 184, 210

Rathbone, Basil 63

Ray, Martha 64

Reagan, Ronald 172, 175, 210, 211

Rebel without a Cause 89

Red Badge of Courage 69, 78

Reddish, Jack 86

Redford, Robert 89

Republic Pictures 186

Republic Studios 71

Reynolds, Debbie 70, 169

Rich Man, Poor Man 73

Richards, Bill 178, 180

RKO 54

Road Agent 70

Road Back, The 64

Robin Hood 184

Rockefeller Center 124

Rockney, Knute 47

Rockwell International 203

Rodriguez, Rod 158

Rogers, Ginger 54

Rogers, Roy 71, 72, 186

Rogers, Will 52

Roker, Al 13

Romanoff, Michael 141

Romanoff's 141, 142

Rome Olympics 144

Romeo & Juliet 13, 63

Romero, Cesar 172

Rose, Murray 115

Rosemary's Baby 204

Route 66 37

Russell, Gail 76

San Juan Islands 195

San Simeon Castle 196

Sande, Walter 171

Sands Dick 219

Sanez, Josephine 168

Santa Clara University 38

Santa Monica Lifeguard Service 42, 119, 121

Scarface 105

Schwartz, Jeremiah 42

Screen Gems 170

Selznick, Myron 70

Shakespeare 47

Shaw, Irwin 73, 74

Shearer, Norma 63, 86

Showboat 116, 117, 123, 133, 147, 150, 173

Shulman, Julius 206

Shurr, Louie 70

Sideways 196

Sidlow, Peter 162, 163, 166, 167, 177, 180, 182, 186, 202, 223

Simpson, O.J. 189

Sinatra, Frank 18, 142

Singleton, Henry 210

Skakel Family, The 179

Skelton, Red 137

Slye, Leonard 71

Small Town Girl 63

Smilin' Ed's Buster Brown Gang 103

Smith, C. Aubrey 63

Smith, Hank 87

Smith, Harley Wright 34, 35

Son of Frankenstein, The 32

Sons of the Pioneers, The 71

Spirit of Notre Dame 45, 48

Sports Headliners 189, 190

Sports Illustrated 85

St. Louis Municipal Opera 133

Stacey, Jim 112

Stack, Robert 23, 69

Stagecoach 13, 17, 66, 67, 168, 169

Stanford Research Associates 188

Stanford University 83, 115

State Department 192

Statute of Liberty 124

Stevens, Connie 112

Stewart, Gloria 54

Stewart, Jimmy 11, 142, 152, 194, 215

Stone, Milburn 171

Strange, Glenn 29, 30, 32

Streep, Meryl 119

Streisand, Barbra 174

Strode, Woody 153

Summerville, "Slim" 45, 62

Sweeney, Bob 173

Tale of a Whale 184

Tallman, Frank 112

Tallmantz Aviation 112

Taylor, Elizabeth 25, 81

Taylor, Robert 25

Tennant, Andy 76

Tennant, Donald 76, 191

Thalberg, Irving 63

Thalberg, Katy 86

Thomas, Danny 135

Thomas, John Charles 132
Thomas, Margie "Marlo" 135
Thornton, Charles B. "Tex" 211
Tilley, William 133
Tiomkin, Dimitri 69
Tipperay, Ireland 37
Titanic 54
Today Show, The 13
Todd, Mike 80, 81, 141
Tone, Franchot 68
Tonight Show, The 171
Tracy, Spencer 155
Trail of the Vigilantes 68
Traveling Saleslady, The 75
Trent, Buzzy 120
Trigger 72
Tropic Fury 68
Trotter, John Scott 64
Troy, Mike 144
Trump, Donald 159
Tucker, Forrest 74
Turner, Lana 25
Twilight Zone 155
Two Rode Together 151
U.S. Information Agency 211
Unitas, Johnny 189
Universal Studios 27, 41, 68, 148
University of Southern California 42, 114, 115, 132, 163
Unser, Al 189
Unser, Bobby 189
Urban Cowboy 204
Van Cleef, Lee 153
Van, Frankie 68
Variety 106
Vaughn, Larry 157
Venice Island Duck Club 133
Verne, Jules 80
Vince's Gym 95, 114
Wake of the Red Witch 76
Wallace, Audrey Faust 124
Wallace, Mahlon 124
Walt Disney Studios 184
Wanger, Walter 27, 28, 66, 70
Ward, Amy 37, 48
Ward, Commander Herman 37
Warner Bros. 54, 105, 113
Watkins, Captain George Washington "Cap" 42, 103

Wayne, John (Marion Morrison) 42, 44, 57, 66, 69, 76, 79, 116, 152, 153, 168, 191, 194, 215
Wayne, Michael 168, 169
Wayne, Patrick 11
Webb, Jack 79, 80
Wellman, Jr., Bill 106
Wellman, William "Bill" 25, 45, 63, 64, 69, 79, 99, 100, 101, 102, 106, 108, 109, 110, 112, 113, 137, 141
Wemple, Dean Emmet 125
White House, The 210
Wick, Charles 210, 211
Wicks, Mary 123
Widmark, Richard 151
Wild Bill Hickok 13, 75, 77, 116
Wilkie, Adele 136
Wilkie, Leighton 136
Wilkie, Michael 134, 135, 136, 139, 142, 184
William Morris Agency 170
Wilson, Ambassador William 210
Wilson, Murray 161
Wings 45
Wizard of Oz, The 54, 104
Wood, Natalie 75, 89
Wood, Robert 186
Wormser, Jack 170, 172, 183
Wrather Corporation 223
Wrather, Jack 211
Wynn, Keenan 25
Yale University 115, 129, 130, 133
Yankee Stadium 123
Yates, Herbert J. 71, 72, 186
Yellowstone 63
Yorzick, William 134, 135
You Bet Your Life 114
You're a Sweetheart 64
Young Lions, The 73
Zahn, Tom 120
Zanuck, Daryl 65
Zeckendorf, William 159

Photo Index

1960 Olympic trials 130

Andy and Dorothy with new airplane 200

Andy and Lon Chaney, Jr. in horse and bear costumes 149

Andy Devine and group on set 47

Andy Devine in *Showboat* 57

Andy Devine on *Andy's Gang* 56

Andy Devine on radio 55

Andy Devine with Arizona football team 39

Andy Devine with Clown Emmett Kelly 58

Andy Devine, age 4 38

Andy Devine, Dorothy Devine and Bing Crosby in blackface 59

Andy Devine, Kellogg's ad 147

Andy Devine, Tad Devine and Dennis Devine 28

Andy Devine, Tad Devine and Dennis Devine in wagon 30

Andy with stuntmen, *Two Rode Together* 149

Andy, Dennis and Dorothy at college graduation 193

Andy's Gang comic book 148

Baseball photograph of Clint Eastwood, David Janssen and Dennis Devine 107

"Cap" Watkins 109

Carole Lombard and Tad Devine 16

Cast of *Liberty Valance* 49

Cast of *Stagecoach* 49

Clark Gable and Carole Lombard 16

Clipping from *Variety* 106

Cowboy Hall of Fame photo 224, 225

Dennis and Dorothy skiing 192

Dennis Devine, age 20 131

Devine Family at Thanksgiving 194

Devine family on location 31

Devines and Wellmans at *Star is Born* premiere 48

Dorothy Devine and Tad Devine 20

Dorothy Devine and Will Rogers 19

Dorothy Devine, Andy Devine and Will Rogers 18

Dorothy with a gaggle of geese 225

Fabulous Frosh article 126

Five freshman with Coach Daland 129

Five freshmen on the floor of the Coliseum 224

Hangar scene *Lafayette Escadrille* 108

Hoagy Carmichael at the piano 60

Hotel Beale on Andy Devine Avenue 39

Jack House Polo Team 201

John Wayne and Andy Devine 10

Ken Murray and Bob Hope in costume 61

National Championship photo 128

Photo mural of *How the West Was Won* 146

Picnic at Gaviota Beach 193

Poster for Andy Devine Days 226

Poster for Philippine Adventure 148

Publicity photo Devine family at barbecue 31

Rancheros Vistadores group 200

Robert Evans, Susan Cox, and Dennis Devine on motorcycle

and sidecar in Beverly Hills 204

Still photograph of Andy Devine 46

Tad Devine, Frankenstein and Dennis Devine 29

Tom Devine, Sr. at hotel 36

Tom Johnson 110

USC swim team 127